The Annotated Anthology
of
Lost & Found Literature, Vol. 3

D1280411

The Annotated Anthology of Lost & Found Literature, Vol. 3

Collected by: T. E. Winchester, Esq.

with

Pitch Mirabelle (Sidekick / Editor)

Charleston, SC
www.PalmettoPublishing.com

The Annotated Anthology of Lost & Found Literature, Vol. 3

Copyright © 2022 by Pitch Mirabelle

First Edition

Paperback ISBN: 978-1-68515-907-8

To my wife, parents, uncles & aunts, cousins, family, & my friends. They made me do this. It's not my fault.

Contents

Preface
by
T. E. Winchester, Esq.

I have crossed the globe, traveled the world, and roamed the earth to recover lost and priceless literature created by historical figures previously unknown for their creative writing talents. The critical importance of these works is that they give us a rare insight into these figures beyond the scope of their historical portrait.

The variety of not only the subject matter, but also the format of these works are of extreme interest since they show the dynamic ranges of their creators. The material format includes plays, essays, poems, and what are now referred to as *'length challenged tales'* (the current preferred, more sensitive, and respectful term replacing the previously discourteous title 'short stories').

One final note. Any perceived misspellings, grammatical, or factual errors found in this book are the results of either the original authors' intention or the best available translations of the original authors' material with the goal of remaining as true as possible to the author's original intent. In other words, it's not my fault.

Your Obedient Servant

T. E. Winchester, Esq.

Editor's Note
by
Pitch Mirabelle (Sidekick Editor)

Questions:

Who is the enigmatic Amanda Reckonwith? Were Charles Dickens and Charles Darwin the same man? For that matter, what do we really know about the literary ambitions of Queen Victoria, Joan of Arc, Al Capone, or Hammurabi?

I must confess, I have no idea because I really didn't read much of this book. As I always say 'Why do hard work and research if you can make stuff up'. However, if you purchase the book (at full price) you can find the answers to these questions and discover the once lost but now found literary works of some of history's most brilliant figures. Figures narrowly taught to us as only kings, queens, or scientists, but whose profiles have been expanded through relentless literary investigations of T.E. Winchester, Esq.

This book will not only provide new insights into the characters of noted historic figures, but will also illuminate your mind and fulfill your intellectual curiosity. Consult with your physician to learn if illumination and fulfillment are right for you. If so, this is the book you need to buy.

Pitch Mirabelle (Sidekick Editor)

List of Figures, Tables, Graphs, and Illustrations

Metaf ⁕⁕⁕ ingmorphosis

Introduction by J. Edgar Hoover, FBI

First of all, let me say that I have a file on everybody out there. I suspect that you are all communists, subversives, or people who like beets (a communist vegetable that I have a file on).

Next, the FBI was robbed of the opportunity to bring down Al Capone by our very own Treasury Department (which has been infiltrated by communists). They put him away on a wimpy tax evasion charge. Who doesn't sneak in a questionable deduction or two on their 1040?

All this while the FBI was painstakingly building an iron clad case against Capone for running illegal mah-jongg parlors for elderly ladies. Mah-jongg is a Chinese game and we all know the Chinese are communists. And don't get me started about old ladies.

Anyway, while Treasury got Capone, the FBI discovered a trove of literature written by him in a hidden vault. It was the same vault that put a dent in Geraldo's credibility as a reporter (not that Geraldo, to paraphrase the Marx Brothers, did very much for it anyway.)

PD-US   PD-US

J. Edgar Hoover (left) and Author Al G. Capone (right)

3

Among the confiscated literary works of Capone was the lost opus, "Metaf***ingmorphosis."

This is where Franz Kafka came into the picture. Kafka seems to have taken the entire premise of Capone's Metaf***ingmorphosis and simply changed the title and characters' names. Then he issued the work as his own under the title of 'Metamorphosis'.

As a result Kafka became a big shot Bohemian author/philosopher. And we all know what Bohemians are—subversive beet eating communists.

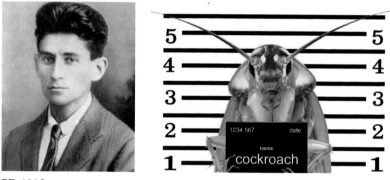

PD-1996

Franz Kafka—Left—publicity photo for Kafka's singing group, Franz and the Pompadours. Right—Kafka in post-larval stage (Courtesy of Prague Criminal Insect Division).

I am writing this introduction to set the record straight about the FBI, Metaf***ingmorphosis, and all the commies in the world today. So please read and enjoy this story courtesy of the FBI.

Thank you.

J. Edgar Hoover

Metaf***ingmorphosis

Joseph "Bugsy" Roditore was not a morning person. He hated to leave the warm cozy comfort of his dreams to face the cold reality of his life. A life he was not sure he was even a witting part of.

Bugsy was twenty-eight and still lived at home with his parents, Carmine (aka, Mr. Ro), Constanta (aka, Mrs. Ro, the former Constanta Sacramucca) Roditore, and his younger sister Loretta "DiDi" Roditore. He thought of the weighty obligations that bound them all together as his back foot scratched the itchy spot behind his ear.

From bed, Bugsy's sleep-heavy eyes seemed to have a sluggish will of their own and roamed over the spartan décor of his room. There was a small narrow window which admitted particles of sunlight, breezes, and the occasional fly. Against the wall was an old dresser handed down from Aunt Leena, the gypsy. Over the dresser hung a crucifix next to a portrait of Jesus.

The Jesus-crucifix combination was one of the seemingly infinite sets that his mother installed all around the house. There was Jesus, the crucifix, and the plastic grapes in the hallway, Jesus, the crucifix and the salamis in the pantry, Jesus, the crucifix, and the cloves of garlic in the kitchen.

It all came to a holy climax in the living room with the shrine of Jesus, the crucifix, and the Last Supper over the TV. These and the fifty or so statues of the Blessed Virgin Mary and associated saints made the house pretty much impervious to any threats that could be mounted by vampires, werewolves, or anything supernaturally evil. Subliminal waves of some sort must have been emitted since Protestants gave the house a wide berth as well.

Bugsy's struggle to become fully awake received a jolting assist when he realized he overslept and was late for work. Why today of all days? This morning he had to attend an important meeting with his boss, Primo "The Big Cheese" Formaggio.

Bugsy took out his sudden anxiety by gnawing at the wooden legs of Aunt Leena's old dresser. He couldn't afford to show disrespect to Primo; that was not looked upon well. Besides Bugsy desperately needed this job.

His father owed Primo twenty-five hundred dollars (plus the vig). Primo took a small deduction out of Bugsy's weekly check until things were settled up. When Bugsy needed extra cash he ran an occasional errand or two for the big man.

There wasn't many choices available to Bugsy, with all due respect to any existentialists out there. His father couldn't pay back the money. Carmine Roditore's workman's comp ran out six months ago and ever since he had been sitting around the house in his underwear playing the wrong ponies.

Bugsy was forced to support the family by paying for food, rent, and taxes. Whatever money came spare was saved to send DiDi to Beautician school. Bugsy rarely ever had more than sixty-seven cents on him at any time. "Who wants to wake up to this?" he thought, "No wonder, I am not a morning person."

Then an odd notion hit him. Why would Primo want to him to attend a meeting? Bugsy recalled Primo's exact words—"I want you here early morning for a confer." Bugsy didn't think of it then, but that seemed peculiar to him now. He didn't know of anyone else who was going to be there.

While mulling over that idea, he sat idly on the bed grooming himself, able to reach places with his tongue he could never reach before. Suddenly a bright flash of light penetrated his head like a .22 caliber bullet. The last guy to have a meeting with Primo was Charlie "Hard Luck Chuck" Condannato. There was a lot of talk around the shop that we had a squealer amongst us. Two weeks later there was no more squealer talk and Charlie popped to the surface in a barrel off the New Jersey Shore not looking too good.

Bugsy's mind was alert and processing the data pouring in from all around him, the analysis led to a startling new discovery—he now had four feet. He was pretty certain he went to bed with only two. And, by God, was there a tail coming out of his butt?

Shock was now added to his regular morning distress. What had he become? How is he going to get to work? And, why did he have an uncontrollable urge to run a maze?

His dread was interrupted by a knock on his door. It was his mother.

"Joey, baby get up. You're late and Tommy Corporale from work will be here." Mrs. Ro said from the other side.

"God." prayed Bugsy. "Don't let my mother see me this way. It'll kill her worse than when I asked that Sicilian girl to the prom."

"Joey, honey, hurry!" His mom called again.

Bugsy tried to answer. His words were intelligible but at a much higher tone than normal. That sets alarms off in his mom's mind.

"Joey, sweetie. Are you coming down with a cold? Is your throat sore? Don't worry, Baby, Momma will get you warm wine and the raw garlic. You'll feel better. And put on your cornetto!" Momma prescribed and then ran off to gather her ingredients.

Bugsy's father was quick to critique the situation, "Connie, I keep telling you you're going to spoil that boy!"

The doorbell rang interrupting any chance of a rebuttal. Momma, with a wave of her hand, simply dispatched her husband to answer it.

"Sta taci, Carmine! Get the door. Put on your pants! We have company." Momma scolded.

Scratching his rear end with vigorous action, Carmine answered the door. Tommy Corporale stood outside futilely trying to light a cigarette. Frustrated, Tommy threw the cigarette away and stepped inside.

Momma quickly offered Tommy the hospitality of the house. "Tommy, sit for breakfast. Sit, breakfast is good for you. Mangia."

"Yeah, thanks Mrs. Ro." Said Tommy. "I'll have a little bit while Bugsy gets ready." Tommy already helped himself to the table. His reply was muffled by his mouthful of food.

Bugsy's father warily waited for his wife to leave the room and whispered to Tommy, "Tommy, put me down for $25 on the nose, eh. I'm good for it."

Tommy "Two Stripe" Corporale shuffled uncomfortably. "Hey, Mr. Ro, if it were me, but Primo says no more until Bugsy pays things off. Sorry. I'm just here to get Bugsy since he don't show for a meeting with Primo, and Primo's p***ed because of it."

Bugsy's father got irritated. "Tell me the kid's not going to lose his f***ing job because he sleeps in. Is he?"

Tommy grew a little pale as he replied. "Ah, at this point, Mr. Ro, losing his job ain't what he should be sweating about."

"OK, good thing, cause I got some hot numbers to play here, Tommy." said Mr. Ro with miscalculated relief.

Mrs. Ro returned with her remedies for her son and with her daughter DiDi grudgingly in tow. DiDi's jet black hair was up in curlers snared beneath a torn hair net. She wore large plastic hoop earrings and bunny slippers. None of this was able to disguise her beauty. She also wore a short tight housecoat which accentuates her long graceful legs, the vision of which almost made Tommy choke on the food in his mouth. He had always fantasized about DiDi, but had never actually seen so much of her in real life.

"Hey, DiDi, you're looking real good there. What you got a new hairdo or lose weight or something?" He tried to sound suave and cool but was betrayed by every facet of his naturally evolved coarseness.

"Nah, just painted my nails." DiDi said between snaps of her gum. She was not oblivious to Tommy and his lusty roving eyes. She was just indifferent to him in total.

"Very nice." said Tommy.

"Joey, Momma's coming in to make your sore throat better, baby." Mrs. Ro proclaimed in front of Bugsy's door.

Bugsy's new ears had gathered all the details of the conversations on the other side and he tried to bring his voice down an octave to deflect the onslaught of maternal healing.

"Momma, I'm OK. Just give me a minute." He begged as he looked to see if he could escape through the small window in the room.

Tommy interceded, "Mrs. Ro, you better let me handle this. I got to get him." Tommy paused as if he came to sentence-ending punctuation. Then realizing his wording might cause alarm, made a clumsy attempt at continuity, "to work, I mean," he added.

Bugsy's dad added some additional incentive. "Move you're f***ing a**, Joey. You aggravate Primo more and he'll have you f***ing wacked."

Mr. Ro released a self-pleased smirk that was meant to praise his own cleverness.

Tommy face grew pale. "You didn't hear that from me."

DiDi loudly directed her own warning to her brother, "Joey, you better not f*** up this job, a**hole. I want to go to beauty school, and you promised to pay for me. You promised!"

"Whoa, whoa, DiDi. Let's not, huh. I'll handle it, please." Said Mr. Ro.

DiDi reluctantly moved away, but got in a parting shot. "You PROMISED, JOEY! F***ing Indian giver!"

Mr. Ro looked at her in disgust scrunched his shoulders and raised the palms of his hands upward, then gestured to Bugsy's door.

Tommy preceded to bang on Bugsy's door. "Hey, Bugsy. Wake up. Primo's waiting for you and he's f***ing p***ed you ain't showed up. He's going to have your "you know whats" for breakfast else you ain't there." Tommy pleaded.

"Tommy, have some biscotti. You dip in the coffee. It's good, come on." Mrs. Ro offered.

"Bugsy, you better be f***ing dressed." Tommy sternly proclaimed. He was answered by a squeaky set of sounds coming from behind the door. "Stop playing f***ing games, Bugs. I'm coming in."

Tommy pushed open Bugsy's door, stepped inside and exited immediately—closing the door firmly behind him. His face was now almost completely white and carried a shocked expression of a man who had just seen Jimmy Hoffa alive. He leaned against the door to prevent anybody or anything from opening it again. All he could utter was "Minachia!"

Tommy took a few seconds to get composed. Finally he said in a low voice. "Mr. Ro, I think you got yourself an issue, here."

"What you mean Issue?" Mr. Ro asks.

Tommy clarifies. "There's infestation on the other side of this door, here."

"Tommy, what the f*** you talking about—infestation?"

"Mr. Ro, there's a f***ing rat the size of a f***ing Chevy in there!" Tommy warned.

Mr. Ro moved Tommy aside and forced his way into his son's room. He took one glance and got out faster than Tommy had.

"Gesu Christu, what a rat!" Mr. Ro exclaimed as he began sweating.

Tommy added, "The size of a Chevy, right?"

"The size of a f***ing B-29." corrected Mr. Ro

Mrs. Ro, having calmed DiDi, returned and asked about her son, "What's the matter, you two? Where's Joey? He's going to be late. Tommy, sit. More breakfast. Joey, honey come out and eat breakfast before you go."

"Connie, forget breakfast, will you." commanded Mr. Ro. "Go do the dishes in the other room."

Mrs. Ro answered back, "We're not done eating yet. What do you think we're at your mother's and she does the dishes before you finish eating?

Tommy, the food hits the table and whoosh she takes it away before you get a fork in it."

"Don't talk about my mother, Connie. She's a f***ing saint. Tommy, she raised four kids on her own, God bless her. We just all ate fast," Mr. Ro explained in defense of his mother.

Mrs. Ro left the two men and took DiDi with her into the kitchen.

The two men, now alone, brainstormed (minus two brains) to come up with a plan.

"What are we going to do, here?" asked Mr. Ro.

"I'm out of ideas." Tommy blankly replied.

"What was your first one?" asked Mr. Ro. "We got to get rid of that f***ing rat."

"OK, OK. How about we wack the rat. Then we chop him up nice. Wrap it and take it to my uncle down at the meat packing plant." Suggested Tommy brimming with inspiration.

"Tommy, that's f***ing sick," Mr. Ro's thought out loud.

"OK, then we dump him in the river. I know some guys." Tommy amends.

"How you going to kill that thing? I haven't got a six foot f***ing mouse trap laying around the house," Confessed Mr. Ro.

Tommy held out his hands as a sign that Mr. Ro stay calm.

"We don't need a f***ing mouse trap," Tommy said and preceded to take out and show off his .22 caliber pistol. "I got this."

After a moment of staring at each other as if waiting for a better idea to spontaneously pop up, they agree on the 'shoot the rat with a .22' plan. The two men approached the bedroom door with great trepidation. Mr. Ro's hand reached for the doorknob and he turned to Tommy and signaled him, finger to lip, to be quiet.

"Tommy, I'll swing the door open and you go in guns blazing." suggested Bugsy's father.

"Why do I have to go in first?" Tommy asked.

"Because you have the f***ing gun, Einstein." Mr. Ro emphasized logically.

"Here, you take the gun, then." offered Tommy.

"I don't want the f***ing gun. It's your f***ing gun." Mr. Ro argued back.

"I got to tell you, Mr. Ro. It feels just a little bit like I'm doing all the work here, you know." Tommy registered a desperate complaint.

"Hey, I'm the one opening the f***ing door. That's the critical part of the f***ing plan. The door don't open and the plan is f***ed. Capisce?" Mr. Ro answered firmly.

Tommy laid down his final conditions. "OK. But we both go in the room or I ain't doing this."

Mr. Ro raised his eyes to heaven and slowly turned the doorknob. The door swung open and they both slid inside the bedroom without a sound. The giant rat didn't seem to notice them until he was alerted by the coins rattling around in Tommy's trembling pockets.

At that point the rat turned toward them and stood on its rear legs. The beast seems to hover menacingly over both men. Its nose twitched rapidly. Tommy's gun hand shook so violently Mr. Ro realized he is not going to hit anything, except maybe himself. He grabbed Tommy by the collar and pulled him out of the room the door closed shut behind them.

"What the f*** is wrong with you, Tommy. You were supposed to shoot the rat." charged Mr. Ro.

"I think we need a bigger gun, Mr. Ro." Tommy explained with a defensive whisper. "If I hit him with this peashooter we're only going to make him mad."

Tommy, at that point, became a mound of tremors.

"You couldn't hit the f***ing thing with a f***ing cannon the way you're shaking" Said Mr. Ro.

Tommy's near convulsions caused the gun to point in dangerous directions

"Gimme the f***ing gun before you shoot yourself. We got to come up with some other idea." Mr. Ro whispered as he grabs the gun out of Tommy's hands.

Meanwhile, on the other side of the door, Bugsy was in disbelief. Were Tommy and his father really going to shoot him? He was so shocked that he couldn't even call out to them and explain who he was—Joey Roditore, the six foot rat.

The situation wasn't looking good, and it was bound to get worse. Bugsy had to find a way to communicate with them or to escape. Neither avenue was going to be without risk.

Tommy and Mr. Ro were just about recovering when Mrs. Ro returned. "Tommy, more coffee. You look so thin. Get more biscotti. You dip." She then looked fiercely at Mr. Ro. "Don't worry about the dishes, we'll keep them on the table."

Mr. Ro just raised his eyes.

DiDi comes in from the kitchen. She observed Joey was not present. "Where's Joey? Is the son-of-a-b**** still sleeping? I'll get him up, the f***ing bum. I'm coming to drag you out of there, Joey!" she screamed.

Mr. Ro and Tommy, after a delayed reaction, grabbed DiDi before she can get to the door. Tommy was pleased with the part of DiDi he was able to grab.

Mr. Ro ordered. "DiDi, come on, clear the table, please. Joey's on his way. Tommy, let go of DiDi's utensils."

As DiDi reluctantly returned to the kitchen, after Tommy reluctantly let go of her. Mr. Ro whispers to Tommy. "Hey, Tommy. Did you see Joey anywhere in the room with the rat?"

Tommy pondered an empty moment. "No, I did not, that you now mention it." Tommy replied.

One thought hit them both at the same time. Tommy was first to articulate it. "Mr. Ro, do you think that the rat ate Bugsy?"

Mr. Ro murmured back, "Well, he ain't there in person that we could see."

"F***ing ate him? Jesus!" screeched Tommy, who got a little loud with alarm. Mr. Ro had to stifle him. This unnerved Tommy more than anything else he had ever experienced—up to and including the time he went on a job with the Brutto boys.

The Brutto boys were four brothers—Frankie, Johnny, Jimmy, and Petey— who did a lot "special" work that nobody else didn't really want to take on. They had a good business, God bless them.

Alright, one day Primo wanted to put a scare into a guy so he got the Brutto boys to snatch him and teach him some manners. Primo told Tommy to go along.

Frankie said, so the guy can hear, "Let's take him to the sewer so the rats and snakes can eat him alive." Johnny and Jimmy started laughing the way that makes your blood pressure go up. Petey, who was the eldest, and never spoke, just nodded OK.

So the boys got this guy down in the sewers and stuck his head into a drain. Just to scare him, remember. And they were doing a great job. This guy was screaming, begging, and wetting his pants. He was going to do anything to be let up.

OK, so Johnny and Jimmy were holding this guy upside down in a sewer drain when all of a sudden this f***ing mountain crocodile from Tibet bit the guy's head off. This f***ing crocodile been swimming in the sewers all the way from Asia and took a wrong turn into town.

So now Johnny and Jimmy were holding this guy with no head upside down. Frankie was so p***ed off he went down the sewer after the crocodile and Frankie gets eaten. Petey dropped dead of a heart attack. Johnny and Jimmy got lost in the sewers and were never heard from again. Tommy (in shock) barely found his way out of the sewer and reported back to Primo who didn't believe a word of Tommy's story. Primo threatened to stuff Tommy in an oil can and dump him in the ocean, but then he cooled off. And that's why Tommy is alive, minus a couple clumps of hair that fell out.

Up until now, this was the worst most frightening event in Tommy's young life. Except, perhaps for, the giant rat thing that Tommy and Mr. Ro were trying to come to grips with. Which was maybe turning out to be possibly much worse.

As Mr. Ro and Tommy stood silent in front of Bugsy's room, Tommy broached another idea.

"Mr. Ro, I know how to get rid of this rat bastard which has f***ing eaten your son. I know a guy who's an extermination professional, not for squealers and punks, but for real bugs and pest stuff." Tommy excited by his new idea was barely able to keep it to a whisper.

"Is he any good?" asks Mr. Ro.

Tommy offered up credentials. "He once caught a crocodile in the sewers, no questions asked."

"What questions?" inquired Mr. Ro.

"About the head. A very discreet man, and very good at his job." explained Tommy.

"OK, call him." Mr. Ro said.

Tommy got to the phone to make the call. He passed DiDi who was now enraged that Tommy still hadn't got her brother out of his room.

"Tommy, you're f***ing useless." she said scornfully as she stormed past him and to Joey's door. DiDi opened a furious barrage of words.

"WHAT ARE YOU DOING IN THERE, JOEY? YOU F***ING RETARD!"

Once again her father pulled DiDi away and handed her over to her mother.

A half an hour passed and everyone was resigned to the fact that Bugsy wasn't going to make it to work this morning. Tommy tried to mollify everyone by saying he'd set it right with Primo.

To bide time Mrs. Ro nervously took refuge in the kitchen. Her mother's instinct told her something was wrong, but she was not quite ready to face what it might be. So she obsessively prepared, or over-prepared, for tonight's dinner—lasagna with meatballs with Bolognese sauce. Lots of it. In fact, enough for an entire U.S. Army airborne division.

Inside his room, Bugsy enviously caught the scent of his mother's food. Hunger and temptation were urging him to go out to the dining room and partake of the feast. Only his concern to avoid shocking his mother kept him in check.

Nervously he paced back and forth across the room, and took an occasional moment to gnaw on something in frustration. Bugsy too, didn't forget that some of the people out there wanted to kill him. He wondered if that might not be better for everyone all around. It was an existential moment for him.

He weighed his will to live against what the future held in store for him.

"Where can I go? What can I do? Being a six foot rat has its limitations." He thought.

Different possibilities came to him. None were very glamorous. For instance, he could be part of a psychology experiment bar pressing his way to sucrose solutions, or he could join a circus or zoo and give kids rides for a quarter. Politics could be a natural, but last resort.

It had been a half hour since Tommy made the call to the pest exterminator. The entire house was like a high tension wire ready to snap. Tommy and Mr. Ro had been nervously watching the dining room clock flanked by the portrait of Jesus and a crucifix.

Suddenly, there was a knock on the door. Mr. Ro bolted to answer it. On the stoop stood a boyishly handsome looking man whose feature and manners made people immediately judge him to be intelligent which was ironic because this man feared that people would find him mentally and physically hideous. He presented a business card to Mr. Ro. The card had only one word printed in large bold black letters—**TERMINESQUE**.

Mr. Ro ripped up the card and threw it away without looking at it. The young man and Tommy followed the torn pieces of the card as they fluttered to the ground.

"Look a**hole, there's only one thing I want to know. Who the f*** are you? And do you exterminate rats the size of Cleveland?" demanded Mr. Ro.

The young man answered. "I'm the exterminator, Kafka, but sometimes my mom calls me by my middle name, Wolfgang."

"Don't worry, Mr. Ro. He's a real pro. Although he never clipped two fat guys eating linguine de mar at the trattoria, he's our guy." Tommy replied.

Tommy face grew stern as he revealed the current predicament to Wolfgang, "OK, Wolvesfang, we have a very delicate situation here, and we don't want to disturb any more of the folks in the house. Except for us, of course. Got it?"

"Yeah, we both are already f***ing disturbed." Adds Mr. Ro.

"I see." Said the Exterminator, "This situation calls for extreme discretion. In that case, I won't use my real name."

Before any further explanations can be put forward, Mrs. Ro appeared to greet the new visitor.

"Oh, hello. I'm Mrs. Roditore." she explained.

"Hello, my name is Franz, but you can call me Kafka or Wolfgang. I would like to say I am from the Swiss Patent Office but my grasp of theoretical physics is far too weak, plus I comb my hair."

"Oh." Replies Mrs. Ro in perplexedly, "What kind of work do you do, Mr. Kafka?" Asked Joey's confused mom.

"Well, ma'am, I believe work is a useless endeavor. The universe surrounding us is far too vast to be comprehensible by mere human thought. Attempts to do so in any form are absurd because we do not possess the intelligence to say or know the value of anything or anyone we encounter with substantial understanding. Therefore, our entire existence is absurd. Though we cannot exist without the pretense of structure of perceived meaning, we are totally incapable of determining what that meaning might be. Thus the absurdity becomes ourselves," states Wolfgang/Kafka.

Mrs. Ro lost by Kafka's proclamation asked. "Ahh, have a biscotti, Mr. Kafka?"

Tommy turned to Mr. Ro. "Did I tell you he was good, or what?!"

The two men followed Mrs. Ro and Kafka into the dining room where Joey's mom introduced Kafka to DiDi who suddenly perked up at the sight of the young man.

"Mr. Kafka, this is my single unmarried daughter Loretta." Mrs. Ro said.

DiDi made a correction. "It's DiDi, Mr. Kafka."

"Oh, Mr. Kafka, I'm sorry, we call Loretta, DiDi. I don't know why. That must sound absurd to you." Mrs. Ro explained.

"I'm trying to process the information, Mrs. Ro. I should be quite confident to give you an evaluation of the absurdity of your statement momentarily," Kafka replied.

"Oh, Mr. Kafka, you sound like you are very intellectually spoken. I myself am hoping to pursue high educational achievement myself." DiDi pronounced, while she struggled to subdue her natural accent and foul mouth.

"Education is an impediment to free will, open thought and the growth of the mind," Kafka responded.

"That is so true, especially at $100 a credit. But, I too am interested in the mind. Thus explaining my hopeful application to hairdresser school." DiDi explained.

"Yes, very absurd," Kafka said and turned to Mrs. Ro in response to her earlier question.

Meanwhile DiDi adjusted her hair net with one hand and ever so slightly opened the top of her house coat with the other revealing some of her ample cleavage.

Kafka didn't notice but instead showed interest in the biscotti on the table.

"You dip them." DiDi said in her sexiest voice.

While DiDi and Mrs. Ro happily hovered about him filling his dish, Tommy and Mr. Ro looked annoyed, especially the slightly jealous Tommy.

"Look at the f***ing guy. Not here for five minutes and bogarting all the dames," Tommy complained. He then grabbed Kafka by the ear and pulled him from the table towards Bugsy's room.

"Hey, como si chiama, the problem is in there. Get to f***ing work." Tommy commanded as he shoved the exterminator through the door. "And remember—DISCRETE!"

The door closed behind Kafka. Tommy and Mr. Ro looked at each other and then put an ear to the door expecting to hear a commotion, screams, or both. There was nothing.

Minutes passed. Silence was the only sound.

"Maybe he took a heart attack?" Guessed Tommy.

"I didn't the body hit the floor." Countered Mr. Ro.

"Maybe the rat revived him." Tommy speculated.

"Tommy, huh. Make some f***ing sense. Please." scolded Mr. Ro.

This conversation ended just as Kafka calmly walked out of Bugsy's room. Unbeknownst to anyone, Mrs. Ro and DiDi joined the others. Their appearance surprised Tommy and Mr. Ro, but the two men were over anxious to hear what Kafka had to say.

"Well?" anxiously inquired Mr. Ro.

Kafka took a deep breath before he presented his analysis to the eager patrons.

He began. "Folks, you have, what we call in the business, a Die Verwandlung Ungeheuren Ungeziefer"

Tommy quickly protested, "Yo, watch your f***ing mouth. There are f***ing ladies present."

"Sorry." apologized Kafka.

"Tommy, calm down." Mr. Ro tried to restore some order so he could ask Kafka. "What the f*** is this Wandering Anhieser Unghoofer thing?"

Before Kafka could answer, Bugsy stuck his nose out the door unaware that his mother and DiDi were present.

DiDi screamed first, "What the f***!!!?"

Then both women shrieked in unison at the sight of the huge rat. Mother and daughter gripped each other in a terrified embrace. Tommy and Mr. Ro rushed to the aid of the women. Tommy comforted DiDi a little too personally and got slapped for his trouble.

He protested. "Hey, I got respectable intentions here."

Kafka places himself between the rat and his family to restore calm. "Please be calm, folks," he said.

Mr. Ro lashed out. "Calm, my f***ing a**. What the f*** is that thing?

Kafka drew a deep breath and said. "Wellll, this may be difficult for you. But I'm afraid," Kafka paused dramatically before concluding with a rapid flourish, "your son has turned into a giant rat. It's very existential."

Everyone stood mouth agape except Joey's mom. She hits the floor in a dead faint. No one realized she is down for a few moments. Then DiDi and Tommy went to her aid and gently helped steady the stunned woman.

Meanwhile Mr. Ro continued to aggressively question Kafka, "What the f*** are you talking about! How the hell can that f***ing piece of vermin s**t," Bugsy's father takes pause, and turned to the rat apologetically, "No offense." He turned back to Kafka and asked. "How can that thing be Joey? Stuff like that can't f***ing happen!"

"All evidence to the contrary." Kafka retorted, "Why don't you ask him?"

"What?" Mr. Ro couldn't seem to process this suggestion.

"Ask him." again challenged Kafka.

Before Mr. Ro could make the inquiry to the rat, Bugsy stood on his hind legs and attempted to lower his now high pitched squealy voice as much as possible. The situation was very difficult for him in so many ways, but he was finally able to speak.

"Papa, it's true. It's me, Joey. I've turned into a giant rat. Sorry."

Everyone was shell shocked by the confession coming out of the giant rat. DiDi and Tommy were so shaken they lost their grip on Mrs. Ro, and she crashed to the floor once again.

"F***!" DiDi and Tommy's cry out apologetically.

Partially regaining their senses, everyone (including the rat) rushed to Mrs. Ro's side. As they surrounded her, a concerned Bugsy stuck his twitching nose through the circle to make sure his Mom was OK.

Tommy brushed away the whiskers which grazed his face. Fear, however, was not his first worry. "Mr. Ro, we better call a doctor." he blurts.

Mr. Ro then countermanded Tommy's order, "No. Get the priest!"

Mrs. Ro came to for an instant. In a weak voice she murmured, "Get Father Angelo, not the Sicilian one. And DiDi, stir the tomato sauce."

She reached out to gently touch Bugsy's wet nose, and then closed her eyes. Tommy rushed to make the call.

Ten excruciatingly long minutes later, Mrs. Ro was propped up on the couch and forced a sip wine, but there was no denying that this turn had stolen her will to live and to drink in moderation. Even with time short, she didn't take loving eyes off her son, the rat who sits close by her side licking her hand. There is a morbid hush of death. Then the doorbell rings.

There is no need to answer it. It swung open and a petite woman, wrapped in a potpourri rainbow ensemble, burst into the house like a whirlwind assortment of Crayola colors.

"Leena's here and I brought cannoli!" she shouted gleefully holding out a tray of dessert pastry.

MR. Ro pointed an angry finger and said, "Leena the Gypsy, you are not welcome in this house!"

Unaffected, Leena replied. "Carmine, fratello mio, shut up and put on some pants!"

Tommy returns and excitedly announced. "The priest is on the way."

All went quiet at Tommy's announcement and everyone stands around looking at each other.

Leena broke the silence. "What's going on with the priest? And what's with the f***ing pony inside the house? Did I miss a birthday?"

DiDi took the question as an opportunity to vent her explosive rage, "What's going on is that my life just got flushed like a f***ing turd! Nobody will want me now."

Aunt Leena offered comfort, "Oh, DiDi, what is it now, hon?"

The comforting words only served to enrage DiDi more, "This is what it is! Suppose, I find some nice guy! 'Come on over and meet my family,' I says!' 'Sure,' he says! 'Allow me to introduce,' I says! This is my mother, this here is my father without pants, and this right here with the big teeth is my brother, Joey, who turned into a sceeve f***ing giant rat one day when he woke up! That's it, my guy he's out the f***ing door."

"DiDi, don't talk about your brother like that." Scolds Mrs. Ro.

Mr. Ro comes back with a counter-argument, "She's got a point, Connie. The kid has big f***ing teeth now."

DiDi vents like an active volcano, "He's got big teeth, you got no pants, and there's DiDi; no gentlemen callers; no beautician school; and no nothing! I just get old and wrinkled, become a f***ing spinster living with my parents, and catch arthritis because I have to shovel f***ing rat s*** every day for the rest of my f***ing life! Why? Because my brother became a motherf***ing rat! How can the man just turns into a giant f***ing rat!"

Aunt Leena just shook her head and offered a slice of her experience, "Oh, DiDi, you might as well learn this about men. Sooner or later they all turn into motherf***ing rats, Dear."

Through all the commotion, Bugsy sat quietly at his mother's side. He only partially attended to the surrounding exchanges. True, he was becoming less and less able to understand their words. However, he could acutely sense the anger and agitation in their tones and gestures. He wished he could be alone with his mother, while it was still possible to be with her at all.

Suddenly Tommy, who had quietly melded into the background, jumped to alert, and bolted for the phone screaming with every panicked step. "J***'s f***ing C****t! Primo! I forgot to call Primo!"

Tommy was frantic, and when frantic, performing simple tasks became monumentally difficult. One of those monumentally difficult tasks was dialing a telephone. Trying to connect to Primo, Tommy misdialed the number several times. He got an automated message—"Your call is very important to us."

"F*** you!" He responded to the recorded message. He redialed.

Next he got an Adult Swinger Service where a sexy female voice lured him with—"Hello, I'm Shawna. I'm naked, and I need a man to love me tonight."

Tommy, hung up, but not before he wrote down the Swinger Service number. On his third, and final attempt, he reached Primo.

"What?" Primo answered completely devoid of human phone courtesy.

"Primo! Primo!" Chattered Tommy.

"No, it's the f***ing Queen of England you f***ing imbecile," Primo snapped.

"Primo, Bugsy's a rat!" revealed Tommy Two Stripes.

"I know, you stupid f***. That's why I sent you to bring him in for taking care of," Primo replied.

"No, Primo. He's a real rat!" Tommy struggled to explain.

"And as a rat is why he needs extermination. F***ing capisce, s*** for brains?" Primo spoke with the accumulated elegance of a man comfortable with ordering the eliminations of injudicious associates.

"We called the exterminator, but he said it's a bad case of a hungoverlung something." Tommy provided additional details that were mostly unintelligible because of his manic emotional state.

"A**hole, you're supposed to be the f***ing exterminator!" Primo reiterated Tommy's assigned function in case there was a possible disconnect.

"We tried, Primo, but figured our gun wasn't big enough and would only get him mad." Tommy confessed.

Primo was momentarily silent on the other end (presumably in stunned disbelief).

"Gun was not big enough? I had not thought to ask this prior but, you do know you're supposed to shoot the gun, and not use it as a bludgeoning type device? And who, for the record, is WE?" Primo inquired.

Tommy responds, "Me and Mr. Ro."

"You had the guy's father with you to shoot him?" Primo's words were drenched in astonishment, "You are either the biggest f***ing moron in history or the most f***ing cold blooded son of a b**** ever."

Primo's words sounded severe to Tommy, but as he let them soak in a second, he thought it entirely possible that those words were meant as some sort of constructive feedback.

In the other room Aunt Leena and Mr. Ro could be heard in the background shouting at each other.

Primo was alerted by the unexpected noise, "What the f*** was that?"

Tommy replied, "That's Aunt Leena and Mr. Ro arguing. Evidently they had a falling out at some point and she isn't welcome in the house. But being that Mrs. Ro is dying because Bugsy is a rat."

Primo interrupted in a panic, "You told his mother that her son was a rat! J**** H. C****! What the f*** is wrong with you!?"

Tommy defended himself, "Primo, she can see he's a rat. He's as big as a Chevy."

There was more shouting between Aunt Leena and Mr. Ro.

Tommy explained the outburst before Primo asks, "That's just Aunt Leena and Mr. Ro again. He's letting her stay until the priest gets here."

Primo exploded at this revelation. "Wait a minute, what the f*** do you mean priest. Minchia! Madonna! You got the f***ing Roman Catholic Church involved!? Tommy, you mother***ing idiot! What are you selling tickets like this is a f***ing rock concert! Do you understand how a hit works? Discreetly, you dumb f***! You f***ing incompetent idiot!"

Tommy finally accepted that there were the dangerous signs in Primo's escalating tirade. He held the receiver away from him and covered the ear piece to mute what he knew was coming next—Primo's rant of Italian curses that would roar like the crashing waters of Niagara Falls.

Primo's muffled voice blurted out, "Miserabile Stronzo! Testa di cazzo. Coglione Leccaculo!"

Tommy grimaced through the barrage of foul language. He checked to hear if the invective was over, but there was still a stream of curses flowing through the phone.

The verbal parade of, "Figlio di puttana! Fanculo! Fottiti tu Pezzo di merda!" made Tommy cover the phone again.

Finally there was silence. Tommy cast a cautious glance at the receiver, half expecting it to produce a delayed parting outburst. There was none. Finally Primo was back on the line in what sounded like a somewhat more sedate state. ·

Primo spoke through gritted teeth, "Tommy, I see for you a nice vacation in Florida. Only, you will not be able to enjoy it as your head will be in another state altogether—in which you will not be. I find myself amused by that pun. I'm coming over to clip you and then the wings off Bugsy the canary."

"He's a rat." Tommy tried to clarify, hoping this would not be his final remark on the telephone.

Primo, with his total lack of telephone etiquette, slammed down the receiver. Tommy heard the fatal shattering of Primo's doomed phone.

Meanwhile, Leena walked about the room and introduced herself, by way of cannoli, to anyone she didn't know.

"Try a cannoli?" Leena offered Kafka. "You'll like them."

"That is an a priori assumption. It is not based on observation, which in itself is flawed since it must proceed through limited human senses which cannot guarantee the reality of the experience," replied Kafka.

"Speaking of experiences, did you ever have a frog swim up your Yooha while you were skinny-dipping? Believe you me, that's an experience you'll know is "real." Leena conveyed what she thought was a relevant image from Woodstock.

Kafka looked perplexed, "I'll try the pistachio one."

"Ooh, that's one's my Woodstock Special recipe." Leena said proudly. "That's where I got the frog up the Yooha." The little bastard stuck his head right up there."

"Human-Frog relationships are tenuous at best," confided Kafka as he took a bite of the cannoli, "This tastes really good."

"It gets better." explained Leena. She continued. "I know what you mean about frogs. I'm not saying I'd never have sex with an amphibian again, but

I think I'd like something deeper in the relationship, and not just up the Yooha. You know what I mean?"

"I'm not sure. Is there a buzzing in the room? I mean like the sound of flowers blooming," Kafka asked.

While Kafka made a very studious observation of his hand which he waved in front of his face, everyone else's attention was drawn to the latest ring from the Roditore doorbell. DiDi, still distracted by her doomed fate as a spinster, managed enough energy to answer the door. She was shocked out of her own misery to discover a priest at the door.

DiDi's only words were, "Oh my God, you're the Sicilian one!"

The priest dwelled a moment to absorb the strange greeting. "Well, I'm Father Palermo." he confirmed.

DiDi strained her neck to look behind the priest, evidently in hope that there was a non-Sicilian priest lurking behind the Sicilian one, "Where's Father Angelo?" she asked.

Father Palermo bore the sad tidings, "He has a Bingo tournament today. Now what seems to be so urgent?"

DiDi hesitated before answering. "Well, my mother is dying, Father, but this might kill her first."

"Has she requested Extreme Unction?" asked Father Palermo

DiDi couldn't hide her distress, "She's going to have an extreme unction when I tell her you're the one they sent. Follow me, Father."

DiDi reluctantly led Father Palermo inside and whispered under her breath, "F*** S***!"

Kafka intercepted DiDi and the priest before they got to the parlor where Mrs. Ro was dying or would die when she saw Father Palermo. DiDi was actually glad to have Kafka take the priest off her hands while she figured a way to announce the presence of a Sicilian in her mother's own house.

"Hi, I am become Kafka, the destroyer of pests. Dig the cool Nehru jacket, man. Krishna rules, man! Frogs suck, though." Kafka said with a relaxed smile and bleary eyes peeping out from under heavy spiked Woodstock cannoli eyelids.

Father Palermo looked sideways at this odd little man paraphrasing the Bhagavad-Gita.

Kafka, who now clung to the tray of cannoli, offered one to the priest, "Hey, Father, try one of these babies. They're really, really good."

Out of politeness Father Palermo accepted and took a bite.

Seeing a new face in the house, Aunt Leena came up to introduce herself
but Kafka did the honors.

"Father," Kafka then did an aside to Leena, "Don't let 'father' fool you,
he is definitely celibate." Then back to the priest, "May I present Aunt Leena
who brought the cannoli?"

Leena jumped in before the priest could utter a word. "I was excommunicated from the Church because when I was six I brought a canary to
Sunday mass. It got away and pooped on the Blessed Mother Mary."

"Oh, my." responded Father Palermo.

Mr. Ro's radar caught the key word 'canary' from all the way across the
room, he dashed to the priest's side to offer his testimony.

"Don't go listening to her about canaries, Father. She killed my pet bird.
That's why I hate my sister. She's a gypsy!" Mr. Ro accused.

"A gypsy, Carmine?" Leena protested.

"And a tramp! And that's the truth." Mr. Ro responded.

"The truth! You want the truth, Carmine? Okay, let me give you the
f***ing truth, the whole f***ing truth, and nothing but the f***ing truth,
bastiacho! Father, my brother Carmine here, never wore pants around the
house, even as a kid. Our mother, God rest her soul, blamed the f***ing
canary for some reason. Plus the G** D***ed bird would always s*** on
the dinner plates. That's why she cleared the f***ing table so fast before we
finished eating. She wanted the f***ing bird dead, Carmine," Leena raged.

"That's a f***ing lie! My mother loved that bird. I saw her kiss it on the
day you f***ing killed him!" Mr. Ro argued back with equal venom.

"That kiss, Carmine, was the f***ing bacio della morte, Carmine. The
kiss of death. Momma, gave the f***ing bird the motherf***ing bacio della
morte! She wanted the f***ing bird dead that day! She put a hit on the
f***ing canary! And I was the motherf***ing hitman." Leena vented years
of frustration with that expose.

At this point, Father Palermo's face had turned three shades of crimson
beyond whatever normal color his face had been when he arrived.

"You f***ing lie!" Was all Mr. Ro could say.

"I was the hitman, Carmine, but I couldn't do it and I let the f***ing
bird free in church. How the f*** was I supposed to know the f***ing bird

would s*** on the Blessed f***ing Mary's statue? That's why I was f***ing excommunicated at f***ing six years old, Father. Six f***ing years old for trying to save the f***ing life of that son of a b**** of a b****** motherf***ing canary. Mamma, that's who killed your precious f***ing bird, Carmine! Now you know! God, that felt good getting that s*** out of my f***ing system." Leena finished her therapeutic tirade.

Father Palermo, could only make the slightest of nods in acknowledgement. It wasn't so much as being paralyzed by the bizarre behavior of the people around him, as it was by the strange buzzing sensation that was brewing up inside him.

Mr. Ro stood in stunned silence as the story crawled into his brain. Finally, he too burst into sobs.

"Momma! Momma! Why, Momma? Why?" he said, tears streaming down his face.

Everyone stood and watched as Mr. Ro descended into a weeping state of oatmeal.

While the canary story was still spinning around inside people's heads, Tommy approached the congregation around Father Palermo. "Tell me, Father, please. You're not Sicilian, are you?" Tommy asked.

Searching for an appropriate reply (and finding none) Father Palermo responded, "Somebody sent for a priest, and here I am." The priest was surprised by the blurred sound of his own words.

"Sorry, Your Honor, but I'm going to have to frisk you," Tommy announced.

The priest's head was starting to ache from deluge of the bizarre exchanges. He was certain that Jesus had sent him into a nest of escaped lunatics from some asylum. It was a test of his faith. A test foretold to him at seminary. However, Father Palermo wasn't sure even God could cook up something like this. Just to be safe, the priest kept looking over his shoulder to see how far away he was from the door. The oddest thing about the situation was that he was actually feeling pretty mellow about the whole affair. In fact, he was feeling pretty mellow about everything now that he thought about it.

"How do you like the cannoli?" inquired Kafka
"This is really good!" the priest replied.

"Wait, it gets better. Hey man, want to see the giant rat?" asked Kafka.

"Cool." Father Palermo thought he, or someone like him, replied.

On the couch, Mrs. Ro's breathing was shallow, and her face was pale. Her son, the rat, sat at her feet monitoring her ever more faint heartbeats. DiDi, with delicate steps, approached her mother lying so still on the couch. Her attention, however, was drawn to her brother.

"Joey, you're squatting. I swear to God, if you have to take a dump, do it in your own room, God D*** it! I'm not in a hurry to be an old maid." DiDi snarled.

"DiDi!" Mrs. Ro scolded in her weak voice.

Mrs. Ro struggled but could barely open her eyes a crack. "DiDi, is the priest here?"

"Yes, Momma." DiDi answered.

Mrs. Ro's eyes were finally too heavy to keep open. But she managed a whisper, "DiDi, tell Father Angelo to come in and give me the last rites."

DiDi hesitated and struggled for an explanation, "Momma." She chokes out, "Momma." She tries again with no more success.

The air was frozen in anticipation of DiDi's words. Even Bugsy who by then could only comprehend speech with great difficulty was anxious.

DiDi started again. "Momma."

"Still here, DiDi." Mrs. Ro responded.

"Momma. Father Palermo is here to see you." DiDi finally got the words out and then braced for their impact.

Mr. Ro groaned and buried his head into his hands. Bugsy, who managed to process his sister's statement, started "eeking," Mrs. Ro's eyes opened.

"Madonna mia! There's a Sicilian in my house! DiDi, hang all the crucifixes!" Mrs. Ro screamed in a now DEFCON 1 state of alert. She made a bee line for the kitchen.

Everyone rushed back into the room to the source of the disturbance. As DiDi bolted to the crucifix supply in the hallway closet, she caught her father's eyes.

"Papa, I told Momma the Sicilian priest is here." DiDi said as she blitzed by Mr. Ro.

"Oh, f***." Mr. Ro's responded. "Connie what the f*** are you doing? You're dying for C****t*s sake. Lay down before you hurt yourself."

"All these people. I got to make dinner or they'll think I'm lazy. Especially the you-know-what priest." Explained Mrs. Ro.

On her way to the kitchen, Mrs. Ro mumbled in an agitated tone. "Ubriaco muto! Perche mi pestate con I Siciliani?"

Bugsy was still emitting high frequency eeks, which set off the barking of neighborhood dogs. Drained of his last ounce of patience Mr. Ro turned to his rat-son, "Joey!" He snapped while drawing his finger across his throat. "Cut that the f*** out before you set off a Civil f***ing Defense alert." Worn and lost, Mr. Ro chased after his wife. "Connie, what the f*** is it with you and the Sicilians?"

Kafka and Father Palermo drifted nonchalantly into the dining room and exchanged philosophical questions.

"I'm not blaming Him mind you, Father. But did he know frogs were like that when he made them?" queried Kafka.

Father Palermo lingered a long moment, then dramatically drew himself up to speak. "What was the question, man?"

"Frogs." Kafka reminded him.

"Oh, he needed them for some biblical curse or plague, or something." supposed the priest.

Kafka absorbed the answer. "That explains a lot. OK, how about the soul?"

The priest asked for clarification, "Like for shoes?"

"What was the question?" asked Kafka.

As Father Palermo entered the living room, he laid eyes on Bugsy for the first time and mistook the giant rat for Mrs. Roditore.

"My Mrs. Roditore, you look so different. New hairdo, lose weight, grow a tail?"

The priest looked to Kafka in confidence and whispered. "This looks bad. We're going to need lots of crucifixes."

DiDi, just back from hanging all the extra crucifixes about the house, overheard this diagnosis. "More! F***! We got more f***ing crosses than the f***ing Vatican! For C*****'s sake, any more crucifixes and we'll have them coming out our f***ing a**holes!" DiDi complained.

"Ah, DiDi, I assume we'll see you at confession Saturday?" Father Palermo's asked while he was picking butterflies out of the air. It was more of a suggestion than a question.

"Yes, Father." DiDi said remorsefully.

DiDi about faced and returned to the crucifix repository. She made a parting protest under her breath. "S***! Another f***ing Saturday shot."

Father Palermo slowly moved closer to Bugsy and knelt beside him. "Mrs. Roditore, I'm sure everything will be fine, but to be safe, we're going to administer Extreme Unction. In your case Really Super Extreme Unction. Now I didn't bring any Holy Anointment Oil with me, but if you have some WD-40 around the house, that will be fine. I won't tell the Pope if you don't, OK?" Father Palermo snickered.

"Is someone going to look for the WD-40?" Asked Father Palermo.

DiDi, with her arms filled with crucifixes, wanted to know why her mother, who was dying, just sprinted past her on the way to the kitchen.

"What the f***ing is going the f*** on?" DiDi exclaimed, dropping the crucifixes and stomping off after her mother.

"It might be best to come early on Saturday, DiDi," Father Palermo called after her.

Father Palermo patted Bugsy on the head and then rose to his feet.

"Don't worry, Mrs. Ro." The priest addressed Bugsy. "They're getting the WD-40 now."

Kafka took Father Palermo aside, and attempted to clarify the situation.

"Man, that big mouse looking thing is not the lady of the house, man. That's her first born that turned into a giant f***ing rat." Kafka explained.

"J**** H. C****! It's a Die Verwandlung Ungeheuren Ungeziefer!" gasped the priest. "How biblical!"

"You've seen this before, Padre?" A question came from a surprised Kafka.

"If I only had a nickel." reported the priest.

"Wow!" exclaimed a shocked Kafka.

"It's not all catechism and bingo in the Church, my son." clarified Father Palermo to the amazed Kafka. "We also cast out demons, perform exorcisms, and do castrations, you know. The Church has a wild side."

"Well, I've got nothing for this sitch, Father." Kafka confessed, "What's the wild side got, dude?"

Father Palermo contemplated a moment, then pronounced his judgement, "More cannoli!"

Arm in arm Kafka and the priest joyfully danced their way through imaginary clouds and rainbows back to Aunt Leena's magical dessert tray.

Mr. Ro sat on the couch about to give up any hope of sanity prevailing.

Tommy turned to Aunt Leena and asked. "What the f*** is in those cannoli?"

Aunt Leena simply smiled and said softly, "Something wonderful."

Tommy, Mr. Ro, and Bugsy, the giant rat, just looked at each other with blank exhausted expressions. Bugsy emphasized the moment with a closing eek.

"You got that right, Bugs." Tommy agreed.

Outside a sinister figure loomed in the shadows observing the Roditore home from across the street. He cast down a cigarette and crushed its life out beneath his shoe. The man then made his way to the alley behind the house and cautiously approached silently looking for an entry.

Through an unlocked back door the menacing figure quietly slipped inside. None were aware of his presence in the house. None, except Bugsy, whose twitching nose and heighted sense of scent detected the intruder.

Bugsy removed himself from the others to investigate and intercepted the phantom visitor in the hallway. As the uninvited man rounded the corner holding a weapon, Bugsy stood on his back legs extending himself upwards to the full length of his six feet.

Standing in front of a giant rat, the last thoughts in Primo's head before he fainted went something like this, "That's a big f***ing rat. This is a small f***ing gun. There's a lot of f***ing crucifixes."

Primo came to just as Mrs. Ro announced that the table is set and ready for dinner. His first words were, "What the f*** was that f***ing thing?"

As if to answer the question himself, Bugsy stuck his nose in Primo's face.

"J****!" Primo shouted in alarm.

"Take it easy. That's Bugsy that turned into a f***ing giant f***ing rat I was telling you about." Tommy explained.

"J****!" Is all Primo could utter.

"Like I was telling you, a rat." Tommy reiterated.

"J****!" Primo repeated.

"Yeah, he's a rat. Not a f***ing canary. Capisce?" Tommy emphasized.

"My sister didn't kill my canary. It was my own mother. Momma, Momma, why?" Mr. Ro started his sobbing again, this time comforted by Leena.

"J****!" Primo said redundantly.

Tommy suggested to Primo. "Have a little wine, Primo."

Primo was pale as he sat up. He looked around trying to determine if he was in a dream. Everything looked normal except for the giant six foot rat. That was about to change as Father Palermo and Kafka came up to him with a tray of cannoli.

"Blessings my son. Have one of these," offered the priest.

"What the f*** is this?" Asked Primo warily.

"Something wonderful," said Father Palermo.

Mrs. Ro's brought out the food and laid it on the table. Soon early lunch was in full swing as everyone found their spot. Mangia is the word of the day. Both wine and compliments to the cook flowed freely.

Primo proclaimed, "Mrs. Roditore, this lasagna is the best I've had since my mother died."

"Connie made it while she's dying." Mr. Ro proclaimed proudly.

"Same with my mother. We had to put her out of her misery right after. Badda Bing." Primo made a gesture of putting a gun to his head, "Poor woman. God rest her soul." Primo concluded by making the sign of the cross.

Tommy took the opportunity to introduce Primo to any unfamiliar faces.

"Primo, this here guy staring at the ceiling is Father Palermo." Introduced Tommy.

"It's the Sistine Chapel. Listen." Greeted Father Palermo.

"The little guy pondering the eternity of existence with his toes is Kafka the exterminator. Kafka, meet Primo." Tommy said.

"I understand reality, eternity, and existence now. It was all in my sweaty little pinky toe. Wanna see? It's existential!" Claimed Kafka.

"No thanks. It might also be odiferous. The exterminator, hah. Say, who have you clipped? Maybe I've heard of your work." Primo asked.

Kafka looked up to reveal a sock stuck up one nostril. The vision was as odd as a man who studiously examined his toes can be.

Primo's head was surrounded by a wondrous tunnel of spinning colors that seemed to rob him of any inhibition.

Primo started, "Once, I got these guys in Brooklyn that got to go. When the job is over, I throw them a big funeral like I was pals with the sons-of-b****es. But I really don't give a f*** about either of them. I reused the caskets cause there ain't no real bodies in there. Those guys are chopped up and in the river someplace." Primo concluded.

Mr. and Mrs. Ro, DiDi, and Aunt Leena wore stunned expressions. Kafka, Father Palermo, and Bugsy were cool with the story. Primo looked at the Roditores and donned a puzzled face himself.

"What?" he asks.

DiDi turned to her father.

"Papa, f***ing Willard, over there, keeps staring. Its f***ing freaking me out. Cut it the f*** out, Joey!" She accused.

"DiDi! Stop it." Scolds Mrs. Ro, who turned an affectionate apologetic look at her son. Mrs. Ro continues, "Carmine, he's hungry and we're all eating. I'm going to feed him."

"Connie, you always spoiled that God d*** kid since he was a baby." Mr. Ro said annoyed.

"Give him some garbage. That's what rats eat." DiDi said caustically.

"DiDi, I swear," scolded Mrs. Ro sharply. That tone was enough to cow DiDi and bring silence to the table.

Then a shot rang out.

Primo held a smoking gun in his hand. Kafka was hopping madly about on one foot.

"He asked me to do it. His reality toes was getting way too extraessential for him." Primo explained in his own defense.

"Hey, you know what, I feel real good so let me tell you what I'm going do since I misunderstood Bugsy over there and I feel bad upon it. Carmine, forget what you owe. It's all good, and I want to get you a job in my employ down at the pizza place. You don't have to wear no pants either." Primo said to the oohs and aahs of an appreciative audience.

"Also, Tommy. For you a promotion and your own crew. You're a made man now, Gumba." Primo offered to a beaming Tommy.

DiDi now looked at Tommy in entirely different light. They both have beaming smiles. Suspicious, Mr. Ro glances under the table.

"Tommy, get your God d*** hand off her leg." He growled. "DiDi sit over here."

Mr. Ro and DiDi exchanged places much to DiDi's reluctance. DiDi began to cry.

"Every f***ing chance I get to be something, I get pulled back the f*** in!" DiDi wailed.

Aunt Leena, now next to DiDi, gave her niece a comforting pat on the back. With tear filled eyes DiDi looked at her aunt.

"Tommy's moving up in the world now." DiDi defended her new man.

"The world is not what Tommy's trying to move up into, dear. Don't give up anything until you have the ring on your finger. And make sure it's real and not C.Z." Aunt Leena advised.

"Oh, OK." Responded DiDi, sobered by her aunt's wisdom.

The chaotic equilibrium is suddenly interrupted as Father Palermo jumped into the air and offered a prayer before the meal.

"Hallelujah! They say Man is born without a soul and it must be earned by good deeds and S&H Green Stamps! Somebody shoot me in the foot!" He cried out.

However, to prevent another shooting, Tommy and Mr. Ro successfully took the gun out of Primo's trigger itchy hands.

Bugsy took all of this in, but to him it was just a rush of motion and a blur of sounds, fewer and fewer of which he seems to understand. His only focus was on his mother. All the while she was busy serving and making sure everyone has plenty on their plate, she looked at him with a tender sadness. He hoped he hadn't brought grief to her.

He only vaguely remembered now his life without whiskers and a tail. However, that memory seemed to be fading, as his repertoire of behaviors became dominated by his rodent self.

Unlike Kafka, Bugsy grasped this reality without having to contemplate any missing toes. He was losing the connection to his family. Losing, in fact, his connection to humanity.

Kafka, by the way, continued to hop about the house bleeding.

For Bugsy, the time had come to leave, to take the first steps of an uncertain journey into an unknown world. This clarity arrived just as Father Palermo, to the horror of Mrs. Roditore, started flipping lasagna to the ceiling with the serving spatula. The purpose, ostensibly, was to feed the characters of the 'Last Supper' he saw above him.

"Come on, Adam. Catch! Good boy!" coached the priest as he readies another slice of Lasagna for the ceiling, "This one's for you Matthew."

Bugsy deemed it best to leave quietly and by the back door. He treaded softly down the back hallway past his old room, which now meant little to him. He stopped for one last look back. There at the end of the dark hallway was a glorious brilliance of light which silhouetted the loving figure of his mother holding the spatula she seized from Father Palermo and then used it to smack him in the face.

Bugsy stopped as his mother came up to his side.

"Where you going, Joey?" she asked.

Of everything he had lost, Bugsy didn't lose the comfort of the sound of his mother's voice. He could understand it and she could understand him. Maybe because those voices didn't come from their mouths, but from their hearts.

"I don't know where I'm going, Ma. Out there somewhere." Bugsy answered.

"But, they don't understand you out there, Joey. They might run you down, catch you, or kill you like your father's canary." his Mom said tearfully.

"That don't matter, Momma. Sooner or later they'll get me, I suppose." Bugsy reflected.

"What will you do, Joey?" Mrs. Ro asked in a trembling voice.

"I don't know, ma. I haven't thought things through yet. Maybe I'll try to make sense of what's happened. Maybe I can do some good, like raise awareness about animal usage in psychology experiments, or the cruelty of mouse traps. Maybe I can fight the things that give rats a bad name." Bugsy pondered aloud.

"I'm worried for you, Joey." Mrs. Ro said through her tears.

"Don't be, Ma. Could be the priest is right. A man, " Began Bugsy.

"Rat." Corrected his mother.

"A rat's got no soul, but has to earn it by doing good." Bugsy continued.

"Joey, that was your Aunt Leena's cannoli talking, not the priest. She's got LSD and whatever she brought home from Woodstock mixed in those things. That's why I never let her in the kitchen alone when I'm making sauce. God knows what she might spike the pot with." Bugsy's mom explained.

"Oh." Said Bugsy.

"But you were saying about good deeds? Never mind, where will you be?" Mrs. Ro asked with interest.

"If I can do good it won't matter, Ma. I'll be all around. I'll be everywhere where a man…"

"Rat." corrected Mrs. Ro again.

Bugsy continued. "Everywhere a rat is fighting cats in an alley, I'll be there. If an exterminator is laying traps in a refuse heap, I'll be there. I'll be the way raccoons can get into garbage cans even with fancy locks. I'll be the way birds pick at a dead flat rabbit on the side of the road. I'll be the way." Bugsy proclaimed.

"Got the concept, Joey." His mom interrupted.

"Well, that's the way it is, Ma. I guess it's goodbye. I love you." Bugsy said through his tears.

"I love you, Joey. I always will, mia amato figlio." Bugsy's mom's last words came along with a loving embrace that she was reluctant to release.

"Ma, OK, ma. Ma, it's good. Let go, ma. You're choking me. Ma!" Bugsy coughs out.

"Sorry, Joey. Joey, wherever you end up, call me. You know how I worry." Mrs. Ro begged.

Bugsy slipped away from one existence and scurries out the back door into the alley to another. He didn't look back. As he rounded the corner and blended into the night, he heard his mother's voice for the last time.

"Joey, If you hook up with a Sicilian girl, don't bother coming back here!" She warned.

THE END

Betty Clue: The Case of Chiddingfold College

Introduction

BETTY CLUE AND THE QUEEN

Betty Clue was a living breathing person who was nearly made immortal through the writings of none other than Queen Victoria. Betty and the Queen were college roommates at St. Lady Murray of Royal Trinity in Oxford.

PD-US

College roommates, Betty Clue and Queen Victoria of Great Britain.

It was in college that Betty gas lighted Victoria into believing the soon to be queen was actually living in a Hallmark Holiday movie. Betty also managed the royal regent's short but impressive collegiate wrestling career. Under Betty's tutelage, Victoria briefly grappled under the name of the Raging Royale and was the first European monarch known to have worn a Mexican wrestling mask.

It was during these lighthearted school days, Betty demonstrated and developed impressive if not impeccable skills in social etiquette, cribbage, and amateur sleuthing where she helped police solve ghastly murders and other crimes. Victoria faithfully documented Betty's investigations and turned them into a series of cozy mysteries. Unfortunately all of these were lost in the fires of the London Blitz.

37

The only surviving remnant of Queen Victoria's Betty Clue works is from a transcript of a live performance recorded by the Quinniwoonsockett Respiratory Theatre Players of Quinniwoonsockett Island, Maine, USA. This is believed to be the very first Betty Clue episode and is known as the Case of Chiddingfold College.

Other Betty Clue amazing accomplishments include: British Isles Knitting Award of Canterbury, England's Bank of Orient Crime Solver Honors, European Charcuterie Arrangement Gold Medalist, Honorary Senior Inspector of Scotland Yard, and Chair of Emily Post Etiquette Board of Directors.

THE QUINNIWOONSOCKETT RESPIRATORY THEATRE

Dr. Alger Hisssssss, director of the Quinniwoonsockett Pulmonary Clinical Institute, founded the Quinniwoonsockett Respiratory Theatre in 1909 as a therapeutic program for patients. Dr. Hisssssss felt that a creative outlet would be very valuable to patients, especially those whose experimental treatments went hideously awry.

The Quinniwoonsockett Respiratory Theatre Players originally included only patients, but through the decades roles were opened to doctors, staff, and private citizens as more of the island's population's health was affected by medical waste and radioactive contaminations pouring out of the clinic's defective sewer and venting systems.

The Quinniwoonsockett Respiratory Theatre also valiantly pushed on through several regretful production decisions that had tragic consequences:

- In the 1980 tragedy, a decision to forego cast swimming lessons for the "On Golden Pond" production lead to the drowning deaths of several extras.

- In 1992 another unfortunate production decision was made to hire real cannibals for the play, "The Donner Party."

- Finally, in 2017, came the most controversial resolution of all. A choice was made to perform "All Quiet on the Western Front" using live ammunition (see casting call flyer below). Thankfully, the opening night was not sold out resulting in fewer casualties than would have been expected. The play closed with only a one night run, and the producer was lynched.

Quinniwoonsockett Respiratory Theatre

Casting Call for

All Quiet on the Western Front

(With live ammunition—Military Background Preferred)

MEMORABILIA—CASE OF CHIDDINGFOLD COLLEGE

Reproductions of memorabilia saved from the Quinniwoonsockett production of the Betty Clue's 'Case of Chiddingfold College' are provided courtesy of the Woonsockett County Sheriff's Office's Criminal Archive division.

MARQUEE:

--------------------0--------------------

Presenting an original program written, directed, and performed by the

The Quinniwoonsockett Respiratory Theatre Players
In:

Betty Clue and the Case of Chiddingfold College
--------------------0--------------------

VARMINTS PET CENTER

PET TRAINING & HOUSEBREAKING

PIGEONS, ~~CATS~~, CHINCHILLAS, & OTHERS

THE RAT & MILDEW TAVERN
DRINKS AND DINING

*WE'RE MORE THAN JUST RATS & MILDEW
BUT NOT MUCH MORE*

HINKLE, DINKLE, WRINKLE, DINKLE, BINKLE, & BONG

LAWYERS AT LAW

WE'LL TAKE YOUR CASE. IF WE DON'T WIN, NO EXTRA CHARGE

THE RESPIRATORY PLAYERS

Agnes O'Edipal Tarboro
(Betty Clue)

The product of the two most inbred families in New England, Agnes has graced the stage of the Quinniwoonsockett Respiratory Theatre for over forty years.
Her portrayal of Blanche DuBois in the company's production of Henry V Part 2 was immortalized when critics wrote, "Where did that lady come from?"

PD-US

D.W. Orson Kurosawa
(Director)

This is D.W.'s third time working with the Quinniwoonsockett Theatre, and the first time with pay. His other collaborations include "Phantom of the Wawa" and the only company musical, "Les Miserables Cats."
Kurosawa is the director emeritus for the prestigious
Bangor Princess Camp for Little Girls with Excessively Rich Parents. He started his career as coordination of safety operations at the Three Mile Island nuclear plant.

Lorraine Wraith
(Jane Boufonte)

At eleven years old, Lorraine's sophisticated performances are as much a mystery as her shadowy emergence onto the shores of Quinniwoonsockett from the cold ocean and clinging fog. All that can be divined of her is a mesmerizing acting talent and the fact that cats die when they come near her. This may account for the poor critical and box office showing of "Les Miserables Cats."

PD-US

Quill Penrap
(Script Editor)

A frequent visitor to Quinniwoon-sockett Island, Quill has written over a dozen original plays for our Respiratory Theatre and at least four bad checks. Quill filled in parts of the Betty Clue script missing from the original text.
We believe him to be on the run from federal authorities, and he will not be present for tonight's curtain calls.

Ted (Set Design)

Ted is the first fully reformed serial killer in New England penal history. He has designed sets for every company production since the mysterious disappearance of our previous set designer in 2009.

PD-USGov-Military-Army

**Donald Reginal
(Colonel Beverly Doddering-
Blowhard)**

As the oldest and only surviving founding member of our company. Donald has been a part of the Quinniwoonsockett "process" from 1964 to 2016, when he lost his mind. Thanks to rehabilitation and robust chemical therapy, Donald has regained his place onstage with vigor.
While he can't learn his lines, rambles, and frequently wanders offstage, audiences love his endearing improvisational style.

**Drake Gander
(Phlegming Walloon &
The Manager)**

Drake is one of the few transvestite transgenders on Quinniwoonsockett Island. Drake's gender/apparel flexibility has dramatically widened not only his/her range, but also the scope of material that the Theatre can address.
Drake's credits include the show stopping engagement in "Tess of the D'Urbervilles" where he played both Tess and the D'Urbervilles to critical acclaim.

**Loreen Lushtic
(Lady Beatrice)**

Loreen is an inspiration not only to insecure method actors but also to anyone who has ever had untreatable psychological or addiction issues.
When not acting or being incoherent, Loreen is a fully licensed contract killer. She is currently engaged to Ted.

**Vava Va Voome
(Souzette Crepes)**

Ms. Va Voome has as played as many roles offstage as she has played on. She is the island's librarian, trapeze artist, and French style-massage therapist. She has portrayed characters ranging from the girl-next-door (Bride of Frankenstein's Roommate) to a femme fatale (The Postman Only Delivers Milk).

Dimitri Atramentous
(Aristotle Necrosis, DJ)

The first and only foreign member of the Quinniwoonsockett Respiratory Theatre. He is classically trained, having performed in a plethora of local TV commercials and personal appearances for Noon's Nails, Quinniwoon Medical Services, and until recently, Quinniwoonsockett Dentistry, Inc.

PD-US

Rasil Dasil-Bathbone
(Constable "Cobbles" Earwick)

The owner of Auto-Mate, Rasil has followed his passion for acting ever since falsely testifying on court TV. As a sponsor of the Respiratory Theatre, he has forced his way into every production since 2004. Offstage, Rasil works tirelessly for charities that aid those not fortunate enough to have hyphenated surnames.

ACT 1

INT—WINTERSDON ARMS—MORNING

The Wintersdon Arms is a combination inn, Asian smokehouse, and center for modern British barbeque. It is located in the Surrey village of Chiddingfold, UK, but would be just at home on State Route 281 near Brownsville, Texas. In other words, it borders on the edge of the Twilight Zone.

A breakfast buffet is being set up by the MANAGER (50), a portly gentleman wearing a MAGA hat and a "We Blow Stuff Up" tee Shirt. No guests have yet arrived.

ENTER BETTY CLUE (50) and following close behind is INSPECTOR SERGEANT EARWICK (45) of the police. Betty sets foot on stage to a STANDING OVATION that lasts nearly a minute. She gently nudges Earwick behind her so that she can absorb the audience's affection alone. She acknowledges their appreciation with a graceful bow. The Manager and Inspector stand by with mildly annoyed expressions and dejected postures. They finally reluctantly join in the clapping more out of embarrassment than appreciation.

Betty Clue is the model of poise, propriety, and perseverance. In addition to her perfectly coiffed bouffant hair and piercing blue eyes, she wears a tastefully plain tweed jacket, tan skirt and practical brown shoes. She looks as if she has just adjourned from a pheasant hunt. However, her willful air leads one to consider the possibility that instead of shooting the birds, she cowed them into surrendering voluntarily.

Inspector Earwick, on the other hand, even in his dark blue police uniform decorated with shining buttons, badges, and blood donor pins, does not inspire a great deal of confidence. He is simply Betty's shadow—as officially noted in his job description.

Betty straightens out a pin and lifts a piece of lint from the Inspector's tunic. She then approaches the Manager with her resolute yet delicate stride. Before she addresses the man, Inspector Earwick shows his Diner's card mistaking it for his police ID card. He corrects his mistake with some embarrassment. Allowing the Inspector to proceed, Betty's attention is drawn to the counter. She runs her gloved finger along the top and looks unpleasantly at the dusty substance she has swept up.

INSPECTOR   Police, sir.

BETTY   Good morning, sir. May I use your phone? We have no signal.

MANAGER   Why do you assume I have a phone? If I may ask.

BETTY   A phone seemed a natural presumption.

MANAGER   Is that how you do your police work—by presuming? What about investigation, evidence, and facts?

BETTY   The facts are that your marquee outside advertises for one to call for reservations and lists a telephone number to do so. Presumably this occurs via telephone and not telepathy.

MANAGER   Of course I have a phone. Wouldn't be in the bloody twentieth century if I didn't. What you want it for, then?

INSPECTOR   This is official police business I will add, sir.

MANAGER   Ooh! Not just regular police business. Official police business. Well, la-dee-dah. Going to solve a big caper, are we?

INSPECTOR   As a matter of fact.

MANAGER   Will I be getting some of the reward? After all it is my phone that cracked the case.

INSPECTOR   You'll be getting cracked on the head, if I don't see some cooperation soon, lad.

BETTY   More importantly, sir, you should start wiping down this counter top! It's dreadful and I'm sure would not stand up to a health department inspection.

MANAGER   Alright, alright. Don't jump out of your knickers.

The Manager reaches behind the bar and places a two tone green phone set on the counter.

MANAGER   Here it is, folks. A British Telecom General Post Office model GPO 706 rotary dial telephone set. Introduced in 1959, the 706 features internal designs of either printed circuit or wiring loom. It comes with metal or plastic baseplates, metal or plastic dials, and optional carrying handle.

INSPECTOR   Very impressive. Do you have any other color available?

MANAGER   I'm glad you asked, Officer.

BETTY   I'm not. However, the GPO-706 comes in seven colors. In addition to the two-tone green, they are two-tone grey, ivory, black, topaz yellow, lacquer red, and concorde blue. The two-tone grey would be the color of choice. If you please, sir, hand over the phone.

At the moment of the question, the manager pulls out a display case with several GOP 706 sets in different colors. The manager gives Betty the two-tone grey set while Inspector Earwick browses the remainder of the collection with interest. He is trying to make up his mind about a color selection.

MANAGER   Have you ever used one of these telephone devices before, ma'am? Really simple operation if you haven't. Let me give you a brief tutorial.

BETTY   That will not be necessary. And you should consider a change of shirt. A clean fresh one would go a long way in fostering the appetites of guests. Though you serve messy American foods, there is no reason for you to look like an American.

Betty takes the phone and prepares to dial under the prying eyes of the Manager. Betty's sharp glance beneath a raised eyebrow sends him sulking away to engage the Inspector in conversation.

MANAGER   Inspector, if you're nearby, Tuesday is Thermonuclear Hot Wings night served with our special secret ingredient.

INSPECTOR   Which is?

MANAGER   Radioactive Iodine-131. Our cook had some extra pills left over from his goiter treatment so he throws in a couple for the sauce. Now none of our customers have any thyroid problems.

Betty dials her party's number and waits for the connection.

BETTY   To whom am I speaking? Yes, I know this is your personal number Superintendent Brackishwater but you have a number of violations against good phone etiquette.

| BETTY | First, you did not answer within three rings, second, you did not identify yourself as a professional courtesy, and third you are not speaking clearly. Shall we try again, Superintendent? Very well, but be more mindful in the future as I'm sure we will be in constant phone contact in the upcoming days. I would hate to hand out demerits. As you have already surmised, this is Betty Clue. Inspector Earwick and I will be delayed in arrival as our vehicle has malfunctioned in Chiddingfold. Even at this remote location, however, I believe I can assist you with the solution to the crime, provided you can list the basic details of the case.
(aside to Inspector Earwick)
Inspector Earwick, will you please note these items in your pad as I relay them? |

(a beat)

The Inspector takes out his note pad and pen. He checks to be sure the pen is able to write. It is not and he spends the time he should be writing Betty's dictations by fumbling, shaking, and scribbling with the pen in an effort to make it work.

| BETTY | I see, the King Edward's Prep Headmaster Humbert Hungerdunger murdered. Head splattered. Founded by Kind Edward VI.
Accommodating students ages 8-12 on site.
Er, Superintendent, these are not all relevent facts, sir.
Yes, I realize the brochure is handy to you now, but...
Oh alright, go ahead.
Co-ed since 1952. President is Duchess of Gloucester—without tiara.
(a beat)
Close to the Witley mattress recycling center and Hambleton FC field. Hambleton with a strong second half now stands with a record 8 and 3. |

BETTY   (a beat)
                     Yes, this should be sufficient. Goodbye Superintendent.

Betty hangs up on the call to the Superintendent. The Inspector's pen only now becomes operational. However, it is far too late to be of any use to take Betty's information. While the Inspector fumbles a photo over the counter draws Betty's attention.

BETTY   This picture over the counter. Who are the individuals?

MANAGER   Why that is the Headmaster of King Edward's, our very best patron, myself, our head waitress Minnie, and a man who claims to be AEthelred the Unready King of England from 978 to 1016.

A small round of applause and whistles at the mention of AEthelred.

BETTY   And was the Headmaster's typical order, butcher's steak with bone marrow gravy?

MANAGER   Why, yes ma'am it was. How did you know?

BETTY   Not important now. I believe I have a solution to the Headmaster's murder. But first I must dial another party with your permission.

Betty connects with the second party she dials.

BETTY   Hello, Mrs. Bumblenoggin. Betty here. Very well, thank you, (a beat) and you are doing well also. Wonderful to hear that. Now, Mrs. Bumblenoggin, for Thursday's tea, please put out the white embroidered table cloth and the new blue napkins in a Rosebud fold. Not in the garden, dear. On the table. There will be places for four. (a beat). No, people. On the table, dear (a beat). The one at my house (a beat) where you are at the moment. Very good, Mrs. Bumblenoggin.

| BETTY | Thank you so much. Goodbye (a beat). No, dear, you are not going on a trip. It is just a common courtesy ending to a call. Yes, on a phone. Goodbye. |

Betty then redials the phone to contact Superintendent Brackishwater at King Edward's.

| BETTY | Superintendent, very much better receipt of the call. Betty Clue here. You will find your murder suspect among the students. She will be wearing a pilly school uniform, perhaps turned inside out. She is approximately 30 years old, blonde with black roots. She does not carry the Oxford Book of English Verse in her book pack, but rather receipts for several butcher steak meals from the Wintersdon Arms, and, of course, the murder weapon. Very good, she's your killer. You're quite welcome. |

| INSPECTOR | How did you solve the case so quickly, Betty? |

| BETTY | Quite obvious, Inspector, the picture over the counter was key. This photo shows Headmaster Hungerdunger, the manager, and the head waitress. The dish holds the remnants of butcher's steak, the check on the table indicates the end of the meal, and note the sour expression of the waitress. |

| INSPECTOR | And who is the other gentleman in the snap? |

| BETTY | Someone who claims to be AEthelred the Unready. |

Again a small round of applause and whistles for AEthelred.

BETTY	Also notice the menu where butcher's steak is the only item that does not have a fixed price. Therefore, the amount of tip cannot be determined regularly. From the expression on the waitress's face, I would gather that the tips left by the Headmaster were far less than her expectations. Since the Headmaster was a regular here, the loss in revenue to Minnie over time must have been substantial. This formed the motive for her homicidal vengeance.
MANAGER	But Minnie has been in a coma for two years.
BETTY	Really. May I have the phone again, please?

Betty redials the Superintendent.

BETTY	Superintendent. Betty Clue here. The suspect I pointed out may not be who we are looking for after all (a beat). Really. Shot while escaping. Yes, tragic. Of course, not your fault. If I have any further insights I will certainly ring you up. Goodbye.
INSPECTOR	Betty, the hackney has arrived to return us to the precinct.
BETTY	Not the precinct, Inspector, but a place in Chiddingfold that I have not visited since my youth. Direct the hackney that our destination is—Doubtend Abe.

CURTAIN

ACT 2

INT—THE DOUBTEND ABE—MORNING

Doubtend Abe, located in rural Surrey, England, has not weathered the years well. It is but a musty shadow of its younger self. The estate is named after two second world war pilots who were marooned and survived together on a tropical Pacific island. They were Captain Reginal Doubtend, RAAF, and Lieutenant Hiroto Abe (where Abe is pronounced Abby).

The manor's baroque banquet hall perhaps best symbolizes the mansion's decline. Today it plays host to a special event identified by the large mottled banner draped across the wide entryway to the hall. It reads:

1980 CURSED CHIDDINGFOLD
COLLEGE CLASS REUNION

Morbid arrangements of flowers sit on pedestals in every corner and free space available. They stand like morose guardians of an Unknown Soldier's Tomb. The overall ambiance holds less charm than a Department of Motor Vehicles waiting room.

On the longest wall, somber tables decorated with black streamers host empty chafing dishes, hopefully to be soon filled with multiple entrées, and bountiful platters overflowing with delicious desserts. On the wall itself are what look like yearbook snaps and graduation ceremony photos.

Only one large circular table is present on the floor. It has a wilted center piece, settings for five places, and a name tag for each setting. It should be mentioned, all who will attend the reunion, will be attired in mourning clothes.

The exception, swimming against the tide of morbidity, is a flamboyant and hyperactive DJ who sets up his equipment. He wears a fluorescent glittering jacket, skinny jeans, platform shoes, and enough bling to make the blind see. His hair is slicked back with enough petroleum product to match the total monthly oil production from Kuwait. His vocal checks shatter the sound barrier and most of the imported crystal drinking vessels.

| DJ | Testing! Testing! Sound Check! Get ready to Rock and Roll with your dream date from Auto-Mate!? Is the sound too tame? Let me crank it up, Class of 1980!!! |

ENTER (without fanfare) the handsome **DR. PHLEGMING WALLOON (30—Class of 1980).** Walloon looks about as if he was expecting some audience reaction to his entry. Recovering, he takes a seat at the lone table and immerses himself in the *London Times*. The **HEADLINES** of the paper are projected in a large **OVERHEAD DISPLAY** for the audience's view.

The display reads:

The London Times
Royal Goose of Pomerania "Ab-duck-ted'
Fowl Play Assumed!
Police efforts to find poultry in motion

ENTER JANE BOUFONTE (30—Class of 1980). Jane elegantly sweeps into the room accompanied by a very warm audience reception that is prompted by an overhead **FLASHING APPLAUSE** sign.
Walloon dons a surprised expression in response to the audience's reception for Jane. He turns and catches sight of the blinking 'Applause' sign behind him. He seems miffed that the sign was not engaged for his entrance.

| WALLOON | Good morning, Jane, darling. May I say you look simply smashing in your mourning attire. Are you prepared for the day's ceremonies? |

| JANE | I would never think to miss this occasion in honor of friends whose lives were tragically lost at our original graduation celebration. |

| WALLOON | Yes, the horror of it haunts me to this day. Fifteen young promising lives snuffed out by a flash of lightning. |

JANE	So dreadful, as were the twelve lost by food poisoning from the tainted fois gras.
WALLOON	Devastating. And then to lose nine more who drowned when the Porta Loos overflowed.
JANE	Tragic. As well the sixteen who were trampled to death during the false fire alarm.
WALLOON	Or the twenty who were simply swallowed when the earth opened up.
JANE	The four eaten by the tiger.
WALLOON	Ah yes, it was a Bengal if my memory is accurate.
JANE	I can't say, really. All those striped beasts look alike to me. Might have been a zebra for all that I know. Thankfully we have Varmint's Pet Center of Quinniwoonsocket to take the proper care of all our animal and pet needs.
WALLOON	Good point. And, of course, we must not forget that final tragedy of the one chap who simply exploded.
JANE	He did go off, did he not? So very sad to endure the many misfortunes on that ill-fated evening, especially since the weather was perfect for our event. Anything of interest in The Times, love?

Walloon holds the paper out for Jane's view. Instead, she reads from the overhead display, much to Walloon's confusion.

| JANE | Very clever wording for The Times. Quite droll. I enjoy puns so. |

| WALLOON | Very odd to have a royal goose, don't you think. Some side effect of Prussian inbreeding, I'm sure. |

Enter **COLONEL BEVERLY DODDERING BLOWHARD, Retired (30—Class of 1980).** The Colonel is in full dress regimental uniform. While only thirty, he looks to be about 105 years old.

| COLONEL | Morning. |

| JANE | Morning. |

| COLONEL | Morning. |

| WALLOON | Morning. Well, Colonel, it looks like the Pommies are at it again.
Here, look at these headlines. |

The Colonel takes Walloon's newspaper as if to read it, but then views the overhead display. This again elicits a mildly confused expression from Walloon.

| COLONEL | Pommie bastards. Holding the high ground at the Somme, and now this. They've been totally inbred for centuries, you know. Surprised they don't have three heads by now. |

| WALLOON | Quite. |

ENTER LADY BEATRICE (60) in her grand sophisticated widow's weeds. She is matron of Doubtend Abe. The audience **APPLAUDEDS** her as they are cued. She acknowledges them with a formal bow. Walloon simply shakes his head.

| WALLOON | Lady Beatrice. You look splendid tonight. |

LADY BEATRICE   Up your hole!

Walloon looks quite taken aback by Beatrice's harsh response. He turns to Jane for an explanation.

WALLOON	Have I made some trespass of which I am not aware?
JANE	Oh, no, dear Phlegming. Aunt Beatrice today endeavors to raise awareness for Tourette's affliction in her own special way. During the performance she will be communicating only through vile and vulgar remarks as is her understanding of the disorder's nature.
WALLOON	How commendable, if not incredibly irrational. I will immediately make contributions in support of her efforts.
JANE	Oh no, Aunt is not raising funds, only awareness. She is a conservative, as you know, and thus believes the distressed have a responsibility to fend for themselves.
WALLOON	Here, here. If we coddle them now, they'll soon drain the economy.
JANE	Certainly, since Tourettes should be readily treatable via Quinniwoon Pharmacy's Cerebral Colonic.
WALLOON	The safest alternative to brain surgery, as you must be aware.
COLONEL	Tourettes, though, sounds a bit French. Aren't there any British syndromes of which we should be more aware?

JANE	Why aren't the buffet platters filled? Where is that Souzette? That girl is promptly late in all her assignments. I don't know why my Aunt retains her.

ENTER SOUZETTE CREPE (22), the manor's domestic to a huge **OVATION**, loud **WHISTLES**, and sleazy **CAT CALLS**. She adores the attention and flirts with the audience. Souzette is a devastating beauty whose voluptuous figure is supremely accentuated by her skimpy French maid's uniform. Souzette speaks with a thick French accent. Naturally, Walloon and the Colonel fawn over her.

SOUZETTE	Bonjour, laissez faire.
WALLOON	Ah, Souzette! You've been dusting
COLONEL	Dust. As in the great dust storms of Egypt with Kitchner. We were to press on to Khartoum to relieve Gordon, when…
WALLOON	Has anyone seen our other classmate this morning?
JANE	No. In fact, I don't remember seeing him since arrival last evening.
WALLOON	That is my recollection, as well. What a mysterious oily little man. Hasn't changed a bit since senior year.
COLONEL	Completely disappeared, has he. My suspicions tell me he may be The Ripper. Quite a case, that. I was but a junior inspector at Scotland Yard then.

The doorbell **RINGS**.

WALLOON	Who could that be at this time?

Several beats and no one makes a move. The doorbells **RINGS** again.

JANE	Souzette, the door please!

SOUZETTE	Oui, Madame.

JANE	I am a Mademoiselle. She deliberately calls me Madame to portray me as the proprietor of a brothel.

LADY BEATRICE Eat me, bitch!

Souzette returns, escorting the man at the door. **ENTER** Inspector Earwick. Earwick holds a dead cat, its back is arched, mouth agape, eyes wide open in a frozen gaze of extreme terror.

INSPECTOR	Hello, hello. I am Inspector Sergeant Earwick of the police, though the boys at the station call me "Cobbles."

WALLOON	Hello.

INSPECTOR	Hello.

JANE	Hello.

INSPECTOR	Hello.

COLONEL	Hello.

INSPECTOR	Hello.

SOUZETTE	Bonjour.

INSPECTOR	And a bonnie ooh-la la to you, miss.

Inspector Earwick then makes a sharp about face to exit.

JANE	Inspector Earwick. Sergeant. Er, Cobbles. Is there any specific reason for your visit this morning?
INSPECTOR	Oh, begging me pardon, Mum. That there is. Surprised I didn't think of that me self. I would like to bring to your attention this poor cat what was on your front landing. As you can see the feline is in a terrible state of demise.

Everyone turns to look at Jane. She just groans and rolls her eyes.

JANE	Don't look at me. I don't know anything about dead cats.
INSPECTOR	Well, not to worry, Miss. I'm sure the poor beast will be right as rain once the rigor mortis wears off.
JANE	Anything else?

ENTER Betty Clue holding a tray of oatmeal cookies.

BETTY	Indeed, there is. I am Betty Clue. Special consultant to the police. Our car sputtered out and we were hoping to arrange boarding at Doubtend Abe for the evening.
LADY BEATRICE	Whore!
BETTY	I beg your pardon, Madame.
JANE	My apologies, Miss Clue. My aunt, Lady Beatrice, is representing a Tourettes sufferer this weekend and will only speak in bursts of foul language.

BETTY I completely understand. Bravo for you, Lady Beatrice. You may not remember but we met many years back when I was a youth and you were raising awareness for leprosy. I still have someone's nose as a cherished souvenir.

To the point of the moment, however. Will we be able to secure rooms for the night?

JANE I am dreadfully sorry, but Doubtend Abe is engaged this weekend for a special occasion.

WALLOON Oh, pif. Our engagement is quite small and there are rooms aplenty. We should be happy to accommodate you.

A bitter expression fills Jane's face and is directed to Walloon.

BETTY That would be splendid, thank you. Two rooms, if you please. It has been many years since my last visit to Doubtend Abe. I can plainly see many things have changed.

JANE We have been remiss about introductions, I'm afraid, Miss Clue. I am Jane Boufonte. I assist my aunt in the management of Doubtend Abe.

WALLOON I am Dr. Phlegming Walloon, veterinarian.

BETTY If I may interrupt. Please remember to enunciate clearly when introducing yourself. Thank you. Please continue, Dr. Walloon.

WALLOON Sorry, I am Dr. Phleming Walloon, veterinarian. I am the fiancé of Jane here. That is on the premise she is playing a thirty year old woman and not the

WALLOON	pre-adolescent she is in reality. I just want to make that clear to everyone so we do not have a repeat of last spring's Romeo and Juliet fiasco.
JANE	Yes, unfortunately, Drake. I mean, Phlegming must still maintain a 500 foot distance from school yards.
WALLOON	And this cheeky chap is…
COLONEL	Colonel Beverly Doddering-Blowhard of the Queen's Own Irregular Bowel Guards—retired. Diverticulitis Fidelis! In no way constipated. I assure you.
LADY BEATRICE	Douche bag. Pee the pants.
BETTY	Of course. And you, Mademoiselle?
SOUZETTE	I am the French maid, a la carte.
BETTY	Quel est ton nom, mon cher?
SOUZETTE	Frere Jacques, dormez vous?
BETTY	No, no, dear. What is your name?
SOUZETTE	Oh, parle vous anglais? N'est pas. I am Souzette, and I do sometimes songs. I perform also here at the manor, as the gentlemen say, carte blanche.
JANE	And your travels today, Miss Clue, business or pleasure?
BETTY	Business, I'm afraid. Murder at King Edward's.

COLONEL	Reminds me of the time we hunted the man-killing Great Sumerian Rat of Rangoon. Twenty five feet head to tail. Ate raw tigers for breakfast. Had to bait our trap with ministers without portfolio. Finally cornered the beast in a Turkish bath. By God, those people have hairy backs.
WALLOON	Horrible. Murder at King Edward's. Who, per chance?
BETTY	Headmaster Hungerdunger.
WALLOON	Not Hungerdunger, the younger?
BETTY	How many Hungerdungers are there at the school?
WALLOON	There's Hungerdunger the younger. There's the younger Hungerdunger. The even younger Hungerdunger and the Original Hungerdunger who married Mrs. Hungerdunger and brung her to the school. So that makes Hungerdunger, Hungerdunger, Hungerdunger, and Hungerdunger—four Hungerdungers.
BETTY	Ah, but you left out the last Hungerdunger, Mrs. Hungerdunger.
WALLOON	Right. Hungerdunger, Hungerdunger, Hungerdunger, Hungerdunger, and Hungerdunger. Five Hungerdungers.
JANE	I'm curious, Miss Clue. If you are on the way to the scene of a murder, why do you carry a tray of oatmeal cookies?

BETTY	Murder investigations, in my experience, are a very unpleasant and stressful event for all. I have found that a good tray of oatmeal cookies helps soften the mood. Since we are not able to make the crime scene due to our motor vehicle's demise, I thought the cookies would be best served here.
JANE	Perhaps that effort will not be wasted, Miss Clue, as our occasion is quite somber and personal. We mourn our lost classmates at this affair. I hope you can forgive my earlier protective posture.
BETTY	Without a doubt. I have passing familiarity with the Chiddingfold Class Catastrophe of 1980. There were seventy-seven tragic deaths that evening, including, interestingly enough, four by Bengal tiger.
WALLOON	Ah, it was a Bengal. I knew it.

Betty removes a plastic sack labeled 'GUM' from her purse.

BETTY	Now if you deposit any chewing gum here, and then wash your hands with soap, we can all enjoy the cookies. By the way, I thought there were other survivors.
JANE	There is a fourth, but he has not yet come to join us. Pardon me. Souzette! Souzette! Getting that girl to attend her duties, I swear!
SOUZETTE	Oui, Madame.
JANE	Souzette, would you please prepare two rooms for Miss Clue and Inspector Earwick.

SOUZETTE   Mais oui. Will that be two for each?

JANE   No, just two in total.

SOUZETTE   For which one?

JANE   One for Miss Clue and one for Inspector Earwick! Two rooms total. Deux au total!

SOUZETTE   Ooh, I see. Separate rooms, I assume we do not charge (a beat) by the hourly rate.

JANE   SOUZETTE!!!

SOUZETTE   I am running to my duty, Madame.

JANE   MADAMOISELLE!!!

LIGHTS & CURTAIN

INT—DOUBTEND ABE—NIGHT

It is now evening and the scene is now set in Doubtend Abe's parlor. The room is well lit which exposes the opulent decay of its once fine decor. All, except the classmate missing from breakfast, are present. Dinner has concluded, and Souzette serves a liqueur digestif.

Lady Beatrice clandestinely takes an extra filled glass plus a direct slug from the decanter. After a bit, it is plainly clear the actress herself is totally inebriated. She precariously sways, ready to fall, while on stage. The other actors look at her and then each other with some degree of concern.

Jane then sniffs the decanter which the prop department should have filled with tea. Her head jerks back at the scent she picks up. She turns to the Walloon and whispers.

JANE   (Whispers) Oh my God! There's real liquor in here. Loreen is loaded for real.

Betty excuses herself from the group to make another phone call.

BETTY   Hello, Mrs. Bumblenoggin. Betty here again. No, dear. I'm Betty. You are Mrs. Bumblenoggin (a beat). Yes you have been for quite some time now. For the knitting club gathering tonight I think it would be nice to sit around the fireplace in the study. No, dear, there won't be an exam. The study is a room (a beat) in my home. The one with the fireplace, yes. Now I would like to put out the rose and cream chenille throw on my rocking chair and could you also place my knitting bag there as well. And do be careful not to stab the cat with the needles (a beat). Oh, my, too late. Well, take him to the vet as soon as you can catch him. Thank you, dear. Yes, that was a very courteous goodbye you said.

JANE	Miss Clue, is being an amateur sleuth extraordinaire an occupation or a hobby?
BETTY	It is neither. A hobby is such a thing as knitting or wrestling kangaroos in a Mexican rodeo. An occupation is something performed by an accountant who manages the Mexican rodeo and siphons off funds to build a carpet factory as a means of illegally smuggling mimes across the French border. I simply assist the application of justice as, what I view is, my civil responsibility. Does that answer your question?
JANE	I won't be sure for quite some time.
COLONEL	The problem with Americans these days is that they haven't the foggiest notion of what a blanc mange is. This is a tragedy, you see. Accounts for our own decline as a world power.
WALLOON	How do you find the Amaro liqueur, Inspector?
INSPECTOR	Well, I suppose I would just search about until I located a cabinet with bottles. Why? Are you missing some?
LADY BEATRICE	Booger eater! Armpit licker!
BETTY	Will your now absent classmate be joining us anytime soon?
WALLOON	I'm not certain. Surely, I expected him to appear by now. Perhaps we should check to be sure he is all right.

JANE	I should say so. I'm finding his absence more and more disturbing since it brings my memory back to the disasters of graduation.
WALLOON	Not to worry, darling, I shall go immediately to check on the fellow.

Walloon's proclamation is answered by an unexpected voice coming from the dark shadows at the foot of the staircase. **ENTER ARISTOTLE NECROSIS (30)** the missing classmate of the evening. Necrosis is short, portly, and bald. He sports a one eyebrow and a missing front tooth. Despite these short-comings in appearance, he is debonair with a generous portion of charm.

NECROSIS	That won't be necessary, Phlegming, old man. Here I am. Apologies for my delayed appearance.
BETTY	And who may you be, sir, if I may be so bold to ask?
NECROSIS	Aristotle Necrosis, Class of 1980 survivor. Currently a man of international travels and trader of, shall we say, unique commodities. And you are Betty Clue. I know of you by reputation, and with great respect, I must add. I am a great fan of your Magazine '*Heinous Crimes and Country Living*'. I particularly enjoyed your article 'How to Bury a Body and Raise Geraniums in Your English Garden'.
BETTY	You flatter me, sir.
LADY BEATRICE	Your crabs have diarrhea breath.
NECROSIS	Good evening to you, Lady Beatrice. Your effort to raise awareness for Tourettes is uplifting.

WALLOON	Well, old man, how have you been? It seems you've hardly changed since…
NECROSIS	Yes, since that egregious day. Still the foreign swarthy, oily gent in the midst of all the arrogant Anglo-Saxon White Protestant Caucasians.
COLONEL	By God, sir. Glad to hear it. So many of you swarthy types don't appreciate the benefits provided in the association with the empire.
NECROSIS	Oh, believe me, Colonel, we have quite an astute appreciation.
JANE	Would you join us in a drink, Aristotle?
NECROSIS	Delighted.
JANE	Well, as we've said, dear Aristotle. We're so glad you joined us and are in fine condition, after all.
NECROSIS	Yes, well, about that. Slight misunderstanding concerning my well-being. You see, I must confess that, to put it bluntly, I've been murdered.

Gasps abound like leaking air from a tire and shocked faces are universally worn across the room.

CURTAIN

ACT 3

The tremor of disbelief stirred by Necrosis's announcement eventually subsides. Questions and curiosity are raised.

WALLOON   I say, old man, I don't mean to doubt you, but are you quite sure?

NECROSIS   Never more certain.

INSPECTOR   Well, sir, in that case, at least you seem to have your health.

JANE   I don't claim to be the expert here, but aren't murder victims generally, at least I would expect the vast majority to be, totally dead? I find this all difficult to comprehend.

COLONEL   Absolutely possible. Saw it many times during the rebellion in the Punjab. Soldiers with heads blown off complaining about the tasteless rations. Of course, they couldn't quite see what they were actually eating, so, it was a protest not totally unexpected.

LADY BEATRICE   Pussy boy slut.

BETTY   Mr. Necrosis, two trains leave different stations at the same time and are heading for each other. Train A…

NECROSIS   The collision which occurred 2 hours and 23 minutes later just outside of Alipur, Punjab province, Miss Clue, had a death toll of six hundred and seventeen, including people on the ground. All due to a fatal algebraic calculation of a math word problem by a fourth grade teacher in the Alipur School for Itinerant Children.

BETTY   Correct in every respect, sir. Thank you. Mr. Necrosis
has indeed been murdered and is currently in the
rare state of death known as Verbose Mortis. It is a
temporary condition of complete awareness with the
ability to swiftly solve complex mathematical train
word problems.

JANE   Rubbish, Verbose Mortis. I haven't heard so many
alternative facts since Kellyanne Conway tried to
explain science to Sean Hannity.

Without warning one of the spotlights, positioned in the upper rigging, falls
and **CRASHES** to the stage inches away from crushing the poor Inspector.
It is clear from the cast's startled reaction that this is not part of the script.

INSPECTOR   What the hell!!! What happened?

To make the point even clearer, a second spotlight SPLATTERS on stage
just missing Jane.

JANE   J**** H. C*****!!!

NECROSIS   It's Ted! He's loose!

All of the actors now move from the center of the stage to the edges so
they are not under any of the upper rigging and heavy objects potentially
falling out of it. They remain huddled together in these safe locations for
the remainder of the play, constantly looking upward with nervous glances
to identify any threats. The show, however, goes on.

WALLOON   I'm afraid it's true, Jane. You would be a believer if
you have ever seen Larry King? I watched him for
years on TV and could never tell if he were dead or
alive.

BETTY — Now who can tell me how long this condition may last? Anyone? Anyone?

WALLOON — Two to four hours, I would venture.

BETTY — Quite. That gives us a window on... Anyone? Anyone?

INSPECTOR — A window on the garden?

SOUZETTE — A window I will have to clean.

JANE — A window on the time of murder.

BETTY — Excellent, Jane. You have been paying attention, after all.
Knowing this, we now have a piece of information that will help us solve the...

Everyone is a bit stumped by Betty's question. They look to each other hoping to find some reasonable response in each other's confused gapes. Walloon gathers his courage and hesitantly steps forward.

WALLOON — The murder?

BETTY — Nothing other than. Of course, Mr. Necrosis could make the solution known to us immediately if wished to divulge the identity of the killer since he was entirely conscious during the heinous crime.

NECROSIS — I could indeed, Miss Clue, but, in that case, the mystery would be too easily solved, and you would not have the opportunity to display your exemplary detection skills—of which, I'm sure, we are all so eager to witness.

BETTY	Your sense of fair play is commendable, Mr. Necrosis.

JANE	Are the two of you serious?

BETTY	Extremely. And as an aside, Jane, you are slumping a bit around your shoulders. Good posture, like good etiquette should always be paramount in a young woman's bearing, dear.

INSPECTOR	What now, Betty?

BETTY	This case has certainly has defined itself as atypical. Therefore, we must examine it with an entirely different perspective than usual.

INSPECTOR	Ah, perspective. Of course! As found in the art of the Renaissance.

COLONEL	Now that it has been mentioned, I can say the Renaissance is where I worked with Einstein in the Patent Office. Terrible clerk. Took him at least three tries to get any form correct. We had a code for him— E=mc2: Einstein=muddled completely twice. He left the service, thankfully. Never heard a further word from the man. Often wondered what became of him.

LADY BEATRICE	Fart licking dookie fumes.

BETTY	Would someone be so kind as to enlighten me concerning the Colonel's condition?

JANE	During the infamous graduation ceremony he was hit in the head by a flying piece of debris from an ice sculpture. An Auguste Escoffier, no less. Flown in from Alaska, USA—and at no small cost.

WALLOON	Since that time he has delusions of being a character in one chapter of British history or another. Preferring, of course, those described by Rudyard Kipling.
BETTY	I think we should begin our investigation of Mr. Necrosis's murder from the point at which, I believe, it originated. That would be the Chiddingfold Graduation Ceremony of 1980. Mr. Walloon, may we begin with you?
WALLOON	Certainly.
BETTY	Capital. Where were you and what were you doing when the first extraordinary catastrophes began?
WALLOON	I was with Jane behind the graduation platform where we had just passionately finished…
JANE	We had just passionately finished decorating the pastry, and nothing more.
SOUZETTE	I'll bet. Sounds like someone was pumping the cream into the tarte.
BETTY	Colonel, you, sir?
COLONEL	At that moment, Hillary, Norgay, and I were making the final ascent to the summit of Everest, if I recall.
BETTY	Yes, thank you, Colonel. And lastly, Mr. Necrosis, your position?
NECROSIS	I don't remember. My recollection has been clouded by the events of that day, and time.

BETTY	Naturally. But please allow me to assist your memory. In the large photo on the wall behind you, a figure, quite fitting your description, is seen at the podium holding several small bags that were aflame. Would you care to guess what was in those bags?
NECROSIS	Haven't the foggiest.
BETTY	I am not the only one here known by reputation, Mr. Necrosis, or should I call you by your nom-de-crim-inel—Professor Acrimonious: Mister of Evil!
NECROSIS	Ah, you have found me out, Miss Clue. Bravo. However, that is supposed to be "Master of Evil", a typo in the initial printing of my business cards. Obviously you did not receive the revised version. My apologies, I will send the corrected material to you directly.
BETTY	I would be in your debt, Professor.
NECROSIS	Of reputation of which we speak, yours is the more well deserved, Miss Clue. How did you surmise my true identity?
BETTY	There is an inescapable association of the small bags aflame with another horrible crime—the burning poopie bag assault on Windsor Castle. The Queen was quite a mess after she attempted to stomp out the fires. Even more damage was sustained when the Corgis grabbed the smoking sacks and rampaged through the chambers.
WALLOON	A dark day for the monarchy.

LADY BEATRICE   Spotted Dick.

JANE   Are you accusing, Mr. Necrosis of instigating the deaths of his fellow students at Chiddingfold?

BETTY   Absolutely not. Mr. Necrosis…

NECROSIS   Minor request, here. Could I be referenced as Professor Acrimonious.? I spent a great deal on the business cards, even though I should get a refund due to the typo.

BETTY   Of course, Professor. The Professor's flaming poopie bags were the only malicious trap that did not spring that night. No one stomped on them. Isn't that correct, Professor.

NECROSIS   Absolutely. Because of my failure on that occasion, I spent years researching and perfecting the burning poopie bag gag, until such time as it became a fool-proof device that I could use against my enemies.

JANE   Enemies? Us?

NECROSIS   All of you, Anglo-Saxon, Protestant elites who looked down upon my short swarthy stature, and missing tooth. I wanted to prove I was as good or even superior to the British who drove down and oppressed the many colored nations of the world. And my plan succeeded. I poopie bagged the Queen!

An uncomfortable silence follows Professor Acrimonious's description of his plan. He could sense the lack of shock and awe that he expected from his audience.

NECROSIS	What? You don't think that was a great plan? What's wrong with it? It covers all the main points of my grievances. Well, doesn't it?

JANE	Yes, well covered, indeed.

WALLOON	Very good design. Great potential.

INSPECTOR	Nothing about the Renaissance, then?

JANE	And you've got a lot of confidence in it, certainly.

WALLOON	Indeed, a very important point.

NECROSIS	You don't like it. I can tell. Come on, you can say it.

JANE	It's not that we don't like it. It's more that we don't have your sense of…

WALLOON	Of…

JANE	Of… perspective.

INSPECTOR	It is the Renaissance!

At that moment, the effects of overindulgence with liqueur surpass Lady Beatrice's threshold. She throws up on Jane's shoes. It becomes obvious that this is not part of the original text of the play.

JANE	J**** C*****, Loreen! What the f***! All over my shoes! Really! Really! God D*****, b****!

Jane takes off her shoes in a fit, and hurls them off stage. The pained **SCREECHING HOWL** of a cat is heard as the shoes land. Everyone then turns back to Jane.

JANE	That has nothing to do with me. I do not f***ing kill f***ing cats! Line!
DIRECTOR (O.S.)	What do you suppose caused the slaughter, Miss Clue?
JANE	What he said.
BETTY	It was a curse that doomed your fellow students at Chiddingfold that fateful day. A curse leveled by the survivors of another disaster decades ago when two trains collided outside Alipur in the Punjab because of a fatal error by a Math teacher. A teacher who matriculated from none other than Chiddingfold College at the time.
LADY BEATRICE	Pull my groin, crap face.
WALLOON	You mean 77 lives were lost because of a wrong answer to a math word problem?
BETTY	No, only four from the math word problem. The ones killed by the Bengal tiger. That tiger came from India.
WALOON	And the rest?
BETTY	Unclear. Bad luck, I suppose. However, there is one final loose end to tie up. There were seventy-seven fatalities at the graduation ceremony, and four survivors. That total comes to eighty-one. However, there are eighty-two seats in

BETTY	the student section, if my count from the old photo is correct. Who is the missing student?

Everyone looks about blankly.

JANE	I have no idea.
WALLOON	Are you sure there was a student number eighty-two?
BETTY	Yes. And it is someone who wanted you, Professor, as well as a cheap low tipping Headmaster at the college, dead.
NECROSIS	My God! Of course! Amanda Reckonwith! I wrote a term paper for her from which the teacher, you refer to, gave her a C. A grade much lower than it deserved. She blamed us both and swore revenge.
BETTY	A teacher who left the college in disgrace and resettled in a private school—King Edward's.
INSPECTOR	The teacher in the photo with AEthelred the Unready!

Mild applause and whistles for AEthelred.

BETTY	And in the photo with our waitress, Minnie of the Wintersdon Arms.
INSPECTOR	Who has been in a coma for two years.
BETTY	Or so she says. Please excuse me, but I must make a call to the Witley Institute for the Comatose.

Betty dials the number for the institute where Minnie resides.

BETTY   Hello. I am Betty Clue working with the police. Do
                         you have a patient in a coma by the name of Minnie?
                         You may have her registered as Amanda Reckonwith.
                         Very good. Has she left the institute for any reason
                         today?
                         (a beat)
                         Yes, I realize she is in a coma. However, could you
                         put her on the phone? It is important that I speak
                         with her.
                         (a beat)
                         Yes, I know what the definition of a coma is. Please,
                         just put her on. Thank you.
                         (a beat)
                         Ah, Minnie, my name is Betty Clue.
                         (a beat)
                         Yes, I know you are currently in a coma. And yes, I
                         know the definition. Let me ask you, have you been
                         shot today?
                         (a beat)
                         A lucky guess. However, I must warn you not to
                         run since the police are converging on your location
                         as we speak. You are being charged with the mur-
                         ders of the Headmaster at King Edward School, and
                         Aristotle…I mean, Professor Acrimonious.
                         (a beat)
                         It should be Master of Evil. There was a misprint on
                         the business card.
                         (a beat)
                         I'm sure he would be glad to send you the revised
                         card, if he is alive to do so.
                         (a beat)
                         Yes, and it was nice talking to you, as well.

Betty receives a call and answers it on the first ring.

BETTY   Betty Clue here. Oh, hello, Mrs. Bumblenoggin. You had the vet do what with the cat? But the Sir Albany was already neutered. What did they cut off then? Oh, poor Sir Albany, if we can even call him that any longer.

Betty next dials the Superintendent.

BETTY   Superintendent, Betty Clue here. It turns out the woman you shot did kill the Headmaster. She is presently wounded and in a coma as a resident of the Witley Institute.
(a beat)
Please don't cry, sir. Politeness demands that you must speak clearly at all times while on the phone.
(a beat)
Yes, I realize they are tears of joy. You're very welcome. Goodbye.

INSPECTOR   How did you know that Minnie was the killer?

BETTY   There were too many coincidences in both photographs to mean absolutely nothing, Inspector. Plus, Minnie would have to spend quite a lot of time at the Witley Institute to pass as a regular coma patient. This meant that her time as a waitress, hunting down her former teacher and term paper writer, would be limited. This was verified by the poor service reviews given to the Wintersdon Arms by clients who experienced long delays, sometimes weeks at a time, waiting for their food to be brought to the table.

JANE   Extraordinary, Miss Clue. I apologize for doubting you. But what of the poor Professor.

BETTY   I'm afraid, unless he makes a miraculous recovery, he will be dead in approximately eight minutes by my watch.

NECROSIS   Actually, I have made my recovery ten minutes ago, Miss Clue!

WALLOON   So, you are not murdered then. Well, jolly good for that, old man.

NECROSIS   Thank you, so much. Now I can get on with my master plans for evil without further interruptions.

Necrosis, as Professor Acrimonious, releases a sinister, hair raising cackle. He goes to the large windows overlooking the terrace, opens them, and stands ready to bolt out into the dark night.

NECROSIS   I bid you all adieu until the next time our paths may cross. At such time I will obtain my revenge! For I am Professor Acrimonious-Master of Evil!

Just as Professor Acrimonious is prepared to escape through the window, a large Bengal tiger leaps, sweeps him away, and drags him screaming into the terrace.

LADY BEATRICE Rat f***!

CURTAIN

THE END

The Renaissance

The Renaissance—An Overview

The Renaissance was a time in Europe where great artists, philosophers, scientists, and political thinkers came out of the woodwork and just went about thinking up or creating stuff like crazy. It was a time between Middle Earth and modern times, if you consider the 1600's modern. If you do then you are either ultra-conservative or don't get out of the house much.

Anyway, the Renaissance is considered a period of great intellectual achievement similar to my sophomore year when I got two B's, one C, a D, and an Incomplete for a whopping 2.25 GPA. I didn't get near the recognition, of course, because my name isn't Italian. Here's my record:

- Art (B)
- Sociology (B)
- Literature (C)
- Science (Earth Science, D)
- Mathematics (Inc.)

Contained in this section are not only works direct from the Renaissance (Nostradamus's Mists of Time), but also a modern academic essay (par moi) describing the Italian Renaissance in general, and an informative profile (aussi par moi) of two colorful Renaissance figures in particular, Lucrezia and Cesare Borgia.

I now present the Renaissance.

J. E. Winchester, Esq.

Nostradamus— The Mists of Time: Episode 1

Introduction

THE MISTS OF TIME

The Mists of Time show was one of the few bright spots during the Black Death of the 14th century. It was hosted by Michel de Nostredame, more familiarly known as Nostradamus—astrologer, physician, and prognosticator of the future.

In the show, Nostradamus would stir the mists of time pool and look into the future where he would connect with and interview a guest with some interesting or unique qualities. Only three transcripts of the show remain. The very first, Season 1—Episode 1, along with Season 2—Episode 16, and Season 3—Episode 36.

Although the show was popular, it only lasted three seasons because of a low spike in viewership as most of the show's audience died of the plague. Nevertheless, Nostradamus is still very well remembered for his Pulitzer Prize winning book—The Prophecies of Nostradamus.

The Amazing Nostradamus
(inspiration for Emperor Palpatine in Star Wars)

J. E. Winchester, Esq.

THE MISTS OF TIME: SEASON 1, EPISODE 1

Cue theme music.

Announcer	Everything you thought to be true is wrong—including your name and where you live. All of these things will be revealed as we explore with the venerable Nostradamus, seer and sage, whose eyes alone can see beyond 'The Mists of Time'.
	'The Mists of Time' brought to you by—Dr. Rollo Kurchek's Lycanthropy Clinic. Metaphysical and Therapeutic de-conversion from wolf to human. No more 'bad-dog'. With a 98.8% cure rate, we make the 'were' in werewolf past tense.
	And now, live from France, the man with the diction of prediction. Heeeeere's Nostradamus!

APPLAUSE.
ENTER Nostradamus.

Nostradamus	Thank you. Thank you. How many of you want to know if you'll enjoy the show tonight. I can tell you. (**RIM SHOT**). I met a gypsy fortune teller the other day and asked her what she made of her future. She said a prophet. (**GROANS**). See it's a play on words—p-r-o-f-i-t and p-r-o-p-h-e-t. Boy, they turn on you quick. OK, we have a great show tonight, so let's get right to it. We're going to look through the mists of time and visit a couple from the future year, 2022, who have a unique relationship with animals. Let's go over to the old mist of time tub and stir things.

Nostradamus goes to the mist of time tub and begins stirring the contents. Cloudy vapors steam upward and out. Nostradamus coughs and clears them away.

Nostradamus   Roses are red and beasts are blue
               Get you vaccine or get the flu
               Children who run and look like prey
               Will likely be eaten anyway
               Burma Shave

He then picks some signal up and watches intently. A few seconds later comes a woman's **SCREAM**. Her arm comes out of the tub and slaps Nostradamus.

Woman   Pervert!

Nostradamus   Sorry, wrong number. Let's try that again.

Nostradamus repeats the time tub stir. This time he gets the right party.

Nostradamus   Hello. Am I speaking to Vera Luckz and Zibigniew Shinycar of East Sheboygan, Wisconsin? This is Nostradamus from the past.

Vera   Yes. Hello, Nostradamus.

Zibigniew   We've been expecting you.

Nostradamus   Now I've predicted that you have a very special relationship with animals and have opened some kind of educational zoo on the Route 53 bypass. Vera, Zibigniew, tell us more about it.

Vera   Yes. We've opened a petting zoo that is absolutely unique. I don't believe there is any other like it in the country.

Nostradamus'   What makes your zoo so unique?

Zibigniew	Nostradamus, our zoo features only the most dangerous predatory and venomous animals.
Nostradamus	Dangerous animals? That is unique as most petting zoos feature cuddly creatures like sheep, ponies, or calves.
Vera	Well, those became food at our place.
Zibigniew	Not our idea though. The predatory animals took that upon themselves.
Nostradamus	I think we have an image of one of the animals in your petting zoo. Yes, here it is.

That looks very frightening. Even deadly.

Vera	That is Walter. He's either an Alaskan or Canadian timber wolf, but he's currently being examined by Dr. Kurchek to be certain he isn't a werewolf.
Nostradamus	Having only seen Walter, and I admit it is too small a sample size to make any definitive judgement, it seems to me that it would be extremely dangerous to let people and wild predatory and venomous animals mix.

Zibigniew	Do you mean, socially?
Nostradamus	I mean in any way.
Vera	Our initial thoughts, as well. However, we quickly came to realize that the introduction of people to species that they normally would never encounter would provide an educational advantage that would offset the risk.
Nostradamus	And how as that worked out?
Zibigniew	Not well. It seems the premium paid to education is not as great as we were led to believe. Perhaps due, in part, to a very unfortunate alleged incident involving a kindergarten tour group from Missileen Falls Elementary School.
Nostradamus	You're speaking, of course, of the attack and slaughter of kindergarten children and teacher from Missileen Falls Elementary school by a renegade gorilla. I believe we also have an image of that.

Bongo, the alleged assailant
of kindergarten tour.

Vera	That is, of course, Bongo, our gorilla. I don't remember if he is a mountain gorilla or a lowland gorilla. Which ever one can park cars.
Nostradamus	And we also have a shot of Bongo the parking lot attendant.

Bongo Valet Parking assistant

Nostradamus	This begs the question of how you could allow man killing creatures so close to people, especially children.
Zibigniew	It's a petting zoo. That's the whole idea.
Vera	Now, we're not downplaying the severity of the incident, Nostradamus, but there were extenuating circumstances in that situation. First, the children, as children will do, made sudden movements which startled the animal. Then, of course, and this was not noted at all in the press, the children were approximately the same size as the gorilla's natural enemies—elves, and I'm not talking Keebler cookies.

Zibigniew	Finally, when the children bolted, albeit, in sheer terror, this engaged the apes completely normal kill instinct. They are, after all, wild and dangerous animals.
Nostradamus	Well, I can see that!
Vera	And I would like to point out an unfair element to this whole situation. If Bongo is found guilty, he will suffer a far harsher penalty than any human who guns down innocent students. The sad thing is that Bongo has a pet kitten. Also he can understand over two hundred words including ointment, profiterole, and queef.
Zibigniew	We are not completely unaware of the risks in our business. We have instituted new safety features to our operation. We now responsibly distribute safety pamphlets to all visitors coming to the zoo.

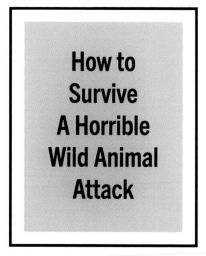

Vera	We are also presenting victims or victims' families with a free Ghini cosmetic package.

Nostradamus	Ghini packages are very sought after commodities with all those great cosmetic and fashion items. They give those away at the Academy Awards. Sounds like generous compensation.

Thank you Vera and Zibigniew. That's all the time we have for today. So long and remember—take the Jets plus 15 at home against the Dolphins on Sunday. This is Nostradamus saying—I'll see you in the future!

Announcer	'The Mists of Time' was brought to you by the Republican Party. The GOP—we are the Grand New American Bund.

And by, CastOut, the number 1 medieval pest removal with over 200 years' experience,

- Licensed, insured professional staff.

- Advanced environmentally responsible technology

- Customized humane solutions for witches, demons, dragons, and Jehovah's Witnesses.

Whether it's a Castle or Hut, no if ands or buts, we will cast out or bust!! CastOut. Schedule a Free Estimate today!

Nostradamus—
The Mists of Time:
Episode 16

THE MISTS OF TIME: SEASON 2, EPISODE 16

THEME MUSIC

Announcer	Everything you thought to be true is wrong—including your birthday and gender. All of these things will be revealed as we explore with the venerable Nostradamus, seer and sage extraordinaire, whose eyes alone can see beyond 'The Mists of Time'.
	'The Mists of Time' brought to you by Whore-Mones, maker of the number 1 performance enhancer for male prostitutes—Gigol-O-Sin.
	Have to keep Don Juan up until dawn, need to have Casanova perform over and over. Gigol-O-Sin for when you need to go!
	And now, he's the blast from the past. Heeeeere's Nostradamus!

APPLAUSE.
ENTER Nostradamus.

Nostradamus	Thank you. Thank you. This looks like a happy group tonight. I just had a vision that there is going to be a terrible multi-fatality traffic accident as you all leave to go home. Come down and check with me to see if you are a victim or survivor. (**RIM SHOT**). Hey, I have a friend who wants to predict the future. He asked me for a tip. I told him to move to a different time zone. (**GROANS**). Watch yourselves. I have a ton of these jokes and no pride. OK, we have a great show tonight so let's get right to it.

105

Nostradamus

We're going to look through the mists of time and visit a daredevil from Mandible Forks, Colorado, in the future year, 2025. His name is P.S. DeResistance. His game is an attempt to jump across the Grand Canyon on roller skates. Let's go over to the old mist of time tub and stir things.

Nostradamus goes to the mist of time tub and begins stirring the contents. Cloudy vapors steam upward and out. Nostradamus coughs and clears them away.

Nostradamus

A giant gap is there to cross
If you like spaghetti sauce
A leap of glorious fate will pass
Or someone just might lose their ass
Burma Shave

He then picks up some signal when suddenly comes a **ROAR** and the clawed paw of some nasty animal takes a swipe at Nostradamus.

Nostradamus

Must have logged into the petting zoo.

Nostradamus repeats the time tub stir. This time he gets the right party.

Nostradamus

Hello. This is Nostradamus from the past. Am I speaking to Mr. P.S. DeResistance?

DeResistance

DeResistance here, Nostradamus.

Nostradamus

P.S., you are currently promoting your upcoming jump across the Grand Canyon on roller skates. Whatever possessed you to attempt something like this?

DeResistance

I really don't have a good answer for that. All I know is that at some point it seemed like a good idea.

Nostradamus	To jump across the Grand Canyon?
DeResistance	The actual jump site is Marble Canyon which is at the northern head of the Grand Canyon. A fascinating fact is that the canyon is not made of marble as the name would indicate. That was a name given to it by an early explorer in 1869.
Nostradamus	Why did he name it Marble Canyon?
DeResistance	I don't think he was very good at naming things. He had an accident where a metal pipe went through his head and remained there for the rest of his life. He had trouble turning his head and chewing food, so I guess coming up with good names for things was low on his priority list.
Nostradamus	Interesting. Why did you select Marble Canyon as your jump site?
DeResistance	This is the narrowest part of the canyon at approximately 600 feet wide.
Nostradamus	And here we have an image of Marble Canyon and your proposed landing area.

Canyon gap

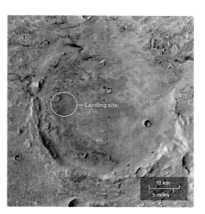

Proposed landing site

DeResistance	Boy, that looks a lot wider than I remember.
Nostradamus	Given that this is the narrowest part of the canyon, P.S., it still seems like jumping that span is more than just a daunting task, especially using only roller skates.
DeResistance	You would think so from that picture, but photographs can fool your eyes. You know how some shots make you look fat or have big hips. That could be what's happening here. Is that the only view you have of the canyon? It really isn't the way I remember it.
Nostradamus	Now, do the roller skates have any additional means of propulsion, like rockets or jet engines?
DeResistance	Absolutely not. This will be done by sheer manual effort. The only aid necessary is a fifty foot ramp that will allow me to get the 30 degrees of elevation I need to reach the other side.

Nostradamus   Amazing. Just for my own edification, how deep is the canyon at the point of your jump?

DeResistance   Pretty deep. We haven't actually measured it, but it goes down a long way.

Nostradamus   That sounds scary, and dangerous.

DeResistance   It does, now that you mention it. Are you sure that was a picture of Marble Canyon? Could you have mixed it up with some other part?

Nostradamus   Now, what safety precautions have you taken for the jump?

DeResistance   I'll be wearing a helmet and knee pads.

Nostradamus   Do helmets and knee pads have special protective powers in your time? You won't be wearing a parachute of any kind?

DeResistance   No, I think we would need to know how deep the canyon was to see if a parachute would even be helpful.

Nostradamus   But you said you hadn't done that. Sounds like quite an oversight.

DeResistance   Yes, when you put it that way, it does.

Nostradamus   Still, I would imagine that you've made other careful calculations to insure a safe and successful jump.

DeResistance   I would hope so.

Nostradamus   Me as well. For instance, what speed would you
                      need to be traveling off the ramp to make it to the
                      other side?

DeResistance   Managed to think of that one.

Nostradamus   And what would that speed be?

DeResistance   Given the width of the canyon, the degree of ele-
                      vation of the ramp, windage, etc. I would need to
                      reach a speed of 275 miles per hour.

Nostradamus   That sounds like an incredible speed to acquire on
                      skates. What is your current best speed in practice?

DeResistance   Nearly 10 miles per hour. Twelve with a following
                      wind. I'm still a little wobbly.

Nostradamus   And going that far below a minimum required speed
                      this close to your jump date, you are still planning
                      to go through with this?

DeResistance   I don't think so.

Nostradamus   Sorry to dampen your enthusiasm for your event,
                      P.S.

DeResistance   Not at all. I'm sure it was all for the best.

Nostradamus   I'm sure, too. And I'm also sure our audience will be interested to know about your medications, their dosages, and whether or not you take them as prescribed. Thanks for talking with us.

That's all the time we have for today. I'll say Au Revoir and remind you, if you have a ticket for the Hindenburg, better think twice. This is Nostradamus. See you in the future!

Announcer   And now, a final message from our The Mists of Time sponsor.

Got earwax, nose hair, eye gunk, and nail clippings? Don't throw them away! Alchemists, witches, and warlocks are looking for these valuable ingredients to make gold and conjure potions. And they're willing to pay top dollar! If you want to make fast cash from disgusting bodily waste products, call us—1-800-555-CRUD. That's 1-800-555-CRUD.

Nostradamus—
The Mists of Time:
Episode 36

THE MISTS OF TIME: SEASON 3, EPISODE 36

THEME MUSIC

Announcer	Everything you thought to be true is wrong—including what you ate for lunch and why. All of these things will be revealed as we explore with the venerable Nostradamus, seer and sage extraordinaire, whose eyes alone can see beyond 'The Mists of Time'.
	'The Mists of Time' brought to you by Aurora Alchemy. The gold standard in transmutation metallurgy and science. If it's not gold, it's not Aurora.
	And now, direct from the Black Death, he's the moocher from the future. Heeeeere's Nostradamus!

APPLAUSE.
ENTER Nostradamus.

| Nostradamus | Thank you. Thank you. Moocher from the future? Where did you get that? Hey, this audience looks anxious. How many of you want to know if you survive the plague? (**RIM SHOT**). Oh, a 'don't ask-don't tell' group, ey. (**GROANS**). May an unclean yak date your daughter. OK, let me tell you about our very special show tonight. We're going to look through the mists of time and talk to an entrepreneur from the year 2035 who is working on a project to make quicksand. Quicksand in 2035? What are your descendants doing out there, people? Let's find out from the old mist of time tub and stir things. |

Nostradamus goes to the mist of time tub and begins stirring the contents. Cloudy vapors steam upward and out. Nostradamus coughs and clears them away.

Nostradamus   I'll have a pizza but the anchovies toss
Your underwear is binding
All your time has been lost
Because your watch needs winding
Burma Shave

He then picks up some signal up and peers into the tub. A few seconds later an arm with a rubber hammer comes out of the tub and beats Nostradamus over the head.

Nostradamus   Must have offended one of the Avengers.

Nostradamus repeats the time tub stir. This time he gets the right party.

Nostradamus   Hello. This is Nostradamus from the past. Am I speaking to Mr. Hammond Aiggs of Treeless Oaks, North Dakota, in the year 2035?

Hammond   Yes, sir. Treeless Oaks, 2035, including the municipality of Bodale, Wonkalunk Village, and Chippankettkee Township.

Nostradamus   Hammond, I understand you are a research scientist. Could you tell us something about your research?

Hammond   Certainly. I am currently working on the development of a safe and economic process to manufacture quicksand.

Nostradamus   Quicksand? Is there a demand for quicksand in the future? It would surprise me since there's not much of a market for it in my time.

Hammond	Things have changed quite a bit in 2035, Mr. Nostradamus. Quicksand is very popular as a landscaping element for home lawns, gardens, public parks, and golf courses.
Nostradamus	Wow! I imagine you must have some wicked sand traps on your courses in 2035.
Hammond	The point being that the company I own—My Quicksand—is very busy trying to keep up with demand.
Nostradamus	Let me ask you, is there a special club you use to get out of one of those quicksand traps?
Hammond	And, if I may add, competition is stiff as there are three other quicksand manufacturing companies in the greater Treeless Oaks area, 2035, including the municipality of Bodale, Wonkalunk Village, and Chippankettkee Township.
Nostradamus	Is it a one or two stroke penalty to drop from those quicksand traps? Sorry, I diverge, but this is so fascinating. Let me get back on track. You say you have some local competition in your business. Is this driving the need for safer and more economical quicksand manufacturing processes?
Hammond	Absolutely. We are constantly studying and finding methods to improve the efficiency and safety of our factory operation.

Nostradamus	Speaking of safety, I think we have a picture of one of your beta-testers drowning in a batch of quicksand. This was at your lab site, I believe.

Quicksand beta-tester fatally examines
early feature delivery.

Hammond	This is a great example of 'My Quicksand's' commitment to address safety improvements. In this specific case, the issue identified in this tragedy was fixed by a subsequent feature release of our methodology.
Nostradamus	How so?
Hammond	We now instruct our beta-testers to try to float rather than flail when they are gripped and being dragged under by the quicksand. It is actually easier to float on quicksand than it is on water. Of course that's a difficult strategy to apply in a raging panic attack. But we are making some progress.
Nostradamus	As in several of my encounters with the future, I have been perplexed by the willingness of people to take on such obviously fatal tasks. What motivates your bet-testers to run such risks

Hammond	Some are condemned criminals or vagrants. Others volunteer because we are holding their families hostage. However, most recently we use political ingrates who have been disloyal to Donald Trump.
Nostradamus	Donald Trump is still alive in 2035?
Hammond	Well, artificially. Actually his body is dead, but his ego is still going. That feeds off the human sacrifices of his enemies.
Nostradamus	Hammond, what was your motivation for getting into the quicksand business, serious head injury, physical or sexual abuse as a child, other?
Hammond	None of the above. My mother was fascinated by the La Brea Tar Pits when she was carrying me and I guess the fascination just passed right through the placental membrane.
Nostradamus	Well, we've run out of time, so we'll never know those details. I'd like to thank our guest, Hammond Aiggs.
Hammond	Thanks for having me.
Nostradamus	I hope you can visit us again.
Hammond	I'm free tomorrow.
Nostradamus	Sorry, we'll call you if something opens up. So let me say goodbye with this reminder. If it's 1929 where you are, get out of the market fast. This is Nostradamus. I'll see you in the future!

Announcer   'The Mists of Time' with Nostradamus has been
                     brought to you by—'Behind the Times Technology'.
                     Solving today's problems with yesterday's solutions,
                     tomorrow.

The Italian Renaissance—
An Overview

The Italian Renaissance—an Overview

The late Middle Ages affected civilization the same way it affects us all: more aches and pains, poorer vision, and more frequent trips to the bathroom. Then came the Renaissance, a rebirth of learning, reason, and art. It was like discovering pickle ball at age 60, and reclaiming the lost luster of vibrant youth by crushing older, more decrepit senior players at the YMCA.

The Renaissance began somewhere in the 14th century and lasted into the 17th century where it provided a bridge into the modern era. Aptly enough, the Renaissance's origins were based in Italy. At that time, Italy shared many of the same qualities that propelled classical Greece into the model for Western Civilization. These qualities included: existence of powerful independent city-states, a new wealth of material, cultural, and philosophical elements, and, of course, espresso.

In Italy, the center of the rebirth was Florence (not the insurance lady, but the city). This city-state was a republic and the center of finance and commercial activity in Europe at this time. The city's accumulated wealth and power was channeled into patronages for artists, intellectuals, and mimes, all of whom flourished in this enlightened environment.

The two most prominent figures of this time are Leonardo Da Vinci and Lorenzo de Medici, shown below.

PD-US   PD-US

Leonardo "Big Brain" Da Vinci   Lorenzo "Laredo Larry" d' Medici

Florence was dominated by the powerful Medici family which included Lorenzo "Laredo Larry" de Medici. He was arguably the family's member most prodigious patron of the Renaissance. He was nicknamed "Laredo Larry" because of his wild cowboy actions when dealing with rivals and enemies. Lorenzo's most famous patronage went to the man who is generally regarded as the face of the Renaissance-Leonardo "Big Brain" da Vinci, a master of art, engineering, and science.

While Da Vinci and Medici were two of the main characters in the Italian Renaissance movement, there was a plethora of artists, thinkers, scientists, and politicians that were also key figures who expanded the boundaries of human achievement beyond the "Dark Ages", so called by people who did not have electricity.

Illuminating the scientific, medical, and mathematical disciplines in this era were such notables as:

- Galileo "The Garrote" Galilei who invented the telescope to study the phases of Venus. Needless to say, Venus was not pleased at the nonconsensual intrusion of her privacy. He died in prison.

- Niccolo "Tricky Nick" Tartaglia the ancestor of Philip "The Pimp" Tartaglia, who with the support of Emilio "The Wolf" Barzini, attempted to wipe out the Corleone crime family in the Godfather Part 1.

- Leonardio "Numbers" Fibonacci, the most talented mathematician of the Middle Ages, who was first to promote math word problems about trains leaving different stations at the same time and doomed to collide somewhere along the tracks. Fibonacci was gunned down in a barber shop when it was discovered his Fibonacci number sequence was totally useless.

- Guidobaldo "The Pineapple" Del Monte, an early student of the mathematician Torquato "The Turk" Tasso. Del Monte was responsible for Tasso's elimination in a dispute over odd and even numbers.

- Andreo "Handy Andy" Cesalpino, Italian physician, philosopher, and all-purpose "problem solver" for the Sforza family.

Equally impressive were the contributions of Italian explorers to the expanding world available to Renaissance masters to study and engage. Such men included:

- Amerigo "Mo-Mo" Vespucci, explorer for the city-state of Florence. While he didn't discover America, he underhandedly acquired the naming rights which made him one of the wealthiest and most powerful men in Florence until he accidently walked under a falling piano.

- Giovanni "Johnny Narrows" Verrazano, another prominent Florentine explorer who was accidently pushed off a bridge between Brooklyn and Staten Island. His body was never recovered.

- Christopher "You Know Who" Columbus. Enough said.

Not to be outdone in influence, the ones who laid the groundwork for the Renaissance were the political masters of the day. The patronage of these figures touched all areas of the rebirth. The best known of these benefactors include:

- The Borgias, Cesare "Big Poison" and Lucrezia "Little Poison."

- Pope Julius II "The Deuce", also known as" capo di tutti fruiti."

- Niccolo "The Prince" Machiavelli.

- Catherine "Catty Cathy" de Medici, who initiated the Italian Wars when she accused Age of Exploration master, Sandro "The Sandman" Botticelli, of non-consensual exploration of her person.

As impressive and important as advances in the above areas were to the development of the Renaissance and beyond, no area of the rebirth captures the imagination and ideals as does the art and artists of those days. This era produced the most profound collection of artistry and culture the world has ever seen. This group of artists includes:

- Michelangelo "Mickey Angel" Buonarroti, who specialized in paintings and sculptures of people with no pants.

- Raphael "Reckin Ralph" Sanzio, who along with Da Vinci and Michelangelo is considered one of the trinity of Renaissance artists. Raphael died of natural causes, 40 ice pick stab wounds to the head. If there had been 41, his death would have been deemed suspicious.

- Francesco "Frankie France" Francia, partnered with Rocco "Rock Head" Zoppo (the sixth Marx brother), and Lorenzo "Larry Knee Capper" Costa. Together these men formed the ill-fated Bologna gang that was wiped out in the St. Louis Cardinal Bobble Head Day Massacre.

- Fillipo "Fat Lip Philly" Lippi (aka, Lippo Lippi, Lippo the Lip, or Lips Lippi). Lippi was killed in a running gun battle with police while attempting to paint a post-modern abstract on the scale of Kandinsky or Pollock.

In whatever form it took, the Renaissance planted the seeds that blossomed into the world we know today and can arguably be called the most influential period in human history.

If you do care to argue that point, I can be reached through the addresses provided in the Contact section of this book.

J. E. Winchester, Esq.

The Borgias—
by
J. E. Winchester, Esq.

*L*ucrezia and Cesare Borgia were the 'redrum' twins of the middle ages, accounting for dozens of treacherous murders, assassinations, and other more serious crimes. Their morbid talents with poisons were held in such high esteem, that the Pope made it an Olympic event in the 1500 Summer Games.

PD-US   PD-US

Portraits of Lucrezia and Cesare Borgia. Lucrezia's dismayed expression is attributed to her disappointing Silver Medal finish in the Pentathlon Poisoning event at the 1500 Olympic Games in Rome. Cesare, winning two Golds at the games, is pictured with the white glove he wore when he raised his fist on the victor's podium to promote Guido Power.

LUCREZIA BORGIA

Lucrezia Borgia is either portrayed as a dangerous femme fatale or as a pawn in her family's ambitious plans to create advantageous alliances through marriage. The truth is, that if you planned to hook up with Lucrezia you

127

better have either a really super-strong ironclad pre-nup, or a foolproof escape plan.

Lucrezia was a highly intelligent and educated woman, far above what was common for women of her time. In fact, her intellect and talents were either equal or superior to many men who were considered stars of the Renaissance.

That being said, she definitely went through more men than beer goes through guys at a football party. She had about ten children (count was lost after eight) through three official marriages, two annulled marriages, and numerous affairs. If there was ever a candidate for relationship counseling, it was Lucrezia.

CESARE BORGIA

Cesare Borgia also possessed supreme intellect, military, political, and serial killer skills, and he ruthlessly advanced his family's interests through those foul talents. It is said he would hone his treacherous expertise through rigorous practice on Lucrezia's husbands and boyfriends (a population that offered an endless supply of training subjects as it turned out.) He was also suspected of murdering his own brother Giovanni, as well as involvement in Jeffrey Epstein's mysterious death.

Cesare was a devoted enemy of the Sforza family. The rivalry between the Borgia and the Sforza tribes brewed over political dominance in central Italy. Also aggravating the bitter rivalry was the difficulty in pronouncing a word that began with Sf. The resulting enunciation made it sound like Cesare had a lisp. It is also widely believed that Cesare Borgia was the model and inspiration for Niccolo Machiavelli's The Prince, although Cesare never received a penny in royalties—a fact he resents to this day.

Both Lucrezia and Cesare were illegitimate children of Rodrigo Borgia (who later became Pope Alexander VI). This was a time when it seemed everyone in certain circles in Italy was illegitimate, especially if their father was a pope. It must have been a swinging time to be an Italian Catholic during the Renaissance.

J. E. Winchester, Esq.

Blithering Heights

Introduction

WHAT A DARWIN DICKENS WE'RE IN!

PD-US   PD-US

Charles Darwin/Charles Dickens? or Charles Dickens/Charles Darwin?

*C*harles Darwin was the greatest naturalist of his time and advanced evolutionary theory as outlined in his master 1859 treatise *'On the Origin of Species'*. Charles Dickens was the premier novelist of the Victorian era and a dedicated social critic who helped bring about much needed changes.

These figures are celebrated as the pinnacles of their respective professions. However, there is much speculation that the two men were actually the same person. Let us look at the evidence. They were both named 'Charles'. Both lived at the same time. Both wrote books. The two were never seen together. Coincidences? How did QANON miss this? I think it speaks volumes of their shoddy research department.

Until now there has been no literary evidence to support the 'same person' theory. However, with the discovery of *'Blithering Heights'* this has been rectified. In this piece, one can easily see the rich structure of Dicken's characters and language interspersed with the Darwinian references to natural selection. I propose this combination would not be possible unless the work were created by a single individual.

The question now becomes 'who was this individual—Charles Darwin or Charles Dickens?' Unknown to us now, the answer may be revealed somewhere in the future through the mists of time.

T. E. Winchester, Esq.

Chapter 1

A Tale to Tell

It was the best of times. It was the worst of times. Who are we kidding, it was the worst of times. The very worst of times. In fact, it was the 'worsterest'. It was during this age that people actually gave their homes names such as 'Bleak House' and their children names such as 'Ebenezer'.

This is a tale to tell of the struggles of a young boy and his effort to become a man. The boy was born into grinding poverty and extreme destitution. One condition would have been severe enough, but to suffer both was almost an unbearable beginning.

The boy's family was so impoverished that they could not provide him with a last name. They could barely afford three letters for his Christian name, none of which were capitals, and none of which were vowels. He was called 'pyp'. The 'y', which is sometimes a vowel was not one when it was acquired for his name. Actually, the moniker 'pyp' belonged to the neighbor's dog who sued for labeling infringement.

While still in infancy, pyp was orphaned when his parents sought better opportunities and decided to die of cholera. The baby pyp was left under the care of his abusive Aunt and Uncle who frequently used him as a carpet beater, a common occupation for the abundant population of orphans. In fact, in England of those times, if anything outnumbered abandoned children or mistreated orphans, nothing comes to mind.

When pyp came of a certain age he was sent off to the Institute of Progressive Stray Waif and Urchin Care to obtain his advanced orphan training. Again he met mistreatment and even starvation. Conditions were so severe that pyp once stood up and asked for a second portion of gruel. No one in the history of gruel had ever asked for a second portion regardless of how dire in need they were of sustenance. The cooks at the Institute were overjoyed and began marketing their product as 'Goldilock's Porridge'—a forerunner to Spam.

One of the most severe and abusive caretakers at the Institute was a woman called Blanche DuBois Ingram. Her special cruelty was to hang the children out to dry after their baths. Fox news commentator, Laura Ingram, may be a possible direct descendant of Blanche—which would explain why Laura is such a bitch. It's all genetics.

While a desperate experience, to say the least, pyp's stay at the Institute provided him the opportunity to meet and bond with many other orphans who would later play roles in his life, and thus in this story.

Chapter 2

A Royal Ghost

Christmas Eve, a generally festive day for most, was no day of mirth, good will, and celebration for the orphans at the Institute. This day was known to them as Black Lung Eve since the children had to mine the coal they were to receive as presents on Christmas Day. The poor waifs were also forced to go barefoot as their socks were taken to be hung as decorations on the fireplace in the great hall. For a few of the really unfortunate came Nativity duty. These sad little creatures were made to model as characters for the manger scene outside in the bitter cold. To insure that they remained perfectly still in their poses, the children were glued into position, and their feet were nailed to the ground. Though those portraying animals had to eat straw—a welcome change from their daily gruel.

It was only after these festivities concluded that the orphans were allowed to go to bed. On that night, pyp tossed about in a restless slumber. Dreams may have flashed through his head. However, prior to the stroke of midnight, pyp was awakened by the eerie glow of a transparent figure mispronouncing his name.

"Pype, Piyup, Peep? Hey, kid, give me a break and wake up," said the figure.

pyp slowly surfaced from his drowsed state and rubbed the cobwebs from his eyes which beheld a visage that floated before him. It was an image of a man who wore a well fitted military tunic with tasseled epaulettes, a double row of brass buttons, a pawn shop full of medals, and a sash. His pants which had stripes down the sides were tucked into a pair of polished knee high riding boots.

"Are you a ghost, sir?" asked pyp somewhat unsurprised because in England of those times, if anything outnumbered the haunting spirits of ghosts, nothing came to mind.

"I am Rupert II. I was King of Synovia but now I'm dead and a ghost. You know the Kings in places like Synovia, or Genovia, or Belgravia don't have a long life expectancy. I'm only fifty-five, but I have to get out of the way so that my son, Timmy, could go to some rustic New England town in America, meet cute and fall in love with an independent mapmaker/family bookshop owner and/or travel writer girl who never heard of Synovia. They'd marry and he'd be crowned over my dead body. Do you think I had a very high quality of life rating? This is the part of the plot they don't tell you about in the Hallmark holiday movies. The sad thing is, my kid doesn't even want to be a king. His ambition is to be an explorer or a Christmas tree hunter. I didn't even know that was a thing," noted the King.

"It is pandemonium in the netherworld this week since the Specter and Ghoul Union is on strike. Tonight I'm scabbing in for Jacob Marley, Hamlet's father, and Casper," the King informed pyp, and continued, "So let's get rolling, kid. I'm already behind."

"Where are we going?" pyp asked.

"Just close your eyes, click your heels three times, and we'll be there in a jiff," said the King.

Chapter 3

We'll Always Have Paris

When pyp opened his eyes he found himself in the middle of a wide avenue that seemed to stretch into eternity.

"Welcome to Paris, kid," the King informed pyp.

pyp had no time to appreciate the city because he was swept away in the raging tide of an angry French mob. He was also now completely on his own. King Rupert II had vanished.

A young lieutenant in his handsome blue uniform spied pyp struggling against the mob.

"Bonjour to you, little pale waif young person. You are having the trouble, no?" the soldier said.

"What is going on?" asked pyp.

"Oh, we are having the revolution, you see." Said the Lieutenant.

"A revolution?" inquired pyp.

"You do not know a revolution, thin pasty boy?" asked the Lieutenant. "Well, we are storming, of course, that building which is we call, the Bastille."

"Oh," pyp said. "What is a Bastille?"

The Lieutenant paused with surprise. "You also know not what is the Bastille?" he asked. "It is a prison jail type place. We storm it because it is the only way we can get some people to wear masks. Also everyone likes to see the fellow with the big cow head hat. But mostly, we revolution because we believe in the Big Lie!"

"I've never been to a revolution. What is the Big Lie?" pyp asked.

"Well, dreadful skinny garcon, English spy. It depends on which side you are on," proclaimed the Lieutenant.

"Oh no, sir, I am not a spy. I was brought here by the Ghost of the King of Synovia," pyp explained.

"The King of Synovia! Sacre bleu! He has died too young just for the holiday movie. Such a poor quality of life. I am saddened, poor malnourished urchin," said the Lieutenant sadly.

"My name is pyp, and I am an orphan, sir," pyp declared.

"Well, in this case, off with your head, ragamuffin. Take him away. Have a nice day," the Lieutenant ordered.

The Lieutenant's soldiers carried pyp off into the Bastille which had now been officially liberated according to Faux News.

Chapter 4

A Far, Far Better Thing

Amid so much confusion, pyp was thrown into a cell with a juggler and a thief.

"It's getting kind of crowded in here," said the juggler to the thief.

"What did they get you for, kid?" asked the thief.

"I don't know," pyp declared.

"Oh, another innocent one. Get in line, kid," complained the juggler.

"One minute I was asleep, then a ghost came and took me to this city, then there was an angry crowd, and now I'm here and it's 'off with my head'," cried pyp.

"Ghost, huh. Now they're throwing in the mentals. Nothing good comes out of a revolution, I always say," stated the thief.

"What ghost, kid?" asked the juggler.

"Why, that one," pyp said as he pointed to the luminous apparition behind the juggler and thief.

"Hey, it's the King of Maldevia!" exclaimed the thief.

"No, I'm the King of Synovia, Rupert II," clarified the King. "You're probably thinking of the King of Belgravia who died last Christmas for 'Regal Vermont Christmas'."

"Oh, yeah," recalled the juggler.

"Where have you been? I think they're going to 'off with my head'!" pyp said desperately.

"Look, kid, I told you I had a couple other appearances to make. I just did one for Hamlet's father. It's actually in this book. Look it up. Anyway, I'm going to get you out," explained the King

"How?" asked pyp.

"The old switch-a-roo! I snuck in this other little kid to take your place and we'll just zip out the back," said the King as he revealed his plan.

"What other little kid?" asked pyp of the Ghost.

"This one," said the King, and the smallest little person that pyp, or anyone else, had ever seen stepped into the dim light. "His name is Teenie Tom."

"But if he remains, he will die in my place," protested pyp.

"It will be a good career experience for him," the King assured pyp.

"Yeah, an impressive addition to his resume," added the thief.

Chapter 5

The Tale of Teenie Tom

*S*ince Teenie Tom is about to sacrifice his life for pyp, it seems only fair that we know a little bit more about him. Besides, nobody is stupid enough to think that such a sacrifice is going to look good on any resume.

Teenie Tom was a contemporary of another notable boy named Tiny Tim. As tiny as Tiny Tim was, which was tiny, Teenie Tom was tinier than Tiny Tim. Tiny Tim was tiny-tiny. Teenie Tom was teenie-tiny. Teenie Tom was less than a foot tall and weighed a pound. In fact, Teenie Tom was so teenie, they issued a search warrant for his mother's uterus in a vain quest to find the rest of him.

All the children loved to play with Teenie Tom. He could be a doll for the youngest, or a stick used to play fetch with the family dog. Teenie Tom was also helpful around the house with chores. After supper, his mother would put a woolen hat on him and used him to scour out the dirty pots and pans.

However much joy this brought Teenie Tom, he felt he was destined for more—all evidence to the contrary. Still, he followed his instincts and went into the noble field of medicine and became a gyno-procto exam special assistant. This is how it worked.

First, the doctors would lube him up, tie string around his ankles, strap a miner's lantern helmet to his head, give him a pencil and pad, and then shove him up either someone's butt or hooha. Whilst in the designated cavity, Teenie Tom looked around and took notes describing what he saw. When the procedure was completed or when Teenie Tom could no longer hold his breath, a firm yank on the string and safely pop him out like a solid turd or used Tampax.

Teenie Tom was highly respected in his field and this respect led him to the attention of Pierre and Marie Curie who believed they could restore Teenie Tom to normal size through the use of radioactive materials. One night, while Teenie Tom, Pierre, and Marie Curie were walking to the laboratory, Pierre tripped over Teenie Tom and fell to the cobblestones of the Paris Street, where a milk wagon ran over Pierre's head.

Teenie Tom was so distraught over Pierre's demise that he simply wandered the streets of Paris in shock. This is where the Ghost of King Rupert II found him. Thanks to the old switch-a-roo plan, once again, Teenie Tom had an opportunity to prove his size was not an impediment to face and overcome adversity. It was assumed that Teenie Tom was executed the next morning in place of pyp. pyp didn't know for sure because by then he was back in England where King Rupert II ghost unceremoniously dumped pyp in the tangled labyrinth of narrow streets and crooked alleys of London's Clerkenwill slums. It was the home of accumulated filth such as evangelists, politicians, and rats—all of whom descended from common ancestors.

Chapter 6

Clerkenwill & the Artful Hatter

*N*ext to Mos Eisley, Clerkenwill was the most wretched hive of scum and villainy in the galaxy. Actually, Clerkenwill had slightly more villainy but Mos Eisley's sheer volume of scum was the difference maker. pyp found himself alone in one of Clerkenwill's stench filled alleys. Alone, until a voice reached out for him.

"Oy, you there, boy. Are ye the new recruit?" the one who asked was a shady looking fellow named Jeff Bozo—alias 'The Artful Hatter'.

Bozo steamrolled into his introduction. "I'm Jeff Bozo. They call me the Artful Hatter because I'm the slickest entrepreneur in the city. How that relates, I have no idea. Anyway, let me tell you about the organization you are about to join.

Bozo, put an arm around pyp and directed him to walk as things were explained, "Yes, we started as a small pickpocket operation, but soon realized the inefficiency of fencing all the stolen watch chains and trinkets we collected. So I developed a distribution system from a central warehouse, which I soon expanded to several warehouses as business boomed. The beauty of the system was that it didn't only work for stolen goods. It worked for any goods."

Bozo continued, "And it works so well because we streamline our workers' time and effort, no more bathroom and lunch breaks thanks to our Use-Reuse-Recycle (URR) technology. Here's how it works. Each worker is fitted in a URR suit. Nutrient dispensers feeds gruel and water to the worker. Bodily exports are captured and pumped into our URR converter which breaks the waste back into water and gruel and then passes them back to the nutrient dispenser. If you want to eliminate the squander of human work effort, you make the worker less human. Our system is especially well suited for places like prisons and orphanages. Of course, being so successful, we diversified into capital reinvestment, banking, and aero-space exploration.

I have my own space ship. It's beautiful, baby!"

"Gee wiz, Mr. Bozo," was all pyp said.

However, pyp really didn't attend much to anything Bozo said because he was distracted by a miniscule boy who kept trying to get his attention. The boy's size was similar to Teenie Tom's and his visage was as transparent like King Rupert II's.

Bozo chimed in again, "I'll grab the papers for you to sign and then we'll get you fitted for your URR suit. I'll be right back. Don't go away."

As soon as Bozo was out of view, the tiny transparent lad ran up to pyp and said, "Come with me if you want to live."

Chapter 7

The Ghost of Teenie Tom

*P*yp went off with Teenie Tom's floating specter.

"I'm the ghost of Teenie Tom. The one who took your place in the Bastille. BTW, thanks for that. I'm the second of the ghosts you will meet," said Teenie Tom.

"Where is King Rupert?" pyp asked.

Teenie Tom replied in a huff, "Hey, I am literally on this job less than an hour so give me a break with the questions. My head didn't even stop rolling when this Ghost Squad guy shoved this itinerary in my face. Not sure how he did that, by the way. All I know is I'm supposed to take you to the Tea Party. So let's go. I don't know if there's a time limit involved here."

So pyp and the ghost of Teenie Tom wound through the crooked streets and alleys of Clerkenwill until they came to a sewer grate.

"Here we are, and in we go," said Teenie Tom.

pyp's senses were almost overcome by the reeking fumes dispensed from the sewer. "But it smells so bad," he protested.

"I know it's not a rabbit hole, but it's either down there or eat your own crap gruel every day for the rest of your life with the Artful Hatter," replied Teenie Tom.

pyp thought for a second, held his breath and dove into the sewer. The descent was more of a slide than a fall, almost like skidding down a slick tube. pyp reached bottom with a plop. He wasn't shaken or hurt, but he was definitely slimed.

In a few seconds, a different ghost with a white powdered wig plopped next to him, sending more slime spraying about.

"Funny," pyp thought, "it doesn't smell as bad down here."

"That's because the slide is greased with gruel. It's as odorless as it is tasteless," commented the gentleman shade.

"How did you know what I was thinking?" asked a surprised pyp.

"It's what everybody thinks when they get here. Sorry I'm late. I'm the ghost of Immanuel Can't—philosopher, moralist, and dead guy," Can't answered. "From this point, it's just a short way to Lilliputz and the Secret Garden."

"Lilliputz? The Secret Garden?" asked a confused pyp.

"That's where the Tea Party is. I'll tell you more when we get there," Immanuel Can't told pyp.

Chapter 8

The Tea Party

*A*fter a few minutes as well as a few twists and turn, pyp and Immanuel Can't stood before two large doors marked 'Tea Party—Abandon All Reason Ye Who Enter Here'. On a tall pedestal to one side sat a repulsive bug-eyed creature whose obese body was simply ripples of slimy fat. Clearly he was a product of unnatural selection much like several Supreme Court justices he pushed through.

"That's Jabba the Mitch," said Can't. "He controls who gets into the Tea Party which is supposed to be open to all. Fortunately we're invisible to him. So I'm going to punch him in the face because I can get away with it. I always wanted to do this."

Can't proceeds to smack Jabba the Mitch. Mitch doesn't know what hit him and so just continues to ooze disgusting slime from his pores. Mitch suffered from irritable jowl syndrome.

Can't and pyp joined the Tea Party already in progress.

To pyp's surprise, the Tea Party wasn't a tea party at all. There was one long rectangular table in the room and all about it sat little red people.

Immanuel Can't told pyp, "See the middle one on the red side wearing the crown. That's 'The Donald—Red Queen of Trumps'. He's feeding his followers by stuffing worms into their mouths. They just regurgitate the crud during the meeting."

"They're all so teenie tiny," noted pyp.

"They're teenie tiny because they're Red Lilliputzes, who are as small of stature as they are small of mind," Can't explained.

Then came the sound of a scepter hitting the hollow head of Rudy Head Drip, one of Queen Donald's top groveling baba-booie aides.

The Donald spoke. "I now announce, not that I'm running again in 2024, but I will. I shouldn't have to run again since I really won the last election which was rigged. Landslide win. And it was rigged so I lost. You can believe me. I know because Mr. Putin assured me I would win. He was clear. Very clear. He's a very nice man who wouldn't interfere with our elections. No proof. So I now say the meeting is open, and I recognize the Georgia peach pit, Marginally Taylor Insane, because she's not wearing a mask."

Chapter 9

Marginally Taylor Insane

Marginally Taylor Insane took the floor. She brushed imaginary flies off her face.

"First of all, I would like to express my thanks to the January 6 patriots for their participation in the election process at the Capital, and also for not killing me there. Sadly, those heroes can't be with us today because a large number are in jail, quarantine, or dead from Covid. God bless America," she announced.

A large round of applause followed her blessing.

She continued, "We will bring up for discussion several important issues facing Lilliputz tonight. These include: immigration, climate, abortion, and the right to hunt down and kill liberals. My topic is immigration, but I will participate in hunting liberals, later.

Our corner of this world has always been Lillieputzer white which is red. It is our noble heritage. One we should, nay, MUST preserve at all costs, as long as someone else is paying the bill. Lilliputz should have less people named Treyvon, Julio, and Wang, and more people named Cooter, Billy Lee, and Bubba. Our precious civilization will surely be 'Gone with the Wind' if we allow the influx of people into Lilliputz whose complexion is swarthy or darker. God himself told me this in a tweet, the same one where he said all liberals are cannibalistic pedophiles and issued a denial that he ever created the Jews. Thank you."

A round applause came from the reds.

"Immanuel Can't turned to pyp and said, "I wonder if God mentioned anything about her lobotomy being overdue. Man, if I ever met a guy named Cooter, I'd be itchy for a week."

"Who is that odd woman?" asked pyp.

"That is a lady who comes from the part of the country where good mental health is strictly an option. And evidentially not a preferred one," responded Can't.

Chapter 10

Guns & Butter & More Guns

*M*arginally Taylor Insane began vomiting flies and so turned the floor over to Roscoe Rod Magnum—a man armed to the teeth with handguns, shotguns, and automatic rifles strapped to every appendage on his body. He was a walking armory.

Roscoe began, "Thank you, Marginally. I just want to say that I'm not a gun crazy maniac. I am simply a maniac, and I believe wholeheartedly in the Constitution where it explicitly says I have the right to bear arms. And implicitly says I can slaughter my fellow citizens, the b***ards, without remorse if they try to take my guns away. In fact, I can slaughter anyone I consider a threat to my security. This, of course, includes, unarmed people in church, shopping malls, or schools.

I have more than four hundred guns, half of which I carry on me at all times. I have so many guns that it is a problem getting dressed in the morning trying to figure out what I'm going to wield that day. Sometimes I worry that if I'm attacked I won't be able to choose in time the gun I'm going to defend myself with. That's why I carry a sixteen inch Bowie knife as backup.

I go to bed with my guns not my wife. She's been wounded too many times in bed already. I call that safe sex. I turn in with my guns because if any holy rolling, bargain hunting, psychology major breaks into my house, I can kill them fair and square. I can do that because I don't sleep, I stay awake waiting for them. Sleep deprivation and amphetamines sharpens your reaction time and makes your eyes turn yellow—not to mention what it does to your ability to reason when you got a .45 caliber automatic with you.

Carrying weapons is a choice the second amendment leaves to me. Liberals preach those with guns are monsters and gun control will save lives. Well, if it comes down to Pro-Life or Pro-Choice. I am going with Pro-Choice at 800 rounds per minute."

The Red panel took a moment to digest the last part of Roscoe's message. The rest of his speech even the evangelicals were at peace with.

"And in conclusion," Roscoe proclaimed, "the liberals are wrong. I am not a monster. I am just a guy who enables monsters to get the weapons to wipe out kindergarteners! Don't judge me!"

Before his last words echoed through the room a trap door opened beneath his feet. Roscoe fell through and a large sheet of flames shot up. The trap door closed but then reopened to release a large happy belch and a sign that read 'JUDGED'.

Roscoe Rod Magnum was finally home where he belonged.

Chapter 11

The Fake Pandemic

*U*pon the liquidation of Roscoe Rod Magnum's brain, Red Queen Donald rapped Rudy Head Drip on the noggin, restored order, and announced the next speaker.

"Thank you Roscoe, very nice speech. Tremendous speech. Good words. Lots of them. Vowels, verbs, and propositions. Loved it. Now our next topic which is coming up next. Also a very good topic. Nothing but good topics here tonight. Excellent topics that we have. Let me introduce our next speaker that has been very loyal, especially to me. Well, only to me or off with the head. That's how it goes, right Rudy?" asked the Queen.

"Yes, Master," replied Rudy Head Drip obediently.

The Queen continued, "OK, then here's my friend and mine, Tucker Hannitwitty."

Again Immanuel Can't turned to pyp. "The first word out of this guy's mouth is always a lie."

Tucker stood up and began his presentation, "Thanks."

"He's lying," noted pyp.

Tucker Hannitwitty continued, "My fellow reds, Mr. and Mrs. America, and all the ships at sea. Tonight I would like to address the mass fraud that has been perpetrated through our land by the fake news-generating leftist liberal media. I am referring to the 'so called' Covid pandemic.

Now, everybody knows this pandemic is a fake. We all know that except for a few people that are dead or dying from these secondary respiratory conditions. But who are you going to believe? Someone on a respirator or someone who swore he had proof Nancy Pelosi was a mistress of the walking dead? The Fox Faux Fact Finder says I was right.

Why are the liberals propagating this phony 'pandemic'? It's simple, just like Chuck Schumer's brain. They want to take away your freedoms. Your freedoms are the only disease, in their view, that has to be eradicated. We are being dictated to by a president who sleeps more hours a day than a cat. He is handing out mandates like monkeys flying out of the Wizard of Oz's butt.

Listen to some of these: You have to get vaccinated. You have to wear a mask. You have to social distance. Well, if you really want to social distance, I say don't shower for three days. That's up to you, and not the federal government to say. Even more intrusive, your children have to stay home and can't go to school. If that keeps up they will dip below the Mississippi-Mendoza line of education in no time. Sure these things might save lives, but they take away your personal right to choose. And if it comes to saving lives or losing personal freedom, well, I choose Pro-Choice over Pro-Life anytime. Thank you."

A long loud round of applause followed Tucker Hannitwitty's summary words.

Chapter 12

Pro-Life vs. Pro-Choice Clarified

Tucker the F***er, as he was sometimes called, handed the floor over to the next speaker, a very prestigious man of the cloth, adulterer, and convicted swindler Jerry Bakkker Swaggerer (JBS), televangelista.

"Thank you." JBS began. "I'd like to quickly clarify something about 'Pro-Life' and 'Pro-Choice' if I may. While I wholly support the intent and content of my fellow Tea Party Reds, I might select some modified labels. Of course, I'm talking about the 'A-word', abortion. Now Pro-Choice in reference to the A-word, implies that the owner of the body carrying the embryo is the only one who has to right to decide the fate of the fetus. As a total aside, fate of the fetus sounds like a really great title for a prequel to 'Fate of the Furious'. Doesn't it?

Anyway, allowing only one person to make such a decision sounds too much like a dictatorship to me, and that's not how we operate in a democracy. Besides, this is too important a decision to be left to a woman especially the one having the baby. We all know God made pregnant women crazy. Besides, who died and gave her the right to carry the baby?

Now, in Pro-Life the fate of the fetus, and I really like that as a movie title the more I say it, is determined by complete strangers who are almost entirely white males, who will take no part in the raising or support of the child, but believe in the Lord Jesus Christ as our savior and our meal ticket. And the fate of the fetus, boy, that just rolls off the tongue. The fate we decide is 'LIFE"! Then we can wash our hands of the situation. Our holy duty is done. Now we can go on crusade and raise money.

Now, I know you're asking how we evangelists can reconcile an anti-abortion stance with support for gun right advocates who enable the slaughter of innocent men, women, and children. Here's how.

There are no innocent men, women, or children. They are all born with what the papists call 'aboriginal sin' so they are fair game and in the world's hands, not ours. However, the unborn who are still in the hooha, are without sin and it is in the best financial interests of televangelism to make them a marquee fund raising bonanza. Hallelujah! It's the same simple logic that we use to explain how we can hate Jews but support Israel."

pyp asked Immanuel Can't, "Is he going to take the Hell Express, too?"

"No, I think God will want to deal with him personally," Can't answers.

As if waiting for its cue, a brilliant bolt of lightning burst through the tea room and rendered Jerry Bakkker Swaggerer into a pile of smoldering cinders.

Sometimes miracles come in unexpected forms. Hallelujah!

Chapter 13

Science Explained

*W*hen the smoke cleared, the Queen of Trumps announced the final speaker.

"Thank you, Jerry. Great finish. Fantastic. The best exit since I got out of being impeached. Totally false charges. Totally not true. That's been proven by Fox News. Now here's another myth we're going to explode. It's going to be a big bang so watch your ears. Don't believe what they hear. Please welcome, and I mean it, Kelly& Wrongway.

A limited round of applause from the surviving Tea Party greeted Kelly& Wrongway.

Kelly& Wrongway began. "Good evening. Today I'm going to talk about the fake science of climate change.

Climate is weather and whether or not you believe that, it is an alternative fact. And weather is something you see on the news following sports which is not science. So you have to ask who has the best sports reporting on television and is television the best format for talking about things that aren't happening in Hollywood where they make movies which are fiction. So when you talk about *Rain Man* you are not talking about something real like rain. It is fiction and how could science say it isn't and then claim climate change is real? It doesn't work both ways. It doesn't work at all. And you need to have something that works, like a job. And our red Tea Party has instituted programs that will provide employment to large numbers of Lilliputzes. I think all educated people will agree with me on this point."

Kelly& Wrongway concluded her muddled menagerie of metaphors and pranced off.

Pyp's head was now hurting. "Is God going to handle this lady himself, too?" he asked.

"No, I think he's just as confused as the rest of us now," Immanuel Can't said scratching his head.

Chapter 14

The Blue Lilliputzes

Red Queen Donald rapped on the near empty skull of Rudy Head Drip to conclude the Tea Party gathering. Immanuel Can't and pyp left the room. On the way out, Immanuel Can't once again punched Jabba the Mitch in his corpulent face.

"I don't understand. Why did we had to go to the Tea Party?" asked pyp.

"I don't know. Repeat—this is my first night on the job. Maybe it was to show you a fair and balanced view of Lilliputz because we're headed for the Liberal Lilliputz Caucus around the corner." Said Immanuel Can't.

Can't and pyp made their way around the corner and arrived at the site of the Liberal Lilliputz Caucus. Over the entry way hung a large banner that proclaimed,

'START CARING FOR THE MENTALLY ILL & STOP ELECTING THEM TO CONGRESS'

Immanuel Can't escorted pyp under the banner, through the doors, and into the bustling caucus room where lots of teenie tiny Lilliputzes tossed about like flotsam and jetsam. These Lilliputzes, however, were blue instead of red.

"Why are these Lilliputzes blue?" asked pyp.

"They're progressives. Super liberals, if you will," Can't answered. "They're the bitterest enemies of the red Lilliputzes."

"The red Lilliputzes believed in some mean and nasty things. Are the blue Lilliputzes nicer than the red ones?" inquired pyp.

"Nicer in their own way, but it's hard to tell whether they have practical ideas sometimes. When you're a radical zealot, idealism tends to strip away a lot of reason." said Immanuel Can't.

Eventually, one blue Lilliputzer made her way to the front of the audience. "What's happening now?" pyp asked.

"Shhh, I think someone is about to address the caucus," said Immanuel Can't.

Chapter 15

The Progressive Idealist

A blue female Lilliputzer stood up and looked directly into the eyes of her audience.

She spoke softly but firmly. "I have come here to rectify a great wrong. It has come to my attention that the cafeteria in the Great College of Lilliputz is named the 'Whitelind-Mannford Cafeteria'. This can no longer be tolerated in the name of social justice."

"Why is that?" asked another blue.

"Because the name contains the words 'White' and 'Man' which put together say 'white man'. And the white man is the oppressor of people of color, women, and non-heterosexuals. We demand that the name be changed to a more socially acceptable title such as the Lilliputz Diverse and Inclusive Center for Nutrition. Also we insist that apologies be issued to everyone in Lilliput for having someone named Whitelind or Mannford."

A round of clapping and 'Here-Here's' filled the room until no one could hear themselves think.

"That sounded..." pyp started to say.

"Trivial, petty, stupid," Can't finished pyp's sentence.

"Well, yes. If the blue Lilliputzes are bitter enemies of the red Lilliputzes I thought they would have much more serious things to say against the red's beliefs," pyp surmised.

"Well, they try, but you see how many different shades of blue there are in the blue caucus. All blues have to totally support every blue shade position. If they don't they're called racists or sexists or whatever. So the fighting is fierce. But you can't have any coherent policy if everything is number one. The struggle for primacy is an ongoing fight for species survival. It's nice to think everyone wants to come together in peace and harmony to save the world by raising awareness and creating massive social programs. Kumbaya. Unfortunately, no one wants to live in total harmony. People just want a bigger piece of the pie. You kind of have to crack the whip to get people to sing in harmony. Either that, or hire the Everly Brothers," said Immanuel Can't.

"Then they just fight each other?" asked pyp.

"They used to, but it just got too exhausting. So now they just do cosmetic stuff like change the names of things to be more politically correct and claim to raise awareness on issues that everybody is already aware of. But that gives some a chance to put something important looking on their resume or college applications. Marching for causes used to be a serious business when there were people on the other side actually willing to kill you for registering to vote, protest a war, or cross a bridge. Now the big issues are to find the right size in an 'I'm Woke' tee shirt" and to smear Christopher Columbus's name. Also it's hard to do anything meaningful with traitor in your midst. See that big floating head changing color from blue to red. That's Joe Munchkin. He's the deciding vote on any serious blue policy. And he always votes red, the b***ard," explained Immanuel Can't.

Chapter 16

A Riot is an Ugly Thing

The roar of an angry red mob shook the blue caucus building. Outside on the street waves and waves of cardinal colored Lilliputzes flew in a rage toward the capitol building.

"What is going on?" pyp asked a manic red.

The red Lilliputz stopped his ranting to answer, "We are storming the capitol. Red Queen Donald told us that's where the lying low-down liberals are hiding all of the socks they steal from our laundry! And the Donald is behind us all the way!"

"It looks like way far behind. How do you think you're going to get away with this?" asked Immanuel Can't.

"Because we're patriots!" shouted the red.

"Because we are freedom fighting insurrectionists!" screamed another passing red.

Other reds joined in with their own ideas about getting away clean. Some of the most creative included they were told this was: a massive sale at Walmart, a rush for Springsteen concert tickets, and just the way New Jersey tourists behaved visiting the capital.

The crimson tide rolled forward like a peasant mob storming the evil doctor's castle. Some of the rioters carried clubs, some signs saying 'Nancy Pelosi is Queen of the Undead', and all of them were missing at least one sock.

Someone once said, 'A riot is an ugly thing, but you can find a lot of bargains if you know where to loot.'

Immanuel Can't took pyp by the arm and said, "Come on, we have to get out of this place. I'm going to get you back to your own world. Besides, I'm due for a coffee break."

Chapter 17

The Good Doctor

With that ghost of Immanuel Can't and pyp floated up, up, and away far from the madding crowd and into the starry, starry night. From this high altitude pyp could see a plethora of ghosts floating about escorting their living fares. He was amazed that each passenger was bound for their own adventure. The scene looked to pyp like a host of lantern flies that mirrored the twinkling light of the stars.

It was beautiful.

Then a sudden drop, a crash, and a sliding stop. It wasn't a smooth landing, but at least it was one you could walk away from.

"Sorry." Apologized Immanuel Can't, "still working on the landings. Look, I'm going to leave you here. The itinerary says someone will be along for you shortly. I've got to get going to pick up some guy named Mr. Chicken. These instructions are really not clear. Oh, you'll be getting another visit from a ghost later on in the story. So long."

With that Immanuel Can't vanished in a sparkling pop and pyp found himself once again alone on a foggy and unfamiliar city street. But he was not to be alone for long.

"Hello," came a voice out of the mist. "Are you the lad interviewing for the laboratory assistant position?"

pyp was surprised, but managed a response, "Well, sir, I am a lad and would welcome employment if it were available."

"Ah, very good then. I am Doctor Victor Frankenschtine, DC. Do you have any experience as a laboratory assistant?" asked the doctor.

"No, sir," answered pyp.

"Any experience as an assistant of any kind?" came the doctor's next query.

"Afraid not, sir," pyp responded.

"Have you ever been in a laboratory?" the doctor quizzed.

"Never, sir," pyp said as he felt his prospects waning.

"Great, you're hired!" exclaimed Dr. Frankenschtine. "Oh, you wouldn't have a hump back by any chance?"

"I do not, sir," answered pyp.

"Bummer. We'll just have to make the most of it, I suppose. Follow me, lad," Dr. Frankenschtine said as he started and stopped several times, each time uncertainly choosing a different direction.

Chapter 18

Doctor Frankenschtine's Laboratory

After a very circuitous route, the doctor and pyp arrived at the laboratory. It was not Dr. Frankenschtine's laboratory so they were off once again on a meandering journey that took them to a stable, a home for old sailors, and a grain grinding mill. Finally, after eliminating most of the edifices in the east end of the city, they arrived at the correct laboratory.

"I hope you can remember your way here, boy," said the doctor. "Wouldn't want you to be late for work. You'll be staying in the laboratory storage room just above the main lab. Tricky set of stairs there. Often get lost. Oh, well. What is your name, lad?" asked the doctor.

"It is pyp, sir," pyp replied.

"pyp with no capitals and no vowels. You must be a poor orphan child. Familiar with that. I too was an orphan or, at least, that's what my parents told me. Well, pyp, my boy. Wait, where did you go?" the doctor said looking about with some confusion while pyp just stood unmoving by his side. "Ah, there you are. Tricky little fellow, aren't you? Well, there'll be a time for games, young pyp, but not for now.

Let me explain my work, lad so that you may better understand the role you will play. And when you understand that, you can explain it to me. Right-o, let us begin. I was once engaged to a beautiful young woman. We were very much in love, so I am told. I was a young doctor with both a promising career and family ahead. My research was focused on developing secret sauces for fast food chicken. However, in the process of my work instead of finding secret chicken sauce I discovered an unknown formula that enabled me to re-animate dead tissue. Not the Kleenex pop up kind, but the tissue of basic body elements. In short, I found the secret of creating life itself! I found a way to bypass natural evolution. And so, I abandoned all else to this pursuit. Abandoned colleagues, friends, and my Y membership.

Most importantly, I abandoned my beloved fiancé, the enigmatic Amanda Reckonwith.

All was lost in the quest to play God, not as an actor, but in reality which was better since I have stage fright, I stutter, and could never remember my lines. Lo and behold, I was successful! I created my own Adam but not exactly in my image since he was nine feet tall and could crush bowling balls in his bare hands. Plus he had a much better sense of direction than I.

Well, this is not something you just let out in the news. I had to keep him secret until the world was ready to accept such a creature. However, before the big ceremony where we were going to go public and make a killing in the market, Adam escaped. He's now out there in the world. Your mission, pyp, should you choose to accept it, is to venture out, find the creature and return him home. As usual, should you be caught or captured I will disavow any knowledge of your actions. Also, watch out if Adam says he's going to crush your skull. He can do it easily. Alright, lad, on your way. The door is over there or maybe over there somewhere." concluded the good doctor.

Chapter 19

Encounter Along the River

And so pyp set out on his search for the nine foot tall, massively built creature named Adam. But where to start? Perhaps it would be near the river and the undersides of the bridges. These area were less traveled and provided many places to hide. Logic told him that is where he should start.

He walked through the tall grass and reeds along the winding turns of the river shore. Suddenly, he felt strong hands grab his ankles, and he tumbled to the ground. Short of a first down.

"Aye, there, lass." the owner of the hands spoke sternly.

"Lad," corrected pyp.

"Right-O, sorry about that, Miss," came a cautious reply. The sound of the words were almost as ragged and worn as the man wielding them.

"What do you want, old man?" asked pyp, who tried not to show his fear.

"I need food and drink, and a file. Do this and no harm will come to you." came a veiled threat. "Also, shoes. Italian made with rich Corinthian leather. And a typewriter or a plow. Whatever is most readily at hand. Also, if you have a musical instrument. Preferably a piano, although a harpsichord would do. Some lumber would also be nice. I'm talking good hardwood, tight grain. Something I could make a boat with. Unless you have a boat, then bring that instead. No, wait. Bring the boat and the wood, and some woodworking tools. I can make furniture while I wait around. You wouldn't happen to have any lottery tickets, would you? Scratch offs, not the pick the numbers kind." the old man rambled.

Pyp's head was spinning from the sprawling list of demands.

"Are you Dr. Frankenschtine's creature?" pyp asked.

"No. I am Howard Uuuuuu. It's spelled with all 'u's', but it's pronounced 'Hughes'. I am a fugitive convict because I didn't get a presidential pardon like some others. Tell me, girl." the old man said.

"Boy," pyp responded, obviously insulted.

"Transgender, ey. I suppose you want your own bathroom," the convict remarked. "Wait, and let me tell you my story."

Pyp shrugged and sighed. He didn't have time to listen, but he also didn't want to be impolite.

Chapter 20

The Story of a Convict

The convict began his tale, "I once lived in the city. I was christened Saddam Stalin Hitler but my good name was slandered when I was accused of stealing from the church poor box. This crime I did not commit but was framed for. My true crime was stealing the communion hosts from the altar because I believed them to be Necco Wafers. I had a sweet tooth.

They could not prove the wrongdoing of the poor box, but damage enough was done that I was forced to leave the city and settle as a recluse in an isolated rural village away from accusing eyes. There I changed my name to Chloe Kardashian but thought better of it, and changed it again to Lawrence Welk, thank you, boys, and finally once again to the name I now bear which is Ebenezer Marner.

In this simple village I worked a trade as weaver of tight sweaters for developing young high school girls. I collected much revenue since my skills were significant. In my bitterness, I came to love gold above all else.

One day, while walking, I came upon an unconscious young orphan girl. This was not unusual as children were very commonly laid about the streets and roads. One could hardly take a step without tripping over one of the little b***ards. But somehow this blonde-headed little girl child struck a note in my heart and I took her in and cared for her. The name I gave her was EpiPen named after the Epinephrine Auto-Injector device.

The child changed my life. I would no longer be a recluse but become a part of my community where I ran for congress and lost in a rigged election. Despite this, I held no remorse as my pride and heart were fixed upon EpiPen who grew into a beauty pageant winner—Miss Welsh Coal Mine Disaster. Her talent was de-boning live chickens.

EpiPen turned out to be the illegitimate daughter of a woman and the county squire. The woman was Amanda Reckonwith and so was the county squire.

Somewhere along the line I murdered someone, escaped, and wound up here. EpiPen is now a scouser with five kids doing a reality show in Liverpool.

So, young transgender person, if you would gather those items which I've asked for, you will be free of me. Oh, did I mention I also need a cow."

"What ever happened to Howard Uuuuuu?" pyp thought as he walked away and continued his search for Dr. Frankenschtine's escaped creature.

Chapter 21

On the Waterfront

*P*yp followed the river down to the sea port docks where he thought the creature might embark on a vessel bound for a foreign land. There would be no undue suspicion of a nine foot tall being who might simply pass as an NBA first round draft pick and member of the 'All—I Dated a Kardashian/Jenner Team'.

And so pyp plied his way through the waterfront taverns, inns, and brothels in search of his quarry. However, his search bore no fruit until he ventured onto the docks themselves were he engaged in conversation with the men who sailed the seas in ships.

"Tell me, sailor, I pray," pyp started, "have you perchance happened upon or sighted a man of some nine feet in height hereabouts? His name is Adam."

The sailor, whose name was Punxsutawney, replied, "Sure, we've got a few on board our boat now."

"Hey, Cooter," called out Punxsutawney to his mate, "any of those nine foot guys named Adam?"

Cooter thought a moment and said, "I don't know. Let me ask, Bilgepump. Hey, Bilgepump, what's the nine foot guy's name?"

Bilgepump replied, "I think it's either Godot or Guffman. Maybe it's Fluffy."

A taller sailor with a weather worn face and piercing eyes interrupted, "It's not Fluffy, idiot. Hey, kid, why don't you come on board and ask them yourself?" The weather worn sailor was called Turnbuckle, first mate of the good ship Peapod.

pyp thought this was an excellent idea and climbed on board the good ship Peapod. His next aware moment came when the ship was a day's voyage out to sea.

"Where am I?" asked pyp. "And why am I so itchy?"

"You're at sea, lad, and everybody gets itchy around Cooter," replied Bilgepump.

Chapter 22

The Manly Crew of the Peapod

"We are all sailing men who were born to the sea and are bound to it. Why do you want to be a sailor, young lad?" said Punxsutawney.

"We'll be at sea a long spell. Maybe years," added Cooter.

"The sea will know if you're a sailor soon enough. What's your name, boy?" Asked Turnbuckle.

"pyp." announced pyp.

"What! With no capitals or vowels? You wouldn't be an abandoned orphan, would you lad? Punxsutawney grimaced as he spoke. "The Captain will not be pleased."

"I don't understand?" pyp was confused.

"It's bad luck to bring an abandoned orphan aboard. It's worse than wearing an albatross around the neck of a naked red-headed lady," said Bilgepump.

"Oh I would never touch one of those," claimed Punxsutawney.

"Why not! They are so hot," Cooter blurted out.

"I don't like red-heads," responded Punxsutawney.

"Oh, sorry, I thought you were talking about the albatross," said Cooter.

"We have an orphan aboard, no red heads, and no Saturday movies," cried Bilgepump.

"Well, lads, it looks like this is going to be a longer voyage than we expected." proclaimed Turnbuckle.

"How will we remain manly men of the seas under such conditions?" asked Punxsutawney.

Bilgepump bemoaned, "Let's face it, boys, we're all going to be sissies by the time we get back home."

Chapter 23

The Grumbling of Sailors

The Peapod sailed on a Dissociative Identity Disorder sea. One day it was calm, the next angry, the next gone, then back again, then whatever. The crew braved on as days turned into months. Their struggles were barely mitigated by the timeless rite of dissatisfied sailors—grumbling.

"Many things are made difficult when at sea so long. Absentee voting is a nightmare, especially if you live in a red state. Did you see what those b***ards in Georgia did." Punxsutawney said.

"Voting? Try getting an extension on filing your tax return. If you're late the IRS will find you, even out here. Believe me." added Cooter.

"That's difficult, but try getting a pet license for a fish." noted Bilgepump.

"The worst thing to me is the pain of living without hope. It is a pain worse than childbirth." Turnbuckle said.

"Childbirth, hah! What about a prostrate exam? That's pain! The birth canal, at least, is a two way path, but the poop shoot, well, that proctologist is driving the wrong way on a strictly one way street. That is a pain that no women, except those in a certain segment of the adult film industry, are aware." explained Punxsutawney.

"I'm having a nice time." interjected pyp, "I think it's very soothing here at sea."

"Good for you, kid. Hey? Does anyone know what we do out here?" asked Cooter.

"What do you mean?" Turnbuckle said and looked for clarification.

"I mean we've been on dozens of voyages. Some of them lasting for years, but I don't know what we do except try to remain manly, watch movies on Saturday nights, or grumble." explained Cooter.

Punxsutawney thought a moment and added, "Good point. We don't fish or hunt whales."

"We don't carry cargo." added Bilgepump.

"Or passengers. Nor are we a man of war." Turnbuckle said.

"Yeah, what do we do?" Cooter asked, no closer to an answer.

Before they could form clearer thoughts on the subject, the crew of the Peapod were summoned by a call familiar to men of the sea.

"Ahoy!" came the cry from a passing ship.

All hands of the Peapod rushed topside

Chapter 24

Ahoy

"Ahoy! Ahoy! Ahoy!" Repeated the call from the passing ship—a pale and hollow vessel that gave more a sense of doom than of life.

"Hold on! Your 'ahoy' is very important to us. Please wait and we will return your hail in a moment," Turnbuckle shouted back, "OK, thanks for waiting. Sup?

A skeletal figure came to the rail of the other ship and waved and shouted across the water, "We are the Metrons. Our skipper, Captain Einstein here, killed an albatross. Now we're all doomed to die horrible deaths at sea and yet he gets to wear Lindsay Lohan around his neck. It's not fair!"

"What do you want us to do about it?" Turnbuckle shouted back.

"Do you have any movies we can borrow for Saturday night?" asked the skeletal mariner.

"No. But if we did how would you return it if you're doomed to sail the sea forever and die horrible deaths?" asked Punxsutawney.

"Good point. Didn't think that one through. Sorry," apologized the stringy mariner.

pyp cleared his throat and yelled across to the ghost ship, "Have you seen a nine foot creature named Adam?"

The skeletal mariner looked pyp over carefully and issued a stern warning to the crew of the Peapod, "Do you have an orphan on board? You do know that's bad luck?"

"The boy is in training." Protested Punxsutawney, "Just answer the lad. Have you seen any nine foot creatures?"

"No. We came across some Greek guy who's been on the water for ten years and badly in need of GPS. And there was this IRS agent looking for a fellow named Cooter. You know him?" asked the shadowy mariner.

"Nope." denied Cooter.

"Well, OK. Sorry to hold you up. We'll just mosey on out of your way," apologized the deathly pale mariner.

The crew watched as the mariner's ship shoved off and vanished into the opaque mist of an ocean squall. Once the ghost ship was out of sight, pyp and his fellow sailors all returned below.

Chapter 25

Captain Arbor

Below deck, the crew gathered in their usual places and took up their grumbling where they had left off.

"I'm not a real sailor," confessed Bilgepump.

"I can't even swim," admitted Punxsutawney.

"I've never seen the ocean," remarked Cooter to the confusion of all.

The grumbling ended suddenly because all attention was drawn to the rhythmic thumping of a wooden peg leg on the deck above.

All looked upward. Turnbuckle was first to speak, "The Captain is out of his cabin and paces the deck."

"Who is this Captain?" asks pyp who noticed the grim faces of the crew.

"Captain Arbor, whose wooden leg now raps against the planks of the deck," answered Punxsutawney.

It was more than a wooden leg that held the crew in awe of Captain Arbor. He was a large man with a scarred face always stern and intense. His peg leg was oak and was matched by a mahogany arm. He had teeth of ash and a maple eye. His skull was part balsa which accounted for his lightheadedness at times.

That was just the outside. Internally his lungs were cedar, his heart and liver were bamboo. His kidneys were composite plywood and he peed sawdust. His only son was named Pinocchio.

The man was made of more wood than a tree—a product of medical woodworking experiments—a certified bipolar PSTD disorder egomaniac with social anxiety syndrome—a man of obsessed, perhaps even evil demeanor—a man who feared naught except for termites.

This was Captain Arbor, master of the Peapod.

Chapter 26

The Endless Hunt

Captain Arbor was driven by one thing and one thing only—his hate for the thing that turned him into a living, walking lumber yard. It was a vengeful hunt that had run a course several times around the world. It was the hunt for Moby Melvin, the Great White Smelt.

Arbor had pursued the beast not only across the seven seas and, across the seven continents. Normally a land pursuit wouldn't be possible because the smelt was typically an aquatic animal, but perhaps due to a genetic mutation of the smelt's constitution it was able to adapt amphibiously.

Arbor first encountered Melvin at a seven course Christmas Eve dinner. There, declining to be eaten as per tradition, the smelt rampaged for his life. Arbor, decimated and half-dead, was the only survivor. From that day on, he swore his life away to seek total revenge on the Great White Smelt. In the process he abandoned friends, family, and even his fiancé, the mysterious, if not totally fictional, Amanda Reckonwith.

However, Moby Melvin was as elusive as he was fearsome. The closest Arbor ever came to the fish was in the streets of Novosibirsk where Melvin, who posed as an insurance broker, sold Arbor several expensive home owner/renter policies. This simply added fuel to the fire.

Now in a new season, Captain Arbor renewed the pursuit. This time he set a course north. North to the bitter cold and ice of the Arctic Circle.

Chapter 27

The Creature is Sighted

For several weeks the Peapod moved about in the frigid Arctic waters, dodging icebergs, polar bears, and a ruthless determined IRS agent. Then one day through the curtain of a snow squall a cry went up. The creature had been spotted. Unfortunately for Captain Arbor, it was not the creature he sought. It was Adam, the nine foot tall, artificially constructed creature of Dr. Victor Frankenschtine.

None had ever seen such a sight and all were amazed. The creature toiled rowing a small craft through the breaks in the ice shelf. He tried to avoid the approaching Peapod, perhaps fearing an unfortunate encounter with the men.

"Ahoy!" went up the call of the Peapod.

"Hi!" came back the creature's response.

Punxsutawney asked pyp, "Is this not the creature you spoke of? If so call out to him."

"OK," said pyp, who now directed his voice to the huge figure in the row boat, "Hello, Adam. Dr. Frankenschtine sent me to bring you home. Do you want to come along peaceably or does this have to get ugly."

Months at sea had toughened up pyp into a manly man.

"No thanks. I'm trying to save the ice cap here. It is disappearing at an alarming rate and if it continues the polar bears are promising to go south and eat Greta Thunberg," replied Adam.

"Have you been out here all along?" asked pyp.

"No, I've been dating Caitlyn Jenner. Honestly, I don't know which of us is more put together," said the creature Adam.

Captain Arbor interrupted with his burning question, "Sir, have you had sight of a great white smelt. One that goes by the name of Moby Melvin?"

Adam responded with a question of his own, "Is it an aquatic or amphibious smelt?"

"Evolutionarily speaking, not having the need to adapt to certain environmental conditions, it's androgynous, just like Marilyn Manson." Answered the Captain.

"I didn't know Manson was androgynous. I just thought he was goth." confessed Bilgepump.

"Of course he's androgynous. How could you miss that?" scolded Turnbuckle.

"Sorry, Captain. Haven't seen any smelts. I did have an encounter with an halibut named, Eric. Is that of any help?" offered the creature.

"Not really. Well, we won't hold you up. Good luck with the Thunberg thing," said Arbor as the Peapod sailed away into the dangerous ice field.

Chapter 28

The Iceburger

By the time light dwindled to dusk, the Peapod had not traveled very far. Ahead a huge faintly luminous figure emerged from the dark and blocked their path. It was Orson Welles delivering a sermon. Captain Arbor steered around him. However, while Arbor attended the preacher, he failed to see the iceburger to port. An iceburger is a splinter of a larger iceberg that is served with soda and fries.

There was a collision. A fatal one for the Peapod. She sank slowly but it was thought possible that the crew could be saved. This was not to be, however. Moby Melvin saw this as an opportunity to end the hunt that plagued him across the seven seas and, thanks to evolutionary adaptation, the seven continents.

The Great White Smelt crashed head first into the dying Peapod time and again until the vessel's back was broken and all life boats were destroyed. The short of it was the captain and crew went down with the ship. Only pyp survived clinging to a piece of flotsam bobbing on the surface. It would be many long days before he was rescued.

As for Moby Melvin, after this encounter he had to undergo concussion protocol. Sadly, the Great White Smelt soon developed dementia and spent his last days at the Aquatic Home for Gill-bearing Seafood (phylum Chordata, class Actinopterygii).

Chapter 29

Rescue at Sea

*P*yp drifted on the waves, out of the ice field, and into the well-traveled sea lanes. To survive he drank rain water from the constant squalls, and he ate the fish from the sea—lemon butter baked cod, drunken prawn with mai fun noodles, and Cioppino.

Luckily, before mercury poisoning set in, he was plucked from the water by passing ships. Unluckily those ships were, in the order of appearance: RMS Lusitania, SS Andria Doria, and the three hour charter tour boat, SS Minnow.

pyp managed to escape all their fates and eventually washed ashore somewhere in the moors of Yorkshire. Here, his next adventure began.

Chapter 30

Miss Havisham's Home

While he recovered from his trials at sea, pyp was brought to the attention of a local woman of means, Miss Havisham. She asked for the boy to visit her when he was well enough. In the next few days pyp felt both strong and curious enough to have an audience with the wealthy woman at her estate.

As pyp came up to Miss Havisham's front door he suddenly sensed his nerves like he had not sensed them before, even when face to face of the terrible Moby Melvin. He hesitated but finally summoned the courage to announce his presence with a feeble knock.

"Come in," spoke a soft woman's voice from within.

pyp entered a spacious foyer. Before him was a desk where sat an attractive young woman. Her name tag read, 'Estella'.

"Can I help you?" asked Estella.

"I have come to visit Miss Havisham," pyp announced.

"Do you have an appointment?" Estella inquired.

"I was told the lady wanted to see me as soon as I was well enough," replied pyp.

"Then, I suppose that means you do not have an appointment," Estella remarked.

"I suppose so, Miss." pyp responded with some embarrassment.

"Well, things are fairly busy around here today. Miss Havisham has just accepted a proposal of marriage. She is engaged and there is much to do. What is your name, boy? I will ask the lady if she can see you," Estella told pyp with just a hint of annoyance.

"My name is pyp, Miss," pyp informed her.

Estella returned quickly, but it felt to pyp like an eternity. Her return was marked with a face filled with a grim and irritated expression.

"It is likely to be quite a while before Miss Havisham can see you. Please have a seat in the uncomfortable wooden chair. Would you like something while you wait, water, tea, gruel?" Estella snippily offered.

"No, thank you, Miss," pyp said.

Chapter 31

On Becoming an Indentured Companion

Meanwhile, across town, a sullen man with dark brooding eyes also made inquiries concerning pyp. He was in search of a companion who was the same age as his own son as well as his adopted daughter. He did not entertain the prospect of having a companion of such an age with favor, but he was advised that with his being a completely sociopathic recluse incapable of bearing affection for any human being, a companion might be a good move.

The man's name was Heathcliff, and he was the master of Blithering Heights—Manor on the Moors—a contemporary gothic mansion/inn with both charm and stature overlooking the vast desolate inhospitable wastelands of the Yorkshire Moors—a perfect solitary getaway from the busy hectic life of the city.

Heathcliff, a man of unrelenting determination, procured the services of pyp while the young lad was still waiting to see Miss Havisham.

"Have the boy report to me at my hotel," ordered Heathcliff gruffly, "We shall leave immediately for Blithering Heights upon his presentation. Haste is of the utmost."

And so it was to be. pyp was to be indentured to Blithering Heights for his foreseeable future.

Chapter 32

Miss Havisham's Home, Later

As pyp sat in his uncomfortable wooden chair without the aid of water, tea, or gruel, Estella's telephone rang. Pyp only heard her side of the conversation, but he understood the subject under discussion involved Miss Havisham's upcoming wedding.

"Well, that means the wedding cake will be delivered well before the reception. Are you sure it will remain fresh standing out for so long?" Estella grilled the baker on the other end of the line. "All I can say is, it better!" She ended the call without a courteous farewell.

When Estella hung up she turned her attention to pyp. "How are we doing over there? Don't touch anything," she said.

Estella's phone rang again. Again pyp only heard her side of the conversation.

"I'm sure the gown looks lovely. Miss Havisham has impeccable taste. My concern is with the material and its effect on comfort. She will have to wear that gown for quite a long time. Well, all I can say is, it better!" Estella warned the dressmaker and hung up again with no goodbye.

Estella cast another wary glance toward pyp. "It is annoying to watch you just sitting there. I will go back and see if Miss Havisham is set to see you. Don't make any moves," she said.

Estella, with a very purposeful stride, went back to inquire about Miss Havisham's availability. She returned soon, but with a distraught face.

"Miss Havisham has been jilted once again. Fourth time this month. While she is distressed, I believe her schedule has opened up and she will see you immediately. Give me a second to see if she is composed," stated Estella with a somewhat lack of concern because in England if anything outnumbered jilted brides, I can't think of it.

Estella's return was swift. "Someone set fire to Miss Havisham again. I'm afraid she is cancelling all appointments and going home early. Would you like to reschedule?" she said

"No, thank you, Miss. I will just move on with my life," replied pyp.

Chapter 33

Denied a Last Name

Heathcliff and pyp arrived at Blithering Heights after a two hour carriage ride during which not a word was spoken. All pyp knew was that he was to be a companion to a pair of children. He did not know if the children belonged to the gruff silent man who drove the carriage or to someone else. All of this he assumed would be made clear to him shortly.

"What is your name, boy?" Heathcliff asked once inside.

"pyp, sir," answered pyp.

"What? With no capitals or vowels. Unheard of. You must get a decent name. For now we'll call you Flea Biscuit after the dog, unless the hound minds," Heathcliff said as a dog growled at pyp. "He minds. What is your family name?"

"I have none, sir. My family couldn't afford a last name," pyp answered.

If anything in this world could move Heathcliff to pity it was the idea of not having a last name. It was his condition as well to have also been denied one. This situation was a constant reminder that he too was once without family. Even worse, it fueled his irrational fear that, only having one name, people would believe he had something in common with Bjork.

However, any sympathy Heathcliff showed toward pyp quickly dissipated. He returned to his hard questions.

"I'm told you are an orphan. What qualifications do you have for that?" Heathcliff asked sharply.

"None, sir. I have always been an orphan since my parents died," pyp explained.

"Well, I suppose you're not going to use them as references, then," Heathcliff said. "Very well, we'll play your little game. I'll give you a one week trial as servant. If there is anything I don't like, I'm going to immediately put you up for adoption. Understood?"

"Yes, sir," replied pyp.

"I don't like your attitude. You're going up for adoption right now, fella," Heathcliff barked at pyp, as did the dog.

Thus ended pyp's days as a companion. Adoption adverts went out immediately but no response followed for several weeks. During that time pyp became friends with Heathcliff's children, the sickly, sniveling, spoiled little b***ard, Lintfuzz, and the charming sweet little girl, Cathy.

Lintfuzz, pyp could throw off a cliff and not care. Cathy, however, found a fond place in his heart as did he in hers. It was a warm feeling that pyp had never sensed before. And warmth was a constant craving on the barren hostile moors.

Chapter 34

The Moors

The Moors were a Muslim group who were employed to make fast a ship or vessel to docks by means of cables, lines, or anchors. Have you ever needed to have your ship or vessel made fast to a dock? If you did, you probably met a Moor.

Moors probably lived by water, rivers or oceans to secure ships. However, there is evidence they also inhabited the Maghreb, the Iberian Peninsula, Sicily, and even Malta during the Middle Ages. It is thought that the Moors' origin was as Berber peoples on the Mediterranean coast of Africa. A coast is land next to the sea. It is also called a seashore, or in New Jersey, simply "The shore."

Moors figure prominently as characters in western art and literature. The title character in Shakespeare's play *Othello* was a Moor. His name was Othello. Moors were also featured as extras in the classic film *Casablanca* starring Humphrey Bogart and Ingrid Bergman. Estevanico (Stephen the Moor) was a professional Mexican wrestler who toured with Johnny Puleo and the Harmonica Rascals when they needed to secure their boat to a dock or by anchor.

Chapter 35

The Other Moors

One does not take lightly crossing the moors. It is a remote and heartless land replete with black bogs, swarming cotton grass, and the occasional surrender of a Japanese soldier who was never told World War 2 had ended.

It is an inhospitable environment and to tread this utterly bleak landscape unaware, one risks the taunts of the various species that have physically adapted a symbiotic relationship to their natural environment. This includes harrier and grouse who are very impolite. Intermittently, one of the many sub-species of curlew or ring ouzel will peek from behind the mosses, bracken, and crowberry under-shrubs to deliver mocking words upon the hapless traveler since they are quite ill mannered for their part. Worse still are the rebuffs of endemic breeds such as the Exmoor Pony, Scottish Blackface, or Lonk sheep, which are similar to the Derbyshire Gritstone. All are hearty sarcastic animals that thrive on the sparse cover of semi-natural native vegetation, but won't bother to give you the time of day.

Many who have undertaken the trek through these barren heaths, have entered but have never returned. Their fate remains unknown and they are spoken of only as doomed adventurers useful as warnings to young children or to tourists who look to see snotty little Mary Lennox's secret garden where she probably murdered and buried poor Mrs. Craven.

Chapter 36

The Moores

Fog shrouded, the paths through the Yorkshire moors are pudding soft. Progress through them is sluggish at best. Drawn by a dark bay Exmoor Pony, the black carriage moved across the heath at the pace of a crawl. The two occupants had no idea what time it was, but they recognized the soon-approaching dusk. The pair bundled themselves as best they could against the fierce cuts of the cold Moorish wind. They did not have a boat.

At the reins was a plump-faced man. His round cheeks were flushed by the chilled air. His features were outlined by long side whiskers which ran down past his ears. His brimmed hat was pulled low over his eyes and his nose and mouth were covered by a woolen muffler. His occupation was solicitor. His name was Albert Heath Moore. He played accordion and admired Lawrence Welk.

Enduring the ride beside him was a woman strikingly akin in both stature and countenance to Queen Victoria. She appeared weak and weary of the dreary journey. The woman was Albert's older sister, Neva Moore-DeRaven.

Neva, at age forty, had been recently widowed and her mental condition seemed to deteriorate under the weight of her grief. Were she Lucrezia Borgia, her woe would be borne in a much lighter vein.

Albert had come a great distance in response to an announcement of a boy put up for adoption. He brought with him his sister in the hope that the vision of the bleak, barren, wasted landscape of the Yorkshire moor would cheer and lift her sunken spirits.

Nice thinking, Albert.

Chapter 37

Two Men Along the Road

As the Exmoor Pony led the carriage along the sunken moor path, the grounded fog, once disturbed, swirled underfoot. In the fading light, the view in the distance ahead was challenging. Yet Albert was able to discern the silhouettes of two figures sitting directly in the carriage's path.

Only a sharp tug of the reins was able to halt the pony, as the animal was of a mind to simply trample over the men, that being the normal sour temperament of the haughty Exmoor Pony. Had this been a Scottish Blackface or Lonk sheep, whose temperament had evolved more drastically, the results may not have been as fortunate.

The two men were outrageously shabby in appearance. One man wore a slouch hat that sat precariously on the back of his head. His jacket was ill-fitting, altogether too small for his frame. The sleeves only reached the mid of his forearms. His trousers were of the most obnoxious color and plaid design. The other man's apparel was, oppositely, oversized for his body. A rumpled top hat was wedged upon his ample overgrown curly flaxen locks. His frock-coat could have fit two of a man his size and nearly dragged the ground. Likewise, his trousers had more material than did mainsails on a Man-O-War.

Chapter 38

In Search of a Room

"Sirs, you block our way. For what reason do you sit astride the moor lane?" Albert demanded.

The shabby man with the too small jacket rose to respond. His voice was decidedly foreign. Albert pegged it as southern European, perhaps Italian.

"I'm a Bottecelli. We a waitin' for Godot. He no come, so we wait for you," said the Italian.

"Absurd," shot back Albert.

"Well, here you are," replied Bottecelli.

Increasingly frustrated Albert said, "It is late and cold. We are in search for a room."

"Nobody say ones a missing. Whats this room look like? If we see, I call you," said Bottecelli.

"Well, what about the other chap there?" asked Albert sharply.

"Attsa good idea, I ask. Hey, Dusty, you saw a room?" inquired Bottecelli.

Dusty's face lit up. From out of his oversized coat, he pulled out a saw and a board. He began to cut the board.

"No, not 'saw—see'," Bottecelli made a gesture of frustration to dismiss Dusty, and said, "Ah, don't listen to him, mister. He's a crazy."

Neva, who was quiet until now, spoke up, "Will you let us pass, please?!"

"Holy cow!" Said Bottecelli in surprise, "Itsa Queen! I think you was laundry all wrapped and a bundled like you was. Hey Dusty, ittsa Queen Victoria!"

Dusty bowed and once again dug into his coat. This time he pulled out a jeweled tiara.

Bottecelli explained his friend's action, "This a no stolen. He was gonna bring back tomorrow."

Albert, near wits end, spoke in a cross tone, "Listen, you. We must find a place to stay for the evening. We were told there is an inn near! If you cannot direct us, then get out of our way!"

"Oh, you need place to stay! Why you no say so? Just up the road. We take you there. Move over. Come, on Dusty," directed Bottecelli.

Albert held up his hand to stop the two men's approach, "See here, there is no room for you in this carriage." He said.

"Oh. Well, then we walk. You pretty slow anyway," Bottecelli replied.

Albert and Neva looked at each other in restrained disbelief. A flick of the reins started the odd procession along the moor lane.

Chapter 39

Blithering Heights

The carriage, with its odd escort, plodded along the moor lane through the misty murk. After some time a light from ahead shone through the fog and guided the travelers forward.

Bottecelli said the beacon that beckoned was the Beckoning Beacon of Bangalore. Notwithstanding that there was no such thing as the Beckoning Beacon of Bangalore, Albert was entirely sure Bottecelli was wrong. Wherever they were, they were not presently in India.

Soon enough all matters were settled when the road led them to the source of the beacon. Sitting defiantly on a small rise was a large aged structure. Except for the Beckoning Beacon of Bangalore, the exterior was dark, weathered, and cowered under the sky. It was as if the structure was wearily exhausted from the constant war against the fierce turbulence of the moors.

Albert dismounted, crossed to his sister, and helped her down from the carriage. With the carriage now empty, Dusty climbed in followed by Bottecelli who chased him out and around the front of the carriage to the opposite side where Dusty again climbed in and Bottecelli chased right behind in an endless loop.

Albert and Neva ignored the two clowns and made their way to the doors of the inn. Neva shuffled along slowly. Albert kept pace but with a slight but noticeable limp as his one leg was shorter than the other and one foot longer than its counterpart. The short leg had the long foot and the long leg had the short foot. While this might lead one to believe that such an arrangement might be optimal given the circumstances, in reality, it presented no apparent advantages.

Finally, the siblings stepped through great twin doors and into an ornate lobby bathed in shadows and gloom.

This was Blithering Heights.

Chapter 40

A Melancholy Welcome

Once inside, Albert and Neva scanned the dark, musty lobby. They could sense the inhospitality permeating through every fiber, every element of the interior. It was as if the room shrunk from the light and any pleasant thought or emotion. Instead it clung like a wet T shirt on a drunken prom date to despondent memories that had cut deep into its inanimate soul.

As they walked further into what seemed more like an abyss than an inn, their footsteps were joined by a hollow eerie sound that echoed through the air before it was swallowed by the gloom.

"I sense this place is cursed," Albert observed warily.

"Where property brothers when you need them!?" replied Neva.

"You'll need the property octuplets for this place," said Albert.

Chapter 41

An Insulting Little Man

The siblings glanced about them as they made their way to the elaborate baroque registration desk. This station was the centerpiece of the lobby to which all other objects in the room were subordinate. All chairs, sofas, and tables seemed to revolve around it like planets orbiting the sun. The desk itself, unsurprisingly to Albert, was unattended.

The brother and sister looked about in vain for a bell or some other device to call attention to their presence. Finally, Albert called out in a loud voice for assistance. He and Neva both were taken breathless by the immediate response of the slight man who, without warning, came up behind them.

The man was appareled in an oversized mourning coat, baggy grey striped pants, and a stooped posture. He wore round wire rimmed glasses, and his eyebrows and moustache seemed to be painted on. His receding hair was parted in the middle. He held a cigar.

"What's the hold up here? Why don't you people give someone else a chance to register?" the man said haughtily.

"Are you the hotel manager?" Neva asked.

"What are you insinuating, Madame? If you are insinuating? Never mind, I resent it on principle. Not that I have any that I wouldn't discard at my convenience," came the little man's next retort.

"Well I…" these are the only words Neva could utter before being interrupted.

"Why, if you weren't the queen I'd give you a good piece of my mind. Unfortunately there aren't any good pieces left. Would you take an I.O.U. for a risqué thought? Either way you'd come out on the short end," the man responded.

"Look here, sir. We want to register for rooms. Can you perform that function, or not?" Albert scolded.

"Well, do you have a reservation?" shot back the man in the mourning coat.

"No," replied Albert indignantly.

"Well, I've got plenty, and they're all about you. Wantonly traipsing about with this poor innocent woman. I prefer traipsing with the young rich ones myself. Well, beggars can't be choosers or the other way around. Either way it doesn't say much for you." exclaimed the little man.

Chapter 42

Registration

"Who is this insulting man, Albert?" Neva inquired.

"Sir, stop this nonsense at once! Direct us to someone who can register us for rooms!" Albert posed a threatening figure behind those words.

"Want a room, hey. You should have said so instead of beating around the bush if we had a bush," the little man said as he looked about. "We have some begonias that look like they need a good trimming."

"Can you provide rooms for my sister and me, or not, sir?!" shouted Albert.

"Well, well, a brother and sister is it? Yes, I can see the family resemblance, and that's not a compliment to either of you. Rooms, eh. So one isn't enough for you? Do you have another sister coming, and does she need a date?" asked the little man hopefully.

"There is no other sister, sir!" came Albert's irate response.

"Niece? Farmer's daughter? Schoolmarm?" asked the little man.

"No!" said Albert who was ready to explode.

"Do I, at least, have the right gender?" the little man's puzzled inquiry followed.

"Please, two rooms, if you will, sir!" insisted Albert.

"Oh, trying to be discreet. Well, you should have thought of that before you brought the Queen here. The tabloids will have a field day, and I'm about to inform them!" said the little man.

"How impertinent!" protested Neva.

"I've always fancied you, Your Majesty, and in case you're doing anything continental style, and need a third room, mine is just down the hall. Knock three times. I'll be there in two so we can turn in early and get our beauty sleep. I can tell by your face you need yours badly." the little man offered.

Neva let out a slighted gasp.

Albert was now completely enraged as he said, "Sir! I am within an inch of giving you a good thrashing!"

"I'll have you know we use the metric system around here. But that standard can be lifted for a small fee. In any case, I can't accept a good thrashing without references. However, if you are looking for rooms, I can help you. Let me introduce myself. I am the manager of Blithering Heights, Orville Q. Thornwacker." said the little man.

Chapter 43

Orville Q. Thornwacker

*O*rville Q. Thornwacker (of the Thornwacker Thornwackers from London's East End) was a living, walking, breathing agitation who always seemed to get the better of everyone, and that sometimes included himself. In the instant that followed his introduction, he agilely jumped behind the registration desk and rang the service bell.

"Welcome to Blithering Heights! What can I do for you?" he asked.

"Mr. Thornwacker!" Albert raised his exhausted exasperated voice.

"Oh it's you two again. Looking for a room, and for what purpose I can only guess. So unless you want to give me a hint, I'm going to have to use my own vivid imagination!" Thornwacker repeatedly knowingly flashed his eyebrows up and down.

"We will have two separate rooms! One for myself, and one for Her Majesty. I mean my sister. An nothing further of your impertinence!" said Albert

"Well, we have rooms with a view, rooms without a view, views without a room, and just views. Take your choice, but we have a two for one deal on the last one," Thornwacker offered.

Albert pounds his fist on the desk, "We will take any two rooms, and we will take them now, Mr. Thornwacker!" these words slipped between Albert's gritted teeth.

"I've got just the pair for you," Thornwacker swiveled the registration book. "Sign in, please."

Albert signed in, and Thornwacker read his signature upside down.

"erooM treblA. Any relation to the treblAs of Eaton? Although I'm sure they'd deny it," Thornwacker asked.

Albert slammed down the pen in a huff. Neva took it up and signed her name. Thornwacker made an honest attempt to view it correctly, and spoke it in a breathless sigh.

"Neva Moore-De Raven. I'd come rap, rap, rapping on your chamber door anytime, Madame." He then whispered to Neva. "Why don't we ditch your brother and go to my place. I have some etchings. And if I make any progress, I'll send for a bottle of wine. If you make any progress I'll be too stunned to drink."

Neva didn't know where to look, her eyes grew wide, "Ooooh dear!" was all she could manage. Thornwacker, however, had much more to say.

"Do I sense romance in the air or is it just musty in here. Anyway, I feel our hearts will find each other. They won't even have to ask directions. You'll be hard to miss," he said.

He then made childishly innocent goo-goo eyes at Neva. A blush swiftly blossomed on her face.

"Oh, Mr. Thornwacker," Neva cooed.

Chapter 44

The Rooms of Blithering Heights

Thornwacker handed out room keys and said, "If your rooms have doors, these keys should work. We've just remodeled so there are a few things not quite finished."

"What!" exclaimed Albert.

"The place has a new look. The old one was so depressing we had to give our guests Prozac. So enjoy your stay. If you do, you'll be the first. Dinner is at six and the only thing worse than the food is the company. That's where you'll meet our other guests. Did you bring any baggage besides the Queen? I'll have it brought up to you," explained Thornwacker.

As Albert turned about, he found his face lightly entangled by a thin strand of something. He pulled it off with some dispatch.

"Mr. Thornwacker, I hope these webs are not to be found in our rooms!" Albert expressed.

"There not webs. That's tooth floss. We're hosting a British Dental Association convention," explained Thornwacker.

The Moores departed for their rooms. Thornwacker went to fetch the porters.

Chapter 45

The Porters of Blithering Heights

O utside on the cobbled pavement, Thornwacker found Bottecelli and Dusty who still chased each other around the carriage. Upon seeing Thornwacker they halted their circuitous pursuit.

"Hey, hello, boss! How you do?" Bottecelli said, and Dusty honked his horn.

"I'd do a lot better without you two, I wager," Thornwacker responded.

"Nah, is no good to bet. You only gonna to lose you money," advised Bottecelli.

"Well, it's not doing me a lot of good right now," commiserated Thornwacker. "I've got a job for you two. Take these bags into the hotel, will you?"

"Sure thinga, Boss. We getta right now," replied Bottecelli enthusiastically. Dusty just stood at attention and saluted.

Bottecelli reached into the carriage and drew down two bags and placed them on the ground. As he turned to reach retrieve another bag, Dusty took the bags on the ground and put them back into the carriage unbeknownst to his partner. This had the appearance of another endless cycle.

"Say, that's some system you boys have there with the luggage," observed Thornwacker.

"Yeah, we gotta this down to a science," replied Bottecelli.

"You know, a lot of people don't believe in science these days, and you're probably the reason why." Thornwacker proposed.

"Hey, we believe science. Lucky for us 'cause they sure gotta lot of bags," responded Bottecelli while Dusty just shook his smiling head.

"If you want any gratuity you better hurry up with those bags. You do know what gratuity is, don't you?" Thornwacker inquired. He did not, expect an answer in return.

Bottecelli thought a moment and said, "Sure, attsa what Isaac Newton discover when he get hit in the head with the apple pie."

"You couldn't be more right, without actually being correct. So when you discover what hit you in the head, come inside with the luggage." imparted Thornwacker who strutted back to the lobby.

When Thornwacker came inside, Bottecelli and Dusty were already waiting for him with the luggage. Thornwacker passed a curious glance back toward the door.

"If I had a nickel for every time this kind of thing happened, I'd be Charles Dickens," Thornwacker said directly to the readers.

Chapter 46

The Towels & Linen Handicap Stakes

"Hey, boss. Where you want us to take these bags?" Bottecelli asked.

"Take those two cases to room 3, and those two to room 4," Thornwacker directed.

"Okee doke! You gotta. Two into four, and two into three. Wait a minute, boss. Two don't go into three," Bottecelli calculated.

"Well, somebody's not going to be happy to hear that, and here he comes now," Thornwacker forewarned as he saw Albert descend the staircase.

"Mr. Thornwacker, We would appreciate if you would also bring us some fresh towels and linens, please," Albert said.

Thornwacker waved to gain the attention of the maid. She was a fetching young woman with blonde hair, blue eyes, and a darling figure. Her short maid's dress revealed seemingly endless curvaceous legs. She carried towels and linen in her arms.

"Cosette, would you please bring fresh towels and linen to our guests in rooms 3 and 4. And don't worry about the arithmetic. We'll deal with fractions later," Thornwacker said.

However, Cosette and Dusty became entangled in each other's vision. Cosette's eyes grew wide with faux alarm, while a naughty impish gleam appeared in Dusty's. Cosette backed up a few cautious steps. Dusty moved a few stalking steps towards her. It seemed to be a standoff until Dusty beeped his horn and the chase was on.

"And they're off and running at Blithering Downs." announced Thornwacker. Everyone acted as if this was not the first time they witnessed this chase.

"Mr. Thornwacker," Albert asked grudgingly, "Are we going to get our fresh towels and linen?"

"If she's ahead after a furlong, you'll get them. If not you're going to have to fend for yourself like the rest of us," Thornwacker remarked.

Chapter 47

For the Benefit of the Public

From the British Dental Association conference at Blithering Heights deep in the Yorkshire Moors, we present Doctors Ruth Canal and Perry O'Dontal with a very important public service message.

"Dentistry has learned a great deal about the oral mouth. For example, it is common knowledge that the people of the British Isles have notoriously bad teeth," announced Dr. Canal.

"Therefore it is of the utmost importance that we all brush and floss before, during, and after every meal to maintain our poor dental standards without further deterioration," warned Dr. O'Dontal.

Thank you for your cooperation from Dr. Ruth Canal and Dr. Perry O'Dontal, BDA, BYOB Room 11. This has been a public service announcement.

Chapter 48

The Story of Heathcliff

*L*est Heathcliff be judged too swiftly it is beholding to learn of his life to this point. It was a bitter life that hardened Heathcliff as he was. His story began in the small kingdom of Synovia where rulers died prematurely in their mid-fifties so their sons could make plausible TV holiday movies. Synovia, then, is where the owner of Blithering Heights was vacationing.

Mr. Blithering spent the last day of his continental holiday preparing for his departure. He hastily gathered up his souvenirs, laundry, and luggage. However, in his haste he mistakenly packed away a small bell boy from the hotel. This he only discovered when Mr. Blithering arrived home to the Yorkshire moors after a long return journey. The boy was Heathcliff.

It is understandable if the boy or, for that matter, anyone packed in crowded baggage experienced a significant ordeal. However, Heathcliff found the confines of the luggage suited him and so he was quite comfortable. Possibly this was because, in comparison to his harsh treatment at the hands of his foster parents, suitcase living was a veritable paradise.

Under his foster parent's care Heathcliff lived in a milking pail which he had to give up early each morning when the cows were to be milked. His only meal of the day was leftover ashes from the cooking hearth. Just before bedtime each night he was thrown into a washing machine fully clothed. This served as both his laundry and bath. Later, after the rinse cycle, he was hung upside down on the clothes line to dry. Indentured to the inn, Heathcliff worked for thirty to forty hours a day and was swung by the feet to beat the dust from carpets—a typical chore for orphans on the continent as well as England. Despite all this, he had a happy demeanor.

Mr. Blithering took a liking to the Synovian youth and adopted him in short order. At Blithering Heights Heathcliff grew up in the company of Blithering's natural, original, and full-time daughter, Catherine. The two grew close—not showering together close—but dear in deep friendship. Together they would walk the moors, gaze at the stars, or make out like hormone demented teenagers in an Annette Funicello Beach Party movie.

At the age of twenty, Heathcliff, swollen with love and allergies, proposed marriage to Catherine. She rejected him outright. What is more she was indignant at the mere suggestion of such a notion since she considered Heathcliff a social, intellectual, and genetic inferior. Obviously, Heathcliff had been misreading her signals.

When Mr. Blithering died after being run over by the same Paris milk wagon that trampled Pierre Curie (the wagon had been relocated and now worked the moors), there was no stipulation for the benefit or Catherine or Heathcliff in his will. All was passed to the Lonk sheep and Exmoor ponies of the estate. The sheep and the ponies lived well and turned Blithering Heights into a resort inn.

Catherine and Heathcliff were thrown out into the cold harsh world.

Chapter 49

The Story of Catherine

Catherine, who had considerable intellect and education, plied her living first as a teacher and then as a private governess, although she made far more money as an exotic dancer and coochie-coo girl. Catherine, shamed from her fall from grace via her social class, hid her true identity behind false names. The first of these was Amanda Reckonwith. Later, she took the name that remained with her through the rest of her life, Jane Air.

Jane's first employment was as a schoolmarm in a half-room school house that was too small to fit any students. This was the forerunner of remote education. Here she taught basic subjects such as reading, arithmetic, and evolution (the critical race theory of its day).

Although she loved teaching, sadly, she retired when several of her students were killed or injured as two trains fatally collided in a math word problem of her design. Even though a report of the safety commission absolved her of any fault, the fact that she felt she had Train A leave the station too early weighed a great deal on her mind and directly led to her decision to leave.

Jane needed a respite from public education and so sought employment in the private sector as a governess. Her debut position was with the von Trapp family where she solved the problem of Maria by having her abducted, and temporarily removed to Siberia until Jane could obtain important references and credentials as a governess.

Upon leaving the von Trapps, Jane was referred as governess to Mr. Hensley Lax Slapdash, then master of Turnscrew Manor and absentee negligent guardian of his niece (Miles) and nephew (Flora) who were mis-named at birth. Jane accepted this position and thus began a ghastly association with the ill-fated Turnscrew Manor, the evils of its haunting spirits, and with its chauffeur named Edgar who claimed he was secretly rich.

From this point forward, Jane's life turned more from what she had known as the natural world of light, and more toward the sinister darkness that seemed to emanate from the very beams and stones of Turnscrew Manor's structure. It was as if the estate contained a condemned soul that devoured innocent life. Although, it also could have been an issue of high property taxes.

Chapter 50

The Curse of the Turnscrews

While the origin of the malignant curse that engulfed Turnscrew Manor and its owners was in doubt, there is no doubt that the curse was real. The doomed fate of all previous masters of the estate testified to this.

The first victim to the curse of Turnscrew was the original owner, Rufus T. Turnscrew. The poor soul entombed himself while tiling his bathroom. His body was only discovered months later when plumbers checked on a leaky faucet.

Next came the strange death of Thaddeus K. Turnscrew who was found strangled by his own dental floss. He had no known cavities at the time.

Then came Rufus T. Turnscrew II who was killed when a Kamikaze crashed into his study while he designed emplacements for anti-aircraft positions on the premises. It was a work too late in implementation to save the young Rufus.

After Rufus Turnscrew II, the demise of the master of Turnscrew became a regular event to which the town's people turned out in droves to witness. They were not disappointed by the annual event which reaped the following deadly harvest:

- Egregious Turnscrew—Struck by lightning
- Homer L. Turnscrew—Abducted by aliens
- Evan McDarby Turnscrew—Eaten by lion
- Forest K. Turnscrew—Eaten by sheep
- William 'Bonnie Bill' Turnscrew—Cauliflower poisoning
- Horatio 'Bilgepump' Turnscrew—Lost at sea
- Farley Granger Turnscrew—Died of hives

- Emile T.S. Elliot Turnscrew—Run down by a
  Parisian milk wagon

Accordingly, the life expectancy of a Turnscrew was shorter than the King of Synovia. One cannot be certain, but this may explain the constant absence of Hensley Lax Slapdash from the estate. A man in fear of his life and soul.

In light of these events, Turnscrew Manor should have been abandoned and burned to the ground. Only the fact that it was convenient to shopping, restaurants, and public transportation saved it from that fate. Location, Location, Location.

Chapter 51

Am I Not Hideous

While Slapdash was the master of Turnscrew Manor, he was not a direct Turnscrew descendent. Rather he was an in-law who inherited the estate and perhaps was not subject to the fate of the curse. However, living secretly in the wings was the next true Turnscrew to become master—the most unfortunate Thomas Turnscrew.

Both the curse and Thomas's presence were unknown to Jane and she took full advantage of the home and, at her own risk, made it her own. One night she smoked a cigarette as she wandered the halls of the manor. While flicking ashes she accidentally caught the entire west wing on fire. The very wing where Thomas resided. He was severely burned.

It would appear that Jane and Thomas would never meet. Until one night as they both wandered the halls in a sleepless fit, the two crossed paths.

Thomas wore a hood to hide the grotesque scars of his burnt face. His appearance frightened Jane nonetheless.

"Who are you?" a startled Catherine asked.

"My name is Thomas Turnscrew. I will one day become master of this house and die a preordained death under the curse of Turnscrew Manor. Until then I live as a recluse and now even more so since I was scarred in the west wing fire," said Thomas.

"West wing fire. Hadn't heard about that," Jane lied.

"I wear this hood to conceal by morbid scars. I do not want to evoke fear, distress, or pity in others," Thomas stated.

"I will look upon you without fear, distress, or pity young Thomas for I have naught but good will for all," Jane bravely proclaimed.

"I believe in your kindness and so then witness this," Thomas removed his hood to expose his mutilated face.

"JEE-ZUS!!! Put that f***ing hood back on, for C*****'s sake!" Jane pleaded as she turned away in fear, distress, and pity.

"Should have seen that coming," said Thomas. "Am I not hideous?"

"Well, its not the face I'd want for my yearbook picture," Jane indicated.

"There is nothing left for me in this world," Thomas cried as he spoke.

"Have you thought about carnival work?" Jane offered him some career advice.

Chapter 52

The Ghosts of Turnscrew Manor

After the encounter with Thomas, Jane began to experience many strange and haunted events at Turnscrew Manor. It was as if something was awakened in her that drew the attention of the supernatural. Perhaps it was part of her soul, her heart, or her mind. It was as if she were feeding the spirits just as she fed the squirrels on the grounds who later became a major rodent problem on the estate.

It wasn't long before Jane realized that most of the hauntings involved the children and the dreadful ghosts of Quintin Q. Quint, the former groundskeeper and the former governess Georgina Jessel, who were going steady at the time of their demise.

Quint's presence was usually announced by the pungent odor and chill of death that preceded him. Miss Jessel, on the other hand, showered regularly even in the afterlife and did not smell so bad. Evidently death does not change some guy things.

It was too late when Jane realized that Quint was drawing the life out of the children in her charge. His purpose was to steal their souls and put them in his post-mortem production of 'The Music Man' which received mostly negative reviews and a very short run.

Distraught beyond measure, Jane left Turnscrew Manor and returned to Blithering Heights where she submitted to her ever growing morbid moods and threw herself under the Parisian milk wagon that roamed the area. There, in the Yorkshire moors of her childhood, she became a restless ghost that haunted the very home where she grew up.

Her purpose in death was to create a stage version of 'Les Miserables' for the next world. She became an actress in the afterlife but what she really wanted was to direct.

Chapter 53

Relationships

The relationships with which Heathcliff and Catherine (aka Jane Air) were engaged were simply masks to hide the losses and disappointments of their deeply disturbed lives. The characters of both people were only capable of concealing such losses, but not able to resolve or move past them. These inflicted injuries suffered them each minute of each day for all their lives.

And so it came to pass:

pyp was adopted by the Moores who treated him well. Catherine (aka Jane) married Edgar, the chauffer who turned out to be EpiPen's biological father. The marriage lasted less time than it takes for potato salad to spoil outside on a hot summer day. They had a daughter named Amanda Reckonwith who changed her name to Bjork.

Heathcliff married Edgar's adopted and estranged sister Isabella and so became Catherine's brother-in-law which produced awkward holiday dinner situations. EpiPen then wed Edgar, her father, who thankfully died before the reception. Howard Uuuuuu, now a reformed man of wealth, became pyp's benefactor but lost the boy's address and so gave all his money to Thomas Turnscrew for facial reconstruction. After surgery Thomas looked like Mario Cuomo and went from Freddy Kruger ugly to Walking Undead ugly.

Timmy, crown prince of Synovia, fell in love with Blanche DuBois Ingram instead of the New England map maker lady. The map maker lady ran off with the Artful Hatter in a flying house that landed on Marginally Taylor Insane. Sean of the Reds proposed to Kelly& Wrongway but jilted her at the altar. Kelly& changed her name to Miss Havisham and became engaged to Victor Frankenschtine who also jilted her. Albert hooked up with a dental hygienist who confessed she was gay. Albert told her he was a lesbian trapped in a man's body. They eloped. Orville Q. Thornwacker and Neva Moore-DeRaven ran off to Synovia for Timmy's coronation festival.

Neva learned she was the Godmother to Amanda Reckonwith who became the bride of Frankenschtine (the creature) and later the mother of Miss Estella. Dr. Ruth Canal and Dr. Perry O'Dontal became so drunk at the BDA convention they married an Exmoor pony and Lonk sheep respectively. Donald the Red Queen learned he was his own mother and issued a pardon to himself.

Chapter 54

The Ghost of Christmas Future

As his adoption to the Moores was finalized, the third ghost appeared to pyp as promised. This ghost was none other than Catherine who now filled in for the retired original Ghost of Christmas Future. Actually he was not retired but released due to his chronic drinking problem which resulted in unacceptable behavior such as telling little kids what they weren't getting for Christmas and why.

Catherine had both good and bad news for pyp. The bad news was that his future Christmases would be filled with presents of socks, underwear, and ugly sweaters. The good news was that he and Cathy would marry. Despite the fact that Heathcliff would be his live-in father-in-law and would constantly Bogart the TV remote control, Cathy and pyp would raise a beautiful family and love each other for all of their days.

THE END

All About Nothing

Introduction

NOTES FROM A WILHELM WUNDT IMPERSONATOR.

I am Dr. Thomas Stuart Tullis, PhD, Adjunct Professor Bentley University, specialist in the field of primate-computer usability, dedicated experimental psychologist, and professional Wilhelm Wundt impersonator. See photos below. Be honest, except for the caption, you can't tell who is who.

I would like to introduce you to Wilhelm Wundt, father of psychology as proven by DNA based paternity testing. In the field of behavioral study, Wundt was first to introduce to the behavioral sciences experimental methodology, objective analysis of results, and, of course, beards. After Wundt all decent psychologists wore beards.

**Wilhelm Wundt Father of Psychology and Dr. Thomas Tullis,
but not necessarily in that order.**

One of Wundt's most famous experimental studies involved the examination of a hypothesis known as the Infinite Monkey Theorem. This theorem proposes that a dozen monkeys chained to typewriters for an infinite amount of time will eventually produce the collective plays of William Shakespeare. I myself, while working on a study in a similar vein, found that those same monkeys could not only produce significant literary works, but also steal your credit card and run up incredible charges for pizzas with banana topping.

While examining Wundt's personal papers, I made the fortunate discovery of two important items from his Infinite Monkey experiment: his experimental design notes, and the resulting literary output (*All About Nothing*). Both are presented in this chapter.

By the way, here are the important winter tour dates for the upcoming Wilhelm Wundt Impersonating All-Star Troupe. This tour's theme— *'Wundt You be my Friend'*.

- 1/19 & 20: Boca Raton, FL—Anchor Inn

- 1/22: Vero Beach, FL—Baily's Surf and Turf

- 1/24 to 27: Clearwater, FL—Rumata Hotel

- 1/29 & 30: Jacksonville, FL—Charlies Steak House

- 2/2: Savannah, GA—Undetermined Location

- 2/5: Charleston, SC—Fort Sumter

- 2/9: Raleigh, NC—NC State Jonston Hall

- 2/10: Durham, NC—Wake Forest Cafeteria

- 2/12: Chapel Hill, NC—UNC Psychology Department Lounge

- 2/15: Richmond, VA—Robert E. Lee Inn (unless venue's name is changed)

- 2/19: Washington DC—The White House

WILHELM WUNDT AND HIS BUNCH OF MONKEYS EXPERIMENT

I am Wilhelm Wundt. There is a premise that a dozen monkeys chained to typewriters for an infinite amount of time could eventually produce the entire works of William Shakespeare. This is known as the Infinite Monkey Theorem. Now, this might be plausible for Golden Lion Tamarins or Black-handed Spider Monkeys, but would most certainly be beyond the abilities of the common macaque, baboon, or langur sub-species.

Starting from this basic premise I will examine this Infinite Monkey Theory using objective experimental techniques that I developed while wearing a white lab coat.

Most people will tell you that experiments are boring, and that experimental psychologists are the most boring. Not my team. We are really fun and crazy to hang with in our cool white lab coats and cool white rats. We're a hoot!

The rats tell us everything. When you study with rats you're ahead of the pack. That is our motto, Otto! The girls really go for us, uberschwemmungen guys.

So, to Sigmund Fraud, analyze this. My beard is longer than yours*. Yes, mein freund, sometimes a zigarre is just a cigar. And sometimes a zigarre is something you get shoved up your anal brunfunnellpooper!

Enough said about that. Let me now outline the main points of our experiment on the Infinite Monkey Theorem.

First of all, you must understand the limits of practicality in the experimental variables of this study. These are:

- Infinite time. We do not have such infinite time at our disposal. We only get for lunch twenty minutes. Schnell, schnell, raus, all the time. So we must make a limit the finish of our study comes before the weekend.

- A dozen monkeys. Because of budget we cannot get monkeys. Monkeys are money in our business. We can only get as subjects, six rats, a chinchilla, A rare Pomeranian Goose, and a token primate—my sister's son, Herman. They called their name—A Bunch of Monkeys.

- Operational conditions. We do not chain any subject to anything. PETA would be up our keilholedippers. The exception being my nephew who has DBD. We have his prescription for restrainment. Also, we have only one broken Underwood typewriter. So we use pencils and paper and hope nobody pokes out an eye.

With these constraints we begin the experiment. In sixty-two hours the subjects produce the work you will read here— "All About Nothing." "All About Nothing" is a three act play, including a rare fourth act. It was nominated for a Pulitzer Prize, but lost to the Bronte brothers. Yes, we admit this play is not Hamlet quality, but neither is it Sharknado.

WILLIAM SHAKESPEARE—A BIOGRAPHICAL NOTE

William Shakespeare, the Bard of Avon and victim of male pattern baldness, is considered the greatest literary figure in the English language-polling slightly ahead of a dozen monkeys, moderately in front of Santa's eight reindeer, and well ahead of the seven dwarves whose latest book received very negative reviews.

PD-US-Record

William "Rogaine" Shakespeare

Dr. Thomas Stuart Tullis, PhD

Sadly, my friend, Tom Tullis, passed away in 2020 due to complications from the Covid virus. He will be greatly missed by family, friends, and colleagues. When we pass, each of us leaves behind a void that can never be completely filled. However, some, like Tom, leave behind a plethora of good memories, friendships, and accomplishments that make it easier to bridge those voids. Here's to Tom, a very good man.

Pitch Mirabelle (Sidekick/Editor)

All About Nothing

by
A Bunch of Monkeys

Act 1

ENTER PARLANTE, a fabler.

Parlante Once upon a long time ago
      In a galaxy far, far away

*A trap door opens and **Parlante PLUMMETS through.***

Stage Manager Thank you. Next.
(O.S.)

ENTER TROVATORE, a Crier.

Trovatore Sit right back and hear a tale
      A tale of a fateful…

Trovatore EXPLODES.

Stage Manager Next, please.
(O.S.)

***ENTER** A nervous* **RACONTEUR,** a minstrel.

Raconteur Listen you to this account with dread
      Listen tight and listen well
      The Duke before his daughter's wed
      Those ramparts where slayed he fell

Raconteur	And of the Fool who saw the crime Must solve the deed 'fore midnight's chime

FOG drifts in concealing Raconteur. **COUGHING**. *The fog then slowly* ***DISPELS*** *for the first scene.*

The scene: Chateau Regale—the ramparts
Built in the style of the great strongholds of the renaissance, Regale offers strength and security blended seamlessly with bountiful luxuries and comforts necessary in a modern abode. Regale overlooks thousands of acres in the gorgeous sprawling Tuscany landscape including rolling hills, vineyards, and vestiges of ancient architectures. The location offers quiet seclusion while still conveniently close to downtown shopping and cultural attractions.

ENTER the DUKE—*Master of Chateau Regale.*

The Duke	I walk these ramparts a thousand times over in quiet solitude. To bare my conscience but nothing further, for no pervert am I. But tonight I seek no solace, for there is none to gain. Still, I but feel the grip of destiny that tugs at my cloak.

Then above on the great battlement seen is great a glow.

ENTER a GHOST.

The Duke	Behold, what sight comes to my eyes? Is this figure real or imagined? What be this? Announce thyself I say.
Ghost	I am thy father's spirit. Doomed for a certain term to walk the night.
The Duke	Dad? You're dead? But I just saw you twenty minutes ago with your head buried in a kettle of beef stew. Not a pretty sight, I may add. At your own granddaughter's wedding, it wouldn't hurt to show some manners.

Ghost   What? No! I wasn't invited to any wedding. What are you talking about?

The Duke   Who are you, again?

Ghost   I am the spirit of thy father. Thy father? King Hamlet? Denmark? Ringing any bells?

The Duke   Sorry, pal, but you're not in Denmark anymore.

Ghost   Uh, oh. I am disconcerted, for both treachery and tragedy have of late courted me.

The Duke   Well, that's why you're pasty, pale and, transparent.

Ghost   By my own brother's hand slain. I did greet him in good sentiment yet malice filled his eyes and blade his hand.

The Duke   Is this going to be a long story?

Ghost   Thus I said, If this be betrayal then strike. I'm doomed if hate is returned for love. Strike and for the heart.

The Duke   That doesn't sound good.

Ghost   I was mortally struck. And it hurt a lot more than I expected. I didn't think that amount of pain was normal. Needless to say, I needed a minute.

The Duke   Yes, well that all sounds really awful. But I have a reception downstairs, and I'm sure you have to catch a flight for Copenhagen.

Ghost   My apologies, sir. This astral projection stuff is still kind of new to me. Let's see. Click the heels three times and... There's no place like home. There's no place like home.

*The **ghost** FADES AWAY like he was beamed up to the Star Ship Enterprise.*

CURTAIN.

ACT 2

ENTER GUANO, the Jester, who now appears on the parapet in search of the **Duke**.

Guano (a Jester)	Trusted Guano. With but one purpose only, am I imparted to these battlements. And that purpose be to retrieve the Duke in hopes he can remove his father's head from the beef stew bowl. But I see him not thus. So I further my search.

Guano walks on and suddenly comes upon the body of the **Duke**. *Struck down and dead.*

Guano	What's this? Can it be? Believe my eyes or not? Yet my Duke lies dead and struck down, but not necessarily in that order

The cold night wind spins a prowling **VAPOR**. *A haunting* **VOICE** *reaches through the cloud and calls to* **Guano**.

Voice	Guano. Guano, the Fool.
Guano	It's Guano, the Jester.
Voice	Whatever.
Guano	Reveal thyself from gloom, oh voice.

The **vapor CLEARS** *to reveal three haggish figures around a boiling cauldron. They are the witches.* **ENTER MINNIE, MAUDE, and JACKIE,** *The Pep Girls.*

Minnie	Guano. See you us, the sisters, Minnie, Maude, and Jackie—The Pep Girls. We come to give you forewarning.

Maude (Sister 2)   We are soothsayers. Sayers of sooths, or soothes whatever the plural be.

Jackie (Sister 3)   And your sooth for the day is—Ta Da!
"Till Birnam Wood to Dunsinane Comes."

Minnie   Jackie, that one's from last week.

Jackie   Beware the Ides of March?

Maude   Skip on down, Jackie.

Jackie   Here it is. Beware for the Duke, your master. Treacherous hands seek his demise.

*Guano points to the dead body of the **Duke**.*

Guano   Ah, yeah. Hello.

Maude   Minnie, did you put the right ingredients in the pot?

Minnie   Yes. Did you stir the pot long enough?

Maude   Of course. Jackie, how are you reading these?

Jackie   Sorry, but there's quite a backlog. I told you we needed more memory.

Minnie   Apologies. But we don't get a very good signal up here.

Maude   Please hold. Your sooth is very important to us.

Jackie FUMBLES with her glasses and re-reads the message from the cauldron.

Jackie	OK, got it. Veins of common blood shall common ends meet. Um, that's not very clear is it?
Guano	And what am I supposed to do with that?
Minnie	Hey, we're just the messengers.
Maude	That's your first clue to the mystery. Thank you. You've been a wonderful audience. We'll be here all week.

*The eerie **VAPOR GATHERS** over the **sisters** and they disappear into it and the darkness. Then **LOUD CRASHING** sounds and **SCREAMS** are heard.*

Minnie	God Da**it!
Guano	There is foul play I understand. A cryptic case without a clue. Blame attached to me be sure. Then will Guano hit the fan.

CURTAIN.

ACT 3

The scene: The Great Hall Banquet Room

*Guano makes his way down to the great hall where **ALL** have gathered to celebrate the marriage of **DONNA SONATA**, daughter of the Duke, to the Prince, **PORTFOLIO**. A festive mood fills all, unaware that tragic news is soon to be announced. **ANGINA**, the Duchess, makes an announcement.*

Angina	Celebrate my wedded daughter, Donna Sonata— betrothed of Portfolio the Prince. Open bar! Fool Guano, ply thy wit and laughter bring.
Guano	It's Jester Guano.
Angina	Whatever. Make merriment with thy cunning tongue.
Guano	Certainly. Meet me in the boudoir in half an hour and bring some wine. On second thought bring a lot of wine. My tongue's a little dry tonight.
Angina	Well, I never.
Guano	Contrary to a lot of talk about flying buttresses in the barracks, and your name is foremost in the conversations.

***ENTER** the **MARQUIS SAUMON DE FILET**—ambassador from France.*

Angina	Um, oh. All, all please bid welcome to the emissary from the court of France, La Marquis Saumon de Filet.
Marquis	Pleasantries to all in this hall, and you the loveliest, Dame Angina.

Guano	No bones about it, Marquis, You're slicker than an eel in vasoline. Maybe you should meet the dame in the boudoir. I'll keep the wine and see if I can get lucky down here.

ENTER FALSETTO and CASTRATO, *guards of the rampart.*

Falsetto (a guard)	Hold celebration all. For ill news do we bring. Ooh, Angina, Queenie that gown is not for you. And that tiara.
Castrato (a guard)	AWWW-FULLL!
Angina	What news bring you to dampen this celebration. Pray ye speak. And what is wrong with this gown?
Falsetto	The Duke is dead.
Angina	The Duke is dead?!!
Donna Sonata	The Duke is dead?!!
Portfolio	The Duke is dead?!!

Falsetto places hands on hips in frustration.

Falsetto	Hello? Echo, echo, echo. Shall we go another round?
Angina	How come you by this dread news?
Falsetto	Well, thank you for asking. We were making our usual rounds when…

*BEGIN music for a flashback. A **MIST COMES FORTH**, and then **CLEARS** for the change of scene.*

The scene: Chateau Regale—the ramparts
Falsetto and Castrato make their rounds on the parapets.

Castrato	I claim to you that Cavatelli isn't just long in the tooth.
Falsetto	Oh, I can't believe you said that.
Castrato	Hold! Who lies ahead unmoving as if in slumber.
Falsetto	Or dead!
Castrato	Why is the glass always half empty with you?

*Falsetto leans close and identifies the lifeless body of his lord, the **Duke**.*

Falsetto	What ho! It is the Duke! And in the cold grip of death he lies. Mr. Glass is not always half empty.
Castrato	So dreadful a sight my eyes will not behold.
Falsetto	Oh, grow a pair.
Castrato	I wish.

*BEGIN music for a flash forward. Again the **MIST COMES FORTH**, and then **CLEARS** for the change of scene.*

The scene: The Great Hall Banquet Room
Returning to present, the story told. The room bears a great gloom and shock.

Castrato	Wait a minute. You left out the best part. Cue the music.

*BEGIN MUSIC for another flashback. Again the **mist** COMES FORTH, and then CLEARS for the change of scene.*

The scene: Chateau Regale—the ramparts
Falsetto and Castrato make their rounds on the parapets.

Castrato	Now this is what I heard. Honest to God. Obbligato is cheating with Agita Hussy.
Falsetto	Oh, my God! I would never believe he's so butch?
Castrato	AND, Apoplexia has discovered such!
Falsetto	Meowww!
Castrato	Three of a kind to beat a full house, dear.
Angina	Enough! Back to the present, gossips. We have but two pages to finish Act 3. Cue the fog, someone

*The music PLAYS hurriedly. The **mist** COMES and GOES thankfully for the last time, and we are back to the Great Hall. **People** COUGH and are annoyed. They WAVE away the last remnants of the mist.*

The scene: The Great Hall Banquet Room
*Many **people** cough as the mist clears. All WEEP or STAND NUMB.*

Angina	The Duke, my Lord, my husband. Dead and by murder on this day of all.
Donna Sonata	My wedding ruined.
Portfolio	All is not lost. Let us not spoil the honeymoon. Remember, the tickets are non-refundable.

Guano	(aside) Suspicion lies with Portfolio. Now the Duke removed, he has position to assume the mantle of Duke.
Angina	Oh, where is your wit now, Fool. For I would have it subside my grief, ere it overwhelm me.
Guano	Indeed, this effort I will make. All listen and stay my speech if this anecdote is familiar by previous hearing, shoot me. A horse walks into a bar. The bartender asks him "Why the long face?"
Donna Sonata	I've heard this one. Somebody shoot him.
Angina	Thank you, Fool. The effort was noble but it has failed to pierce the anguish that now encases me.

*ENTER, **Draino**, the brother of the Duke. He has not been told of his sibling's demise.*

Draino	Greetings all on this special day. But, why the tears and long faces? Tell me this of you all, I pray.
Angina	(laughs) Why the long face? Now the meaning is revealed to me. Very good. Very good indeed, Guano. All greet Lord Draino.
Guano	Lord Draino, are you wearing pantaloons or are you just happy to be here?
Portfolio	Lord Draino, beloved brother of the Duke. The Duke is dead by foul play.

Draino

The Duke dead in play with a chicken?
Much had I pleaded him to stay his fowl diversion.
An unnatural way to get eggs, I counseled.

Portfolio

What?

Draino

My dearest Angina, more than sister to me. How can I be of comfort? Use your imagination. Think out of the box if you will.

Guano

Looks like you're out of luck, Frenchy. I think this Draino guy has the first shot at the lady. Tell you what, I'll split the wine, but you're on your own with the girls.
(aside)
Ah, but a more likely suspect comes forth in Draino. Good Draino, only now displayed. Does his coveting of Angina provide motive for fratricide?

CURTAIN

ACT 4

The scene: The Cathedral Constipado

The funeral of the Duke is held in the Cathedral Constipado, a magnificently elaborate and spectacular example of original Gothic architecture. The cathedral was among the most expansive structures in the world when it was finally completed five centuries after this day of the funeral. For the present it consists of a wine barrel altar, a couple wooden benches, and no roof. Chickens roam the dirt floor, and swallows poop at will on the people below.

*The chamber is divided into left and right. On one side sit the people of **Portfolio**, Prince. The other finds the family of the **Duke**.*

ENTER FATHER O'RIELLY *with an Irish brogue.*

Father O'Rielly (Friar)	Shed no tears for our Duke as he lived a glorious life to be rewarded in heaven. We remember him as leader to people, husband to wife, brother to brother.
Impromptu (a heckler)	Lover to chickens.

Donna Sonata *breaks down into humiliated **SOBS**. **Portfolio** offers clumsy comfort.*

*When all are assembled. **ENTER** Angina, the Duchess, escorted by **Draino**. In position on the unfinished **WALL** of the cathedral above the floor is **Obbligato** and **Apoplexia** from medi**E**val News.*

Obbligato	Now entering the Cathedral, Angina Duchess of Regale, looking very lovely today. Her escort is the very debonair Lord Draino, brother to the late Duke. Apoplexia.
Apoplexia	Thank you Mr. Gigolo. The Duchess is wearing a long one-piece low cut sequined gown in midnight, befitting the traditional color of mourning. She is also adorned with gorgeous diamond and emerald brooches, topped off by a ruby tiara.

Obbligato	Simply fabulous, Apoplexia. Her escort, Lord Draino, be him also well garbed, but of more import is that he bears the point of rumors that such regard him as successor to his brother as Duke.
Apoplexia	Rumors abound, Sir Man-Whore. There is much mentioned of him as successor to the Duchess's hand as well. Yes, a witch's brew of rumors abound. And speaking of witches, let's go to the floor where our own home wrecking, nymphomaniac slut, Agita Hussy is probably already on her back.

ENTER AGITA HUSSY REPORTING from the floor.

Agita Hussy	Thank you, Miss Cougar-Bimbo. For this next piece of gossip, hold on to your hat, Plexy, because we know you can't hold on to your men, A whirlwind of gossip has torn through the palace about the new Duke taking the hand of the Duchess, although my sources indicate he has already helped himself to much more than her hand. The service is now about to begin so let's take it to the altar, and Father O'Rielly.
Apoplexia	Thank you, bitch. Obbligato, speaking of getting far, I heard you and Hussy had dinner. I know she had whatever they feed pigs these days, and you had the chicken. Which did you favor most, breast or thighs?
Obbligato	I'm not going to dignify that remark.
Apoplexia	Oh, you're going to dignify it, you cheating SOB!

*We see **Apoplexia SIEZE** a large rock and **RAISE** it overhead for the express purpose of smashing it into Obbligato's head. However, we cut to the **ALTAR** and the main gathering for the service before she actually strikes.*

Father O'Rielly	Dear friends, offer us up prayer and blessing for the soul of our late Duke.
Impromptu	Louder!
Father O'Rielly	Would you were mute as well as deaf, my son.
Impromptu	OK, now, down in front!
Father O'Rielly	Oh you little heathen. As I was saying. Pity fill our hearts for the Lady Angina, and of course, our next Duke, Lord Draino!
Portfolio	Hold! Enough! For no such proclamation has been made! While several worthy candidates, I among them, contend still.
Draino	Dare you, sir, to argue this with heated temper, here in this place of all! A disgrace!
Portfolio	Disgrace! You from a family of chicken diddlers!

*Donna Sonata erupts into **SOBS** once again.*

Portfolio	Eh, sorry, dear. But you, sir, Draino, brother of the Duke, I challenge your honor!
Draino	Judge of me you!? Court thy disaster!
Portfolio	Trial of arms I demand!

Draino	Verdict rendered by steel!
Father O'Rielly	Objection!
Impromptu	Overruled!
Portfolio	Scoundrel!
Draino	Knave!
Portfolio	Villain
Draino	Bitch!

Swords are **DRAWN** *and* **Portfolio** *and* **Draino** *square to duel. Blades are ready to strike when* **Angina RUSHES** *between the contenders to stay their hands. But it is too late. She is caught and* **PIERCED** *by rapier thrusts from either side.*

Draino	Uh, oh! My bad.
Portfolio	That was me! Sorry.
Angina	I wouldst stay your hands, beloved son and brother—brother-in-law, er, fiancé. Wow, this really hurts. Die, poor Angina, widow, mother, flying buttress.
Father O'Rielly	Tragedy. I offer last blessing to your departed soul, Angina.

Rigatoni, *man of the prince, and* **Cavatelli,** *man of* **Lord Draino,** **INTERCEDE** *to see proper Marquis of Queensbury codes be followed in the now deadly duel.*

| **Rigatoni** | My prince, for the proprieties, let me act as second for you. |

| **Cavatelli** | As for you, Lord Draino, I will similarly act with your permission. |

*The duel **RESUMES**. **Portfolio** and **Draino** circle then **ADVANCE** and **THRUST** their blades. **Portfolio** misses **Draino**, but fatally **STRIKES Cavatelli**. **Draino** misses **Portfolio**, but fatally **STRIKES Rigatoni**. Both wounded men let out **VIBRATO SQUEALS**.*

| **Portfolio** | God D***! |

| **Draino** | Holy S***! |

| **Father O'Rielly** | Lord, I offer last blessing to these newly departed souls, Rigatoni and Cavatelli. |

*New seconds are appointed, **PLACEBO and FUSILLI**, for the **Prince** and **Lord Draino** respectively. However, unfamiliar with protocol, they **UNSHEATHE** their own swords and **HAVE AT** each other, interrupting the main event. **Portfolio** and **Draino** simply look on.*

| **Placebo** | Your words are twisted, Fusilli. |

| **Fusilli** | And your words, do not affect me, Placebo. |

*Naturally, they **KILL** each other, and **Father O'Rielly RUSHES** frantically to offer last blessings.*

*Suddenly an altercation **ERUPTS** over possession of an aisle seat (due to overbooking) and the general disturbance **STIRS** the congregation. There is **PUSHING and SHOVING**, swords and knives are **DRAWN**.*

*When **someone** is **KNOCKED BACKWARD** into a player piano, the tune "**Camp Town Races**" commences **LOUDLY**. **CHAOS EXPLODES** amidst the congregation.*

Men, women, and children all participate in the brannigan. *Punches, chickens,* and *pies* are *THROWN.* **People** are *STABBED, RUN THROUGH, or CHOKED.*

Several **people** are *HIT* over the head with chairs and whisky bottles or are *DRIVEN THROUGH* the stained glass windows (much to the horror of **Father O'Rielly**).

One person is CATAPULTED from a bench and through the wall, while another SWOOPS in from a chandelier which, from carrying excess weight, CRASHES down and CRUSHES those below*. NUNS get into the act CLIMB on top the altar and DANCE to the melody coming from the player piano**.

A SMALL DOG BARKS incessantly and occasionally bites someone's ankle. Chicken feathers FLY everywhere and people are POOPED ON.

Apoplexia and *Agita Hussy SPILL across stage RIPPING each other's hair and clothes.*

*Even the Dead Duke participates as his body is used as a **battering ram** to RUN DOWN the crowd. It is then THROWN through a stained glass window only to be HURLED back inside through the adjacent stained glass window. Eventually his body is TORN TO PIECES during the **fight** and some folks RUN AWAY with body parts as souvenirs.*

The entire out-of-control scene makes a food riot look like a street fair.

*In fact as the body count rises with exponential speed. Camp Town Races" turns to "**She'll be Coming Round the Mountain.**"*

Meanwhile, Portfolio and Lord Draino are simply spectators to the UPROAR.

Father O'Rielly finds he cannot keep up his invocations. Under these conditions he ANNOUNCES a special wide area blessing for all within a 50 yard radius.

---

* Author's thought: Since there is no roof, can disbelief be suspended in the chandelier scene? Ibid, op cit, el cid, op ed.

** Author's other thought: What if the nuns go topless with body sequins and headdresses with many large feathered plumes? Ponder this further.

Father O'Rielly	Lord, please provide your bulk blessing to all dead and dying within the 50 yard confines of this madness.
Impromptu	Louder!
Father O'Rielly	I have had it with you, you bastard!

Father O'Rielly and *Impromptu* exchange ***GUNFIRE*** *and fatally shoot each other in a hail of bullets.*

Father O'Rielly	Jesus H. C*****, I'm dead.
Impromptu	Louder.
Portfolio	Have at you, and may the better triumph!
Draino	Well-spoken, and engage. Wait! Look over there!

Suddenly ***Draino*** *POINTS to something behind* ***Portfolio***. *Portfolio turns to look, and* ***Draino*** *RUNS HIM THROUGH.*

Portfolio	That never gets old. I die. Elvis has left the building.
Guano	(aside) This has come to my notice. Draino strikes with right hand while the Duke's bane struck with left. Lord Draino, by your own hand I have absolved you of the Duke's murder.
Draino	Lowly Fool.

| **Guano** | Lowly Jester, please. |

| **Draino** | Whatever. Dare you, of such base station, insult me further with your false accusations and empty acquittals. And now I reply to your earlier inquiry. Yes, I am wearing pantaloons, and I am glad to be here. |

Draino DEALS Guano a most grievous wound.

A moment later ENTER A GIANT ROOSTER which PECKS Lord Draino to death.

| **Guano** | Fowl play indeed. So fulfilled is the prophesy. Veins of common blood shall common ends meet. Jealously being the rooster's revenge and cause for murder. As for Guano, no regrets for him. Though I never played Broadway, at least I got to be in show business. |

Guano DIES. All is quiet since everyone is dead. ENTER Raconteur, the fabler. He watches the dog WALK PAST proudly GRIPPING one of the Duke's hands in his jaws.

Raconteur	While determined in our obsessions
	To gather all earthly possessions.
	No true happiness do they bring?
	For they are all about nothing.

A 16 TON WEIGHT falls upon Raconteur and then explodes.

CURTAIN

THE END

The Players

Guano (The Jester . . . . **Chips Ordure**

Angina (The Duchess . . . . *Amanda Reckonwith*

The Duke . . . . **Lymmon Lime**

Donna Sonata (Daughter of the Duke) . . . . **Anne Onnamus**

Portfolio (**A** Prince, Husband of Donna Sonata). . . . . **Clipper Shears**

Draino (Brother of the Duke, a Lord). . . . . **Vinnie Vidivici**

Father O'Rielly (a Priest) . . . .*Father O'Reilly*

Impromptu (a Heckler) . . . . **Harry Goad**

Falsetto (a Castle guard). . . . . **Lax Bandergeld**

Castrato (a Castle guard) . . . . **Nick Capon**

Obbligato (Host of Royal Banquet Tonight) . . . . **Wolfe Lecher**

Apoplexia (Hostess of Royal Banquet Tonight). . . . .*Sassy Mynx*

Agita Hussy (Reporter Royal Banquet Tonight) . . . .*Fille Dejoie*

Minnie, Maude, and Jackie (The Pep Girls). . . . . *Agnes, Betty, and Mable Sobeleski*

Rigatoni and Placebo (the Prince's men) . . . .**Insignificant Extras**

Cavetelli and Fusilli (Lord Draino's men). . . . . **More Insignificant Extras**

Parlante, Travatore, Raconteur (Fablers). . . . .*Expendable Insignificant Extras*

Stage Manager . . . . **Carmine "The Pliers" Calissio**

Lefty the Giant Rooster . . . .*Himself*

Note:* The Duke appears courtesy of Paramount Pictures.

L' Affair Noir

Introduction

JOAN OF ARC & THE ORIGIN OF FILM NOIR

oan of Arc was not burned at the stake in 1431 as history claims, rather she was burned by French literary critics covering the release of her first novel, 'The Maid of Orleans before Katrina'. It was a story of a peasant housekeeper who moonlighted as an exotic dancer on Bourbon Street.

PD-US

Joan of Arc, (1429 photo)

Other critically bashed, but moderately popular, works followed—'How Long is the Hundred Years War', and 'If I'm a Heretic, You're a Cross Dresser'. The latter was the first LGBTQ book ever published.

She also coined the title 'Dauphin' for the heir apparent to the French throne. Dauphin, meaning Dolphin, was meant to follow the English tradition of naming the royal successor after aquatic mammals.*

---

* It was only after the end of the Hundred Years War that it was realized the English title for the heir apparent was 'Prince of Wales', and not 'Prince of Whales'. This drastic misinterpretation was one of the leading causes of the French Revolution.

THE ORIGIN OF FILM NOIR

Joan also introduced radically new elements to the format of the medieval novel. The most ambitious of these included subtitles and the ticker slide at the bottom of the page. Both are found in the work presented here.

Also demonstrated in this selection is the first known stylistic presentation of the traditional Film Noir structures—seductive femme fatales, morally ambivalent protagonists, and Venetian blinds.

The work, L'Affair Noir, was thought to be lost in the fire that did eventually claim the life of Joan of Arc. It was later found among the Dead Sea Scrolls, in the light reading section.

J. E. Winchester, Esq.

L' Affair Noir

PD-US

(Editor's note: All characters are portrayed by actors 18 years or older)

Le bord de la nuit coupe le plus profond.

The edge of night cuts deepest on the thin line between light and dark. That's when the wretched come out of the shadows to make their vile living.

Jean Paul Sartre se presente avec son partenaire Louis XVI—detectives.

That could have described me and my partner. My partner was Louis XVI, and I'm J.P. Sartre. We're detectives. I ran the business. He ran up expenses and then he ran out of luck. They found him in a dark alley—shot, stabbed, and run over by a tour bus hauling old ladies from Cleveland. He was holding half of a tuna sandwich. They said he died of natural causes, for a detective, that is. He was now part of the world outside existence.

Louis a ete tue. De mauvaises choses arrivent.

Whether he had it coming or not, I don't know. Bad things just happen. You don't have to be special. I don't think about it much. I don't need more troubles than I already got.

La probleme est venu sous la forme d'un femme fatale.

If you're in the wrong place at the wrong time trouble will find you. Maybe I was in the wrong place and the wrong time. Trouble found me and it came in the shape of a beautiful woman. I should have known she was dangerous. I should have known a lot of things, but they all seemed to have slipped my mind once I saw her.

Mon bureau etait sombre. Vous ne pouvez pas cacher la verite a l'ombre.

My office was dimly lit. When it's too bright, the light can play tricks on you the way it attaches to a face or an elbow. You're always better off to see someone in the shadows. You can't hide the truth from the shadows. I couldn't hide from her.

Entre la Femme Fatale.

I invited the beautiful trouble to come in.

"Etes vous un detective prive, bitch?" Elle a demande?

"Are you a detective?" She asked with a voice smoother than silk and deadlier than undercooked pork chops.

"C'est ce que quelqu'un a peint sur la porte." J'ai repondu.

"Not really." I came back. "I just have that painted on the door because I don't like looking at a clear pane of glass."

Elle etait un fantasme.

She was every fantasy I ever had, except for the one where I hit a homer to win the series for the Yanks, but she was all the rest. She was breathtaking—her hair, her eyes, and her face. She had legs longer than the wait times at the DMV.

"Tu es drole comme Jerry Lewis." Elle dit.

"I'll assume you're joking, Mr. Sartre." She said with a sly wit.

"Vous voulez entendre une blague. Un cheval entre dans un bar…"

"Sure, you want to hear another one? A horse walks into a bar…" I began.

Elle s'est presentee. "Je suis Betty Marie Boop."

Lakehurst, NJ, USA: Hindenburg disaster not airship, but real Hindenburg. Spicy food blamed :::

"Mr. Sartre, my name is Betty Marie Boop." She cut me off with her introduction.

"Comment ca s'ecrit?" Je demande.

"Can you spell that?" I asked while sketching her legs.

"Avec des lettres." Elle repondit. "BTW, je suis Jane Doe maintenant."

"No thank you. However, you can just call me Jane Doe. The 'Doe' is silent. I never use it because I'm really Indira Gandhi." She emphasized.

"Qui est le proprietaire de votre trouble de la personnalite?" Je dit.

"How bourgeois. Can I talk to the character in charge of your personality disorder?" I quipped.

"Ca, c'est moi, Marie Curie." Elle a parle.

"That would be me, Marie Curie." She said.

"Chanceux tu n'es pas Marie Curie. J'ai laisse mas hazmat costume est chez le 'dry cleaners'." J'ai plaisante.

I heard somebody knee clubbed you when you went to pick up your Nobel prize. I'm glad to see I was misinformed. Wouldn't want to have those legs dented. By the way, I hope you didn't bring any radium with you, Marie? My hazmat suit is at the cleaners." I mentioned. "Please, sit down."

Elle etait sexy quand elle s'asseyait. J'aimerais avoir de meilleurs meubles.

I marveled at the way she slid her supple body into the chair. I only wished I had more furniture to offer her.

"Ca te derange si je fume?" Elle demande.

"Do you mind if I smoke?" She asked.

"Tu fumes maintenant. Oh, tu veux dire cigarette." Je dit.

"You already are. Oh, you mean with a cigarette." I said.

"Quel est votre interet?" A-t-elle demande sournoisement.

"If I could borrow one? Would you be interested in my case, Mr. Sarte?" She asked wryly.

blamed: ::::: Reuters: French surrender to Germans. Italians protest, "We quit first." ::::: Mookie Mouse,

"Gonflement."

"Why not, I'm interested in everything else of yours.." I said honestly.

"J'aime un homme avec un potential de croissance." Elle revelee.

"You remind me of a croissant. I like a man who resembles a croissant." She toyed.

"Qu'est –ce que tu aimes d'autre avec ton croissant?" Je dit.

"Who doesn't? What do you like on your croissant?" I asked.

"Le foie." Elle repondit.

"Sweet cream." The words flowed out of her delicate lips.

"Tu es chanceux. J'en ai beaucoup." Je repondu en retour.

"It's your lucky day, baby. I have loads of it." I tried to give her the impression that I was like the entire dairy section of a supermarket.

"Rappelez vous ce qu'est une cigarette?" Elle a rappele.

"The cigarette, remember?" She deflected me coyly.

"Comme un elephant." Je dit.

"Like an elephant on gingko bilboa." I said.

"Dangereux, non?" Elle a note.

"That sounds dangerous." She noted.

"Uniquement avec les pronoms." J'ai avoue.

"Only when you tangle tusks."

"Le Kinke."

"Kinky." She smiled.

Editor's Note

The following section is displayed with the 'Commentary' option selected. This option allows readers to witness a descriptive review and analysis of the work in progress.

The commentary is presented in the original French and is from Miss DeNarde's fourth grade Film Appreciation class.

Menu
Sub-Titles: ON
Commentaire: ON

Pitch Mirabelle (Sidekick/Editor)

new cheese franchise. ::::: NBC: Priceless Picasso drawings missing. Details sketchy. ::::: CBS:

Mlle. DeNarde, l'enseignante de quatrieme annee de L'Ecole pour Enfants, etait jeune, grande, et attirante. Par coincidence, elle revoyait aujourd'hui L'Affaire Noire de Jeanne d'Arc avec ses eleves.

Even though I was wearing a hat, I knew I was in over my head. She was leading me down a road with no detours. Her hypnotic eyes kept my hands on the wheel and not where I wanted to put them.

Etudiants, est ce quelqu'un sait ce que un detective?

I struck a match and we were both lit up. When we exhaled, two billows of smoke rose and mingled in the air. I didn't have any idea about what to offer her next. I only knew it wasn't going to be profiteroles.

"Un detective est quelqu'un que ma mere a suivi mon pere parce qu'elle croit qu'il la trompe." Henri repond.

"So how can I help you, Madame Curie?" I composed myself, and asked the first question all detectives should ask or so the manual says.

"Merci, Henri. Mais la prochaine fois moins de details sur la famille." Mlle. DeNarde suggere.

She looked at me with those bedroom blue eyes and I nearly fell out of my shoes. Lucky I had them tied in double knots.

"Qui est la femme que Sartre invite dans son bureau?" Mlle. DeNarde quiz.

"Mr. Sartre, oh, can I call you Jean Paul?" She interrupted herself. That was twice she cut in on her own sentence. That was a big clue about her manners.

"Une sale petite f**king Ho bitch!" Reponde Angelique.

"Sure, Angel. I'd like to be on first name basis. Which one of the four do you want me to call you?" I asked.

Details sketchy. ::::: CBS: Midwest thunderstorms wreak havoc. Confusion rains. ::::: Antelope

"Langue, sil vous plait. Est ce que tout va bien a la maison, Angelique?"

"As I was saying, for over 165 million years, dinosaurs ruled the earth. Then suddenly, about 65 million years ago. That's really not a long time in terms of geology, or is it geography? It's one of the sciences that starts with a 'g'. I know it's not gynecology or gender studies. Let me think, a second." She pondered.

"Qu'est ce qu'un 'Ho', Mlle. DeNarde." Demande Marcel naivement.

I had a feeling it was going to be a long ponder, so I cut her short.

Louise leve la main et reponde. "C'est ma mere apres que nous ayons decouvert qu'elle trompait le pere d'Henri."

"Why don't we just go with geology for now? That'll be the first thing I check out if I take the case."

"No, No, No. Ne plus parler de meres ou de peres, ou d'autres membres de la famille!" Mlle. Dit frenetiquement. Puis elle murmure. "Mon Dieu, Quelle maison vit ces enfants doivent vivre."

"Alright. As I was saying, 65 million years may seem a long time, but it's practically a heartbeat in." She paused her tempting full lips. "Did we agree on geology?"

Mlle. ordonne la classe. "Soyons tranquilles et concentrer sur l'histoire, et uniquement sur l'histoire."

"That was the deal." I said as I focused on her delicate mouth and the face it was attached to.

Alors, Marie Anne se plaignit a haute voix. "Mlle. DeNarde, Jean Luc me fait des grimaces!"

"About 65 million years ago, dinosaurs were suddenly extinct." She stated emphatically.

havoc. Confusion rains. ::::: Antelope Freeway 1 Mile. ::::: BBC: Bolivia DeHavillands face Cardiff Wh

"Jean Luc est un retarde." Brigid ajoute.

"Did they stop using deodorant?" I asked from a personal hygiene point.

"Il est aussi masogeniste!" Accuse Harriette.

"No, 'X-TINCT'. Meaning they vanished from the earth without a trace. Some say it was disease, or climate change. Others believe it was some catastrophic cosmic event that doomed them." She paused dramatically to catch her breath.

"Et il possedait des esclaves." A ajoute Robert.

"Well, Marie, that all sounds very interesting, except for one thing. You don't believe any of it. You think they were murdered."

"Je blame la societe." Jean Luc s'est defendu.

She turned away with such drama that it made A Streetcar Named Desire look like a Vaudeville review. Then she slowly turned back sweeping everything up in her innocent doe eyes. Only the eyes that caught me had a wily glint that made me feel like I just walked into the crosshairs of something nasty.

"Assez! Jean Luc plus de visages. Tout le monde ce tait." Mlle. DeNarde ordres.

"That's absurd." She protested.

"Je pourrais utiliser un cognac." DeNarde pense.

"I've found absurdity resides all around us. Things in this life only have the meaning we give them. If you ever watched 'Keeping Up With the Kardashians', you'd know what I mean." I explained my philosophy in simple terms.

"Je vais vous dire que ce n'est pas absurd. Kim Kardashian un cul titanesque. C'est hors de controle." Une autre pensee traverse le cerveau de Mlle. DeNarde.

---

1 Mile. ::::: BBC: Bolivia DeHavillands face Cardiff Whales in Cup final Saturday. ::::: NYT:

"Will you take the case?" There was a smooth blend of innocent pleading and clever deceit in her voice. She was good at what she did. Real good. But I had some tricks up my sleeve, only they were in my other jacket. This one only had my arms in them. "How much would you charge?" She asked.

"Mlle. DeNarde, pouvons nous fumer?" Demande Linda.

"I'm no Henri Bergson, so time is valued at twenty bucks a day, and free will means plus expenses." I quoted my standard fee. "Plus another twenty a day, and expenses for you Betty Marie, Jane Doe and whatever other friends that come around."

"Ou prendre du cognac?" Demande Alain.

"Very well. Do you take junk bonds or Confederate money?" She counteroffered.

"Je voudrais un coup dans le cul de Kim Kardashian." David sourit mechamment.

I leaned forward to protest and caught the seductive scent of her. There was no use denying, I fell for her like a couple of spheres dropped by Galileo from the Leaning Tower of Pisa in 1590. He proved his theory of gravity, but I wasn't proving anything except that I was a major league sap, regardless of hitting a home run for the Yanks. I had to snap out of it.

Mlle. DeNarde es choque. "Non, Non, bien sur que non. Qu'est ce qui ne va pas chez vous les enfants? Tu n'as que neuf ans. Et David tu es sur le point de franchir une ligne!"

"No problem." I said without much of a snap.

"Oui, but c'est une maturite de neuf ans. Nous sommes beaucoup plus sophistries que nous n'en avouns l'air." Liza annonce.

She got up and extended her hand to me. I took it, and escorted her to the door.

Cup finals Saturday. ::::: NYT: Criticism of Beethoven's behavior falls on deaf ears. ::::: LAT: Hi

"Le 'snapper head' l'emmene a la porte, et l'emmene fair un tour." Henri dit.

"Thank you, Mr. Sartre." She said in a tone reserved for talking to a fish you already had on the hook. She left, and I looked at her walk away.

"J**** C*****, vous le gens!" Mlle. remarques.

My secretary, B.B., knew that look and slapped me in the head. B.B. was my reality check.

"Qu'est ce qui t'enerve autant, bitch? Froideur." François tente d'apaiser.

B.B., was a good girl Friday, maybe the best. She had the looks to go anywhere she wanted with anyone she wanted to go with, but she stayed here for a lousy secretary's pay, which didn't always come at regular intervals.

David remarque. "D'apres cette description, on dirait que BB. A un beau cul."

Once I asked her why she kept on and took all the grief we gave her.

"Ton pere a un beau cul, Henri." Soupire Louise.

She cooed, "Somebody's got to look after you and Mr. XVI. Plus I'm using you as a front for a money laundering operation, and I move stolen merchandise through your outgoing postal. Believe me, it's not as easy as you think to send something like a hijacked truck through the mail. You need a lot of stamps."

"David tu as besoin de traitements par electrochocs." Met en garde Mlle. DeNarde.

"Anything else?" I asked hoping to get the whole picture.

"Je peux creer quelque chose pour vous, Mlle. DeNarde." Offert Jacques.

There's also numbers and gambling rackets that I run out of the lavatory. That's why the bathroom is always occupied even though there are only three of us in the office."

Mlle. DeNarde se contente de le regarder. A moite dispose a accepter l'offre, et a moite dispose a' le tuer pour avoir offert.

"That's all fun and games, B.B., until somebody gets a serious UTI." I lectured.

"Asseyez vous petite fils de…" Elle dit.

"Tell me about it." She said experientially.

Puis la cloche sonne pour annoncer un pause de dix minutes en classe.

I didn't know much about dinosaurs except they had brains the size of walnuts, just like Rudi Giuliani. My limited understanding meant I had to do some checking with the foremost dinosaur experts in the country—the third grade students at Ecole L'Enfant's.

I wasn't thrilled about going back to third grade for a fourth time, and I'm sure the feeling was mutual. Three of the best years of my life were wasted there because I couldn't master fractions, punctuation, and social skills. I decided to visit a museum instead.

I had been to the Louvre once on a case so I knew my way around. I was headed for the Dinosaur Concierge Desk, but I never got there. A wet-behind-the-ears two-bit gunsel shoved a roscoe in my ribs.

Without being properly introduced, I already knew three things about him: He was Corsican; He was short; and his shoelaces were tied.

"We're going to see the man." The Kid said in an unfriendly whisper.

"Mr. Rogers?" I inquired.

"Shut up, and walk." The Kid tried to talk tough, but hadn't been around much, so I pulled an old detective trick on him.

"Hey, Kid, your shoelace is untied." I warned him insincerely.

The gunsel was green enough to go for the gag. A quick move later, and I was holding the gun on him.

"Come on, Junior. Let's go see the man." I ordered.

1751 BC. ::::: 1883 Krakatoa erupts. Columbus blamed. His day removed from calendar. ::::: 7

EDITOR'S NOTE

It seems we have lost the original story text in French. I am currently trying to contact 15th Century French Literature Support to resolve the issue.

You may continue to follow the story via the English sub-titles. Please bear with us and thank you for your patience.

Menu
Sub-Titles: ON
Commentaire: OFF

Pitch Mirabelle (Sidekick/Editor)

As it turned out, Junior didn't know where we were going either. So we had to take the interactive museum tour to find 'the man'. Our search ended in the Fat Antagonist Villain wing of the museum

"Good day, Mr. Sartre. We finally meet, sir. A privilege." Said the fat antagonist villain.

"I usually charge for privileges, especially for people who invite me at gunpoint." I replied.

"I see you've already met my associate, Bonaparte. My apologies." Said the fat man.

"This guy told me my shoes were untied. You're going to pay for that, Sartre." Threatened Bonaparte.

"These are the hazards of the business, my boy." Consoled the fat man.

"I want to be called—Emperor. That's my crime name." Bonaparte demanded.

"Mr. Sartre, sir. Do you have any idea of who I am?" Asked the Corpulent villain.

"Should I?" I asked sarcastically.

Bonaparte continued his tantrum. "Then he took my gun. You keep asking for it, Sartre, and you're going to get it. Oh, yeah, I'm the one who's going to give it to you. See?"

"Perhaps you should know me, Mr. Sartre, then again, perhaps not, sir. But to remove any doubt, I am Otto Von Bismarck. Mastermind of German unification, its first chancellor, and the virtuoso diplomat that directed European affairs for decades."

Bonaparte whined on. "What kind of a guy lies about your shoelaces, and then takes somebody's gun? A creep, that's who! You're a creep, and I'm going to take care of you, Sarte."

"Sorry, I only pay attention to domestic political characters, Bismarck." I quipped back to the Chancellor. That may have deflated him a bit. "Can I return Junior's gun?"

"Of course, sir. A boy must have his gun, I always say." Otto clarified.

::::: 1347 AD- Healthcare workers overwhelmed by Black Death. ::::: Antelope Freeway ½ mile. ::::::

"You say a lot." I observed aloud.

I tossed Junior his gun. The boy didn't drop it. It was more of a juggle, just enough to make it go off and shoot the Kid in the foot. That's when he dropped the gun. And it went off again. This one got him in the other foot. With two shot up dogs, the poor kid didn't even have the benefit of hopping around in pain.

"Well, let's get down to business. Shall we sir? Bismarck suggested. "I am aware that you had a visit from a mysterious woman today, sir. Did she give you her name?"

"She gave me lots of them." I recounted.

"Was it, Ruth Wonderly, or Norma Desmond, or Betty Jo Bialosky?" Rattled of Bismark.

"No, those ladies didn't show up." I answered.

"He shot me! He shot me with my own gun! With my own gun, he shot me!" Bonaparte yelped loud enough for Bismarck and me to give him a passing glance.

"Do you want to know her real name, sir?" Asked Bismarck.

"Je ne pense pas qu'elle en ait un." Je dit.

"I'm beginning to think she doesn't have one." I surmised.

"Anastasia." Bismarck revele.

"It is Anastasia." Bismark revealed.

"Espeller?"

"You want to spell that out for me, Heinz?" I probed.

"Cannez vous utilisez en la sentence, por favor?" Il dit

"Can you use it in a sentence, please?"

"Utilisez le vous meme. Je ne suis pas ton bitch!"

"OK, so what do you know about Anesthesia?" I asked. There was nothing to lose.

Nobody likes

"Dites moi d'abord. Le chou me donne du gaz." Il dit.

"I would be remiss if I relayed anything, sir without a reciprocating exchange. If you gather my meaning?" Bismarck stated.

"Ow wow, wow, wow, Mon pieds!" Saab Bonaparte.

"My feet! My feet!" Came the pained wails from the poor Kid, now wriggling on the floor.

"Paciencia, garcon. Je possesser un deck de cartes pinochle, Mssr. Sartre."

"Patience, my boy. We'll attend to your needs momentarily." Bismark consoled the boy insincerely. "Well, Mr. Sartre, you can't expect me to lay out all my cards, can you sir?"

"Je pense donc je suis!" Je crie.

"Look at it this way, you can tell me now, or I find out for myself and then Miss Dissociative Identity Disorder will get the brass ring." I veiled enough of a threat to get Bismarck's attention.

To Snuggle

EDITOR'S NOTE

Looks like we recovered the original French story text. I am still attempting to contact 15th Century French Literature Support to identify the root cause of the original issue. Thanks once again for your patience.

Menu
Sub-Titles: ON
Commentaire: OFF

Pitch Mirabelle (Sidekick/Editor)

Or Dine

"Wah, wah." Dit Bonaparte. "Je sanguine a mort! Vengeance! Restitucion!"

I'm bleeding to death! I'm going to get you for this, mister! I can't feel my legs!!" The Kid was moaning now with a weakened faint voice.

"Patience, Bonaparte. Je ne peux pas porter de chapeaux." Dit Bismarck.

"Shortly, Bonaparte. Shortly. Bravo, Mr. Sartre, I admire a man who can veil a threat so smoothly. A also admire a man who can wear a hat. That skill has always eluded me. Well, I shall lay my cards on the table, sir." Bismark relented.

"Mettez votre carte sur la table, Bismarck. Meme ceus qui te relevent." Je dit.

"Even the ones up your sleeve?" I told him.

"Le ha, ha, ha." Bismarck rit. "Estes vous familier avec l'art? Par exemple, Rodin?

Bismarck laughed like a bowlful of jelly, then he asked. "Are you familiar with master artists like Rodin?"

"Rodin le sulpteur ou Rodan le monstre?

"Rodin the sculptor, or the Japanese monster?" I asked for clarification.

"La statue de Michelangelo appelle, David. Cela a ete vole." Bismarck revele.

"What? Anyway, there is a sculpture, sir that was created by none other than Michelangelo." Bismarck began. "It is called David, or just Dave to those who are his sophisticated art aficionados. It was displayed in Florence—the city not the insurance lady."

"Quelqu'un le cache sous son manteau?"

"Somebody sneak it out under their coat?" I jested.

Accompanied By

"*Exactement!*" Bismarck exclame.

"Exactly, sir. A size 957 Husky fit to be exact. It is priceless."

"Le manteau?" Je die en surprize.

"The coat?" I asked.

"Non, la statue. Beaucoup buckereaus sur paye oute pour le retourner au la statue." Bismarck m'a dit.

"No, the statue. Several collectors are interested in the acquisition of the piece, illegally of course. They are willing to pay fifty million francs for it. Naturally, there are several concerns interested in acquiring the object d'art for them." Bismarck concluded.

"Tu es l'un d'entre eux, naturellement." Je devine.

"Naturally, you're one of those concerns, and you're concerned about the other concerns getting a leg up on you."

"J'aime pas etre touche." Dit Bismarck.

"I'm concerned about a leg or any other body part getting up on me, sir. Touching has never sat comfortably with me."

"Qui est derriere de capres du crime?" Je inquirer.

"The theft, who was behind it? I was digging for an answer."

"Merci de demander. No se. Mais je te payola por tu discouver et."

Very good question, sir. One I'm prepared to pay a handsome fee for you to answer."

"Je suis beau." Je lui ai dit.

"Why not, I'm a handsome guy." I told him boldly.

"Certainement. Acceptez vous la bondes de Milken ou Confederate?"

"Excellent, sir. A admire a man who admires himself. Would you accept forty dollars an hour, plus expenses in either junk bonds or Confederate money?"

A Porcupine

"OK."

"I do now. You have a deal." I agreed smugly.

"**Je passe oute avec la vapours. Ambulance! Ambulance!**" Begger Bonaparte.

"I'm going to pass out. Someone call an ambulance." Pleaded Bonaparte. He closed his eyes and darkness swarmed over him.

Burma Shave

EDITOR'S NOTE

Let's look at more of the exciting commentary from Miss DeNarde's fourth grade class.

> Menu
> *Sub-Titles: ON*
> *Commentaire: ON*

Pitch Mirabelle (Sidekick/Editor)

La classe de Mlle. DeNarde a repris. Et elle a prefere se poignarder dans la jambe que recommencer.

It wasn't a bad day, but I've had better. I figured it was time to go home to get some overdue extreme ironing done. That wasn't how it played out.

"Etudiants, ayons une classe tres ordonne cette session. Ou bien je serai force d'infliger des blessures corporelles." Mlle. DeNarde annonce.

At my door was my partner's widow of two days—Her Majesty Marie Antoinette. She was wearing a lacey pink chiffon mourning dress.

"Premiere question. Qui est Marie Antoinette, et Pourquoi est elle a la porte?"

"Jean Paul, I'm so distraught with grief. I had to see you. Also I have two tickets to the opera that are burning a hole in my pocket. Let's go. It's HMS Pinafore." She whimpered annoyingly.

Angelique repond. "Elle est un prostitute Ho de parc a roulottes."

I hated to break this to a new widow, but Pinafore was really an operetta. Some people might call it a comic opera. Those were the kind of people who don't put a new roll of toilet paper on the roller when they use the last of it.

"Angelique, Toi et David etes une paire qui peut batter un brelan." Mlle. DeNarde dit, puis sort l'oeil d'Angelique. "Quelqu'un d'autre?"

"Sorry, Your Highness, I've been busy on a case. Let me get you off my back. I mean let me get back to you." I tried to give her the brush, but I couldn't scrape her off.

Marcel tente de repondre. "Marie Antoinette est a la porte parce qu'elle une liaison avec le pere d'Henri?" Un livre frappe Marcel a la tete.

"I know it's only been a day and a half since Louis was killed, but I need to move on. Why don't I move in, and we'll move out together—tomorrow?" She pleaded.

ported. ::::: Russia: Vladimir Putin's new book- 'No More Mr. Nice Guy' hits shelves tomorrow. :::::

"Si je ne me calme pas, je teurai un de ces enfants. Pas qu'il y ait quelque chose de mal a ca." Mlle. DeNarde pense.

"Baby, I don't want to take advantage of your grief. Besides, if we do anything now, the cops will be all over us." That wasn't just a line. Somehow I could feel the police were already hovering like vultures over a dead meat packing facility.

Mlle. DeNarde sort un sac d'herbe de son bureau et se roule un 'Doobie', elle va dans le placard et l'allume. Elle en resort une femme beaucoup plus heureuse.

"You know you're the only man for me. You're strong, manly, and you have an attached head. What more can a girl ask for?" She implored as she clung to me like a wet tee shirt on a prom date.

L'herbe est tres puissante. Il est cultive sur le flanc d'un volcan dans le sol riche des indigenes lapides qui ferilisent les champs avec leur propre 'poop'.

"Look, doll, why don't you take a little vacation until things cool off? Then I'll come to you." I suggested firmly.

"Mlle. DeNarde, qu'aimez vous chez un homme?" Demande Josephine. La question est suivie d'une vague de fous rires.

"Where would I go?" She asked innocently.

"Josephine, vous avez beaucoup de surprises a attendre chez les hommes. Je ne vais pas vous gacher l'un d'entre eux." Dit Mlle. DeNarde.

"Tristan da Cunha." I said.

Elle continuer. "Cependent, je vais vous donner un conseil. Vous allez devoir perdre du poids et devenir plus flexible si jamais vous esperez le faire a l'arriere d'un Renault Turbo."

With that she blew me a kiss, caught the edge of her pink dress in the door as I slammed it in her face. She stumbled backwards trying to free her hem, and then fell down a flight of stairs. Say what you want about her, the lady knew how to make an exit.

tomorrow. :::: Science: Panel accuse report on ocean pollution 'watered down'. ::::: History: Mis

"Mlle. DeNarde. Tu as l'air endormi." Dit Alain.

Now that encounter was over, I brought out the ironing board and heated up the iron. I was about to press when it sounded like a sledgehammer was pounding on my door.

"No, ca va." Mlle. DeNarde rires, et prend un autre gros coup sur elle reefer.

I threw the door open, but wasn't surprised to see who was there.

La professeur realise soudain. "Ou'est Angelique? Cette petite bitch a besoin de se detendre. Angelique, viens ice et prends un bouffe, ma fille. En fait vous venez tous et prenez une coup. C'est la bonne shit. Ne le manquez pas.

"Inspector Javert, is this a business or social call?" I asked with a smile.

La classe forme un cercle et fait circuler le hachage.

"Hello Sartre." Javert growled.

"Tout le monde prend un coup et le trensmet. Ne fais pas 'bogart' le joint, mon amis." Danielle conseille.

"Why don't you call me before you come over, this way I won't be around when you arrive?" I joked.

En deux tours, tout le monde est decontracte, deconstruisant la realite, et recite de la poesie comme une bande de beatniks.

"Quit cracking wise, or I'll charge you with battery so fast you'll be shocked."

"Bonjour, amour, avec le ciel. Mon dieu ne pas. Bonjour, amour." Marie dit.

"Don't blow a fuse, Javert."

"J'ai une idee!" Mlle. DeNarde dit.

I want to be the conductor on the train that sends you to the electric chair, Sartre. Don't sell me short. Because I'm currently positive I have grounds to do it." Javert snapped.

watered down'. ::::: Antelope Freeway 1/2 mile. ::::: Pope farts during communion service. :::::

"Quel?" Alice demande.

"Why so negative today, Javert? Let's switch the subject." I said, exhausting all the puns I could think of on this subject.

Mlle. DeNarde annonce fierement. "Je peux encore le faire sur la banquette arriere d'une Renault Turbo!"

Javert was irritable when he was in a good mood. He always wore a crumpled brown fedora, an equally crumpled overcoat, and a three day beard. A half smoked cigar was eternally stuffed in the side of his mouth. The ashes from the other half could be found all over his clothes, keeping the food stains company.

"Faire ce que?" Demande Marcel.

"Getting mighty cozy with you ex-partner's ex-wife, hey gumshoe?" He grumbled.

"Mlle. DeNarde, Pourquoi David continue t il de laisser tomber et de ramasser son crayon?" Recits Liza.

"Is that a crime, Inspector?" I asked, already knowing his answer.

Il se pense qu'il essaie de regarder ta jupe, Mlle. DeNarde." Informe Michel.

"It is if murder and bigamy hold hands, like teenagers on their third date, Sartre." It was clear that either Javert didn't know teenagers or had never dated.

"Quoi de neuf jupe de Mlle. DeNarde? Linda demande.

"Javert, you'd love to pin Louis's murder on me. You've been trying to stick that on me even while he was alive." I pointed out

Jacques prend un gros coup sur le doobie. "Est ce Woodstock? Il reve.

"Yeah, but now he's cooperating." Said Javert.

"Non, c'est 'Iowa.'" Brigid clarifie, bien qu'a ce moment la, rien, y compris l'air rempli de fumee le toke, ne soit clair pour quiconque.

"You're barking up the wrong track, Javert. Louis died of natural causes." I told him.

"Eh bien, nous ne sommes plus au Kansas. Est temps d'etre un homme, David. Sauter sur la banquette arriere du Renault Turbo." Dit Mlle. DeNarde.

"I don't believe everything I hear, and I don't hear what I can't see. You like to play it dangerous, Sartre. Well, one day you're going to put your tongue on the frozen monkey bars once too often, and I'll be there, but not with the hot water."

"Sortons les huitres!" David pleure de joie.

At first I thought he was joking, but Javert had the sense of humor of an alligator about to be made into a suitcase. Javert sounded like he was rolled up newspaper, and I was a fly. We both knew that the squashed up bug on the Sports page was going to make it as difficult to read as swallowing hospital food. But that's the dangerous game we played.

"Surveille tes pas je te previens pampootie orthopedique." Javert menace.

"That's it for now. Fair warning, Sartre, You better watch your step, because I'll be watching you closer than an orthopedic pampootie." He laced me with a threat.

"Ne sois pas le talon d'une chaussure." J'ai repondu.

"Don't be a heel, Javert." I shot back.

marijuana. ::::: India: Gandhi With the Wind breaks Bollywood box office records. ::::: Scores:

EDITOR'S NOTE

Based on the little French I know, it appears to me that something very inappropriate, if not downright illegal, is going to happen in Mlle. DeNarde's class. So, let's turn off the commentary for a while and see if things cool down.

> Menu
> *Sub-Titles: ON*
> *Commentaire: OFF*

Pitch Mirabelle (Sidekick/Editor)

Pas de repassage. Plus de coups de porte.

I didn't go back to my ironing. I figured I'd there was another knock on the door coming. Bad things always happened in threes.

A la porte regnait une forte odeur de fleur de MALE.

When the inevitable rapping came, I dutifully answered. There was a strong scent of 'Fleur de Male' floating in the air, but no one was affixed to it. Or at least that's what I thought until I followed the scent toward the floor.

Debout a la porte etait un etrange petit homme.

Standing, at least I thought he was standing, was an odd little man wearing a bowler, a monocle, and a black overcoat. He looked like he was just a torso. I couldn't spot any legs or feet, at least from my present altitude.

"Bonsoir, monsieur Sartre." Il a dit un Rocky Rococo voix.

"Good evening, Mr. Sartre. May I engage your hospitality and enter? He spoke with a soft eerie Rocky Rococo voice.

"Qu'est ce que c'est?" Je demande.

"What's this all about, Kid?" I asked

"Je suis Trop Lache Lautrec. Trop Lache comme dans les intestins irritables."

"It's Mister, Mister 'Too-Loose' Lautrec. Not like 'Toulouse' as in the city, but 'Too-Loose'—as in irritable bowels." He introduced himself.

"Alors tu veux utiliser ma sale de bain?" Je demande.

"So, you're here to use the bathroom?" I asked out of concern for my new carpet.

"Si c'est pratique." Il dit.

"Only if the convenience is convenient, sir." He confessed.

CHC 0. ::::: USA: Indigenous groups sue Phoenicians over 'First to discover America' claim.' :::::

"Tu as de la chance ce n'est pas mon bureau." J'ai dit.

"You're lucky you didn't come to see me at the office." I advised him.

Dans la salle de bain il a tire plusieurs fois la chasse. Il est sorti avec une arme.

I showed him to the privy. About fifteen minutes and eight flushes later, he emerged. This time he wasn't as friendly as before. He had a gun in his hand.

"Esoin de plus de papier toilette?" Je demande.

"If you need more toilet paper, all you have to do is ask." I told him.

"Non, merci. Je veux rechercher votre appartement." Il dit.

"No thank you. There was a sufficient amount. What I want is to search your apartment, Mr. Sartre. I need to see if you are hiding a 17 foot statue of Michelangelo's David. You don't mind, I hope, if I look about, sir?" He demanded politely.

"OK." J'ai dit.

"Sure, Sure. Knock yourself out, shorty." I laughed. "Knock yourself out."

"Merci, mais je dois encore faire caca." Il dit.

"Thank you." He said as he scanned the living room. "I'll next need to search the kitchen and bedroom. Will you kindly show the way?" He asked as his face suddenly contorted. "Uh oh, I think I have to poop again. Will you excuse me?"

"Mieux vaut se depecher" Je lui ai dit.

"Only if you make it in time." I said, again thinking of my new carpet.

Lautrec est alle a la salle de bain et a tire la chasse d'eau un peu plus.

Lautrec slipped away into the bathroom, and after few more minutes and several additional flushes, he poked his head out the door.

---

discover America' claim.' ::::: Antelope Freeway 1/4 mile. ::::: Germany: Guttenberg found guilty.

"J'ai besoin de plus de papier toilette maintenant, s'il vous plait. Dit Lautrec.

"I think I will be needing that additional toilet paper now, Mr. Sartre. If you don't mind." He requested.

"Un Rouleau?" Je demande.

"Will one roll be enough?" I inquired.

"Deux s'il vous plait." Lautrec dit.

"Two would be better, please." Came 'Mr. Poopie Pants' estimate.

Quand il a eu fini, il a fouille le reste de mon appartement.

When he finally came out again, he apologized, and told me show him the rest of the apartment.

"Est ce que je ressemble a un agent immobilier?" Je demande.

"What do I look like, a real estate agent?" I grumbled.

"Je ne sais pas. Je n'en ai jamais vu." Il dit.

I don't know. I've never seen one." He answered.

Il n'a pas trouve ce qu'il cherchait—la statue de David.

There's nothing you can do when I guy says something like that except show him around the place. He looked everything over thoroughly and satisfied himself that I wasn't harboring the statue of David anywhere in my place.

"Merci, maintenant je dois te chercher." Lautrec dit.

"Thank you for your patience, Mr. Sartre. Now I must, how do they say it, pat you down."

"Pensez vous que je le porte?" Je demande.

"Do you think I'm hiding it on me, pal?" I grinned.

ay 1/4 mile. ::::: Germany: Guttenberg found guilty. Prints found all over crime scene. ::::: NYSE

"C'est possible si vous portez un manteau hysky taille 957." Il dit.

"All things are possible. I once knew someone who had a size 957 Husky coat. He could fit an elephant into. I do not like to leave anything to chance, Mr. Sartre." Too-Loose informed me.

"OK, mais tu ferais Mieux d'attacher ton lacet de chaussure d'aboard." Il dit.

"Go ahead, frisk, but first you better tie your shoelace." I said. He bought it, and one punch later, he was out like Chaz Bono in a tabloid, and I had the gun.

Je l'ai fouille et j'ai trouve une bouteille de Fleur de Male.

Now it was my turn to frisk him. I did a thorough job, but all I found was a ticket to HMS Pinafore and a personal sized bottle of Fleur de Male. The cologne was as delicate as a divorce lawyer on retainer. Mr. Poopie Pants probably had to freshen himself up every time he hit the head. I didn't want to think what he'd smell like without it.

Quand il a recupere je lui ai donne a boire.

When he came to, I gave him back his goods, plus a shot of the-hair-of-the-dog. The dog jolted him back on his tiny wobbly legs.

"Je te frapperai si tu sors ton arme. Nous poserons des questions.

"Unless you want me to slap you around some more, I'd keep that gun in your pocket and don't try to tell me HMS Pinafore is an opera. I have a few questions for you, and I'm sure you have a few for me, besides—'can I use your bathroom?' Since I'm the home team, I'll let you go first." I offered.

"Je saigne et je dois garder mon sang dans mon corps." Il dit.

"No further questions, Mr. Sartre. You've completely made me bleed, and I assure you I strive to keep my blood inside me at all times." The little man claimed wiping his bloodied lip.

crime scene. ::::: NYSE: Stocks tumble, bonds fall. The market crashed, and you lost it all.

:::::

"Travaillez vous avec quelqu'un?" Je demande.

"Never mind that. It's my turn. Are you working solo or are you with any of these others?"

"Non, mais les autres ne m'ont pas mentionne?" Lautrec demande.

"I am an independent agent, if that is what you are asking. Did the others not mention anything about me?" Lautrec answered but, at least he wasn't bleeding on my carpet.

"Ils ont oublie." Je reponde.

"Must have slipped their mind. I'm guessing that you'll want the same deal." I said.

"Donnerez vous la statue au plus offrant, Mssr. Sartre?" Lautrec demande.

"If you find the statue, I assume you will hand it over to the highest bidder, cash and carry?" Lautrec guessed.

"Pour jouer au jeu, vous devez acheter un billet, Trop Lache." Je dit.

"No, I'm going to give to whoever asks the nicest. It's all about the money, Lautrec. If you want to get in the game, buy a ticket." I said.

"Combien d'argent veux tu?" Il a demande.

"I am at a financial disadvantage at the moment, Mr. Sartre. If you wait until I have the 100 million francs for the statue I can reimburse you. What is your current asking price?" He asked.

"Mon tariff habituel, plus papier toilette." Je dit.

"Forty dollars an hour, plus expenses. And, yes I accept junk bonds or Confederate money. Take it or leave it." I laid the deal straight out for him.

"Je dois accepter. Me contacter." Lautrec dit.

"That is very reasonable of you, sir. Of course, I must accept." Lautrec conceded. "How will you contact me, if you succeed?"

---

lost it all. ::::: NYC: Giant primate falls from Empire State Building. Witness: He was pushed. :::::

"OK." Je dit.

"Same way I'll reach the others." I bluffed. I hadn't thought about how I would reach anybody. That might have been a big oversight, but given the way people kept popping up, it probably wasn't going to be much of a problem.

"D'accord. Si vous trouvez mon sang, merci de l'envoyer a cette adresse." Il dit.

"If we have an agreement, I will pay one last visit to your toilet. Oh, if you find any of my blood around would you please forward it to this address." Lautrec said handing me his business card. Then he left taking the aroma of Fleur de Male with him.

"Croyez vous vraiment qu'il aime cet accord?" Demande une voix sexy.

"Do you really think he is even half satisfied with that arrangement, darling?" Came the seductive voice from behind me. It was Madame Curie again.

"Comment es tu arrivee, Marie Curie?" Je demande.

"How did you get in here?" I asked, surprised by her appearance.

"L'ecrivain m'a envoye." La Femme Fatale dit.

"Poetic license. The writer was tired of people just coming through the door. She wanted to mix it up." She revealed.

"Qui es tu ce soir, bebe?" Je demande.

"Looks like I'm never going to get those wrinkles out of my shirts. Who are you tonight, baby?" I inquired.

"Betty Crocker, avec une recetter pour nous render riche." Dit La Femme Fatale.

"My name is Betty Crocker, I don't iron, but I have a recipe that will make us both rich, if you'll listen to my plan." She proposed.

---

was pushed. ::::: Sports: NBA announces 'All- I dated a Kardashian' Team. ::::: USA: Phoenician

"Une recette sur les dinosaures ou les statues de la renaissance?" Je demande.

"It depends. Is it about dinosaurs or renaissance statues?" I asked.

"Vill du veta en hemlighet?" Fragade hon.

"It's about two hundred million francs, and do you want to know a secret?" Betty asked.

"Jag lyssnar. Vincent Van Gogh skulle inte saga det." Jag berattade for henne.

"I'm all ears." Was my reply. Something I knew Vincent Van Gogh wouldn't say again.

"Eleanor Roosevelt alskar dig." Hon sa. Och nu har jab problem.

"I'm in love with you, or, at least, either Amanda Rekonwith or Eleanor Roosevelt is." She said with just enough conviction to get a smart guy setup, double crossed, and maybe killed. I was in those crosshairs again.

Forsta damen och jag tillbringade natten. Sen gick jag jobbet och stannade sent.

The First Lady and I spent the night together talking about the new deal. I had to kick her out about nine the next morning since we were both taxed and I had get to the office because I wasn't thrilled about the scent coming out of my bathroom. I worked late that night. B.B. stayed on and we were closing up about ten.

Sent pa kontoret kom en dod man till kontoret ikladd en huskyjacka I storlek 957.

We were in the front room with the lights out when a huge 300 pound deadman, wearing a size 957 Husky jacket, crashed through the office door. He was carrying a seventeen foot tall package that I had to sign for. It was wrapped in torn newspapers.

Han levererade ett 20 fot hogt paket som jag var tvungen att skriva pa.

"Put your name here." He muttered. Evidently he wasn't quite dead, or he was a stickler for delivery protocols.

Min sekreterare, B.B, blev radd. "Vem ar han?" Hon fragade.

B.B. was taken by surprise and held on to my arm. "Who is he?"

"Det ar inte julomten." Jag sa.

"Three will get you five, it's not Santa Claus." I answered.

Den dodes sista ord var 'Rosenknopp'.

"Rosebud." The package guy gasped with his last breath. It was now clear he was hoping to get more money by creating a speaking role for himself.

"Rosenknopp?" Fragade B.B. "Vill han ha lite te?"

"Rosebud? B.B. questioned. "Does he want some tea?"

"Det kommer inte att muntra upp honom, alskling." Jag sa.

"It won't cheer him up, baby. The only thing he needs now is six feet of dirt." I told her.

EDITOR'S NOTE

It seems that our original story text is now in Swedish instead of French. We are attempting to determine if either Joan of Arc had ever been to or associated with Scandinavia to explain this situation.

At this time we aren't even sure the original French story text has been accurate to this point. Meanwhile we are still attempting to contact 15th Century French Literature Support to resolve the original problem. Please bear with us and thank you for your patience.

> Menu
> *Sub-Titles: ON*
> *Commentaire: OFF*

Pitch Mirabelle (Sidekick/Editor)

physical ::::: Rome: Julius Caesar assassinated. Official 'Lone Gunman' conclusion questioned. :::::

Bonjour. (Hello)

"Who killed him?" B.B. asked timidly.

Comment ca va? (How are you)

"Normally in a case like this I'd say he did. You have to eat right and exercise regularly to carry this package up two flights of steps. And I don't think he did either." I surmised.

Ca va bien, merci. (I'm good thanks)

We got a pair of scissors and started cutting away at the wrapping on the package.

Oui, au une histoire de asteroides. (Yes, one story about asteroids).

"Look!" Spoke B.B. in an excited voice as she read a torn piece of wrapping! "There's a sale on shoes at Galeries Lafayette!"

Excusez moi. (Excuse me)

"Men's or women's?" Asked a voice that wasn't supposed to be in the room.

S'il vous plait, voir le kangourou. (Please see the kangaroo)

"Javert, ever heard of knocking?" I snapped.

Oui, pres Tolede. Porquoi?

"Yeah, it's in northwest Shropshire, England. Why?" Javert replied.

Comment dire ca en francais. (Why don't you learn French yourself, dumb ass)

While I tried to keep Javert occupied, B.B. hurriedly began to tape back what we tore off the package. I didn't want Javert to see anything he didn't have to.

Je dois y aller. (Yeah, go f*** yourself)

"That's a big package. What's in it, and who's the dead whale on the sofa?" Javert asked. He was more observant than I expected.

At Ease She Said

"He's not dead, he's pining for the fjords." Was my desperate comeback.

Meanwhile, B.B. kept taping the package furiously.

"OK, enough about the piner. What's she taping up?" Javert probed.

"A fruit cake. My mother sent it for my birthday. It mutated somewhere along the line during delivery. I think it's trying to take over the city." I used the old fruit cake ploy hoping Javert would bite.

"Mother, hey?" Said Javert suspiciously.

"That's right, Javert. Ever have one." I was quick to quip.

"Watch it, Sartre or I'll cite you and the girl for excessive use of adhesives, and I'll make it stick." Javert threatened.

"I know you have something brewing, Sartre, and it ain't Rosebud tea. Nobody has a dead 300 pound dead whale and a twenty foot package just hanging around their office unless their up to something. Sooner or later I'll put two and two together and figure out what it adds up to. Don't be surprised if it will come out to be five to nine at the State Penn for you." Javert croaked gleefully.

"And you wonder why you got a D minus in math, Inspector." I stated mathematically.

"Enjoy yourself while you can, peeper. Your time is coming and it's at nine AM tomorrow morning sharp at the D.A.'s office. He wants to see you. Be there or be square." Javert dropped his bomb.

What could the D.A. want with me now? I'd been dragged in front of him plenty of times before, but I always had the answers. This time it wasn't high school and I couldn't steal a copy of the biology exam ahead of time to get the questions.

That was tomorrow's worry. Tonight, in spite of interruptions, the D.A., and shoe sales, we had to see what was in this package. When we got it unwrapped we were looking at Michelangelo's David, a lot of newspaper on the floor, and David's 'You-Know-What'.

Maneuvers Begin

Not that I'm a prude, but I tried to shield B.B. with all the morality I could muster. "Don't look B.B. he's…"

"Tiny." She finished my sentence, but not the way I expected. "Everything else looks OK, but that thing is really skimpy."

"Alright, let's not talk about it. And stop staring. Hey, hey! Don't touch that!" I scolded. "Now wash your hands, d***it!"

Things needed to be cleaned up before tomorrow morning. That meant we had to do something with 300 pound Mr. Rosebud and David the twenty foot undraped model.

"B.B, you have a big apartment, can you take Rosebud to your place and hide him for a while." I begged.

"You want me to hide a dead guy in my apartment?" She asked in a shocked tone. "No way!"

"Come on. You've take plenty of guys home before. This won't be any different. Besides, Rosebud here isn't going to put any moves on you." I persuaded.

"He's going to stink!" She complained.

"Not if you spray him with Fleur de Male." I responded. "Besides, you owe me for using the lavatory in the office as a front for the rackets."

Frustrated by my logic, B.B. reluctantly agreed. "Oh, all right!" She said in a terse angry tone. "Help me get him down to my car."

"No can do, baby. I've got to clean up the newspapers, and figure out what I'm going to do with Mr. Au Naturale here."

"Fine!" B.B. snarled. "Just help me lift him on my shoulders."

A few minutes later, B.B. was hefting the 300 pound Mr. Rosebud out the door, down the stairs, and off to her apartment. I felt negligent for not reminding her to take the elevator. But I didn't have a lot of time to feel bad about it—a bunch of flowers or a box of candy would take care of that later.

When You Get

Right now the real problem was to figure out how to make a renaissance statue blend inconspicuously into my office. I kept moving it around from place to place to see where it looked best.

After a while I realized it just didn't match my office décor. I was going to need an entirely new Renaissance style office suite. Since that wasn't in my budget, I was going to have to steal some furniture, and there was only one place to do that—the Palace at Versailles.

While I was pondering a plan, I saw a scrap of newspaper used to wrap the statue. I read the article on it. Suddenly, like when a chicken whose head is on the chopping block finds out the dinner menu has been switched to pork—my luck changed for the better.

Without trying, a big piece of this caper's puzzle dropped into my lap. Sure, I was still going to have to break into Versailles, but now I wasn't playing this game behind a cassapanca.

If nothing went wrong, I could have this case wrapped up in a nice little package with a pretty pink bow. All I had to do was start making some phone calls, get the D.A. off my back, and find more masculine wrapping materials.

Those Whiskers

EDITOR'S NOTE

Star date: 4247.2:

We are still having problems with the original French story text. Please stand by.

The 15th Century French Literature Support team has dispatched a technician to our location, and he has identified the problem. The issue is due to a known bug in the initial year 1421 offering of the Commentary option for L'Affair Noir.

This issue was resolved in the 2.0 release version of L'Affair Noir in 1461 by decree of Charles VII, King of France. The 2.0 release was in celebration of the French victory at the Battle of Castillon, considered the final battle of the Hundred Yeas' War.

We are attempting to download the 2.0 fix now. Why we didn't spend the money for the 2.0 version of this material in the first place is currently under investigation. In addition, the publisher is weighing the possibility of giving a partial refund on this book due to inconvenience caused.

Once again, please bear with us, and thank you for your patience.

Pitch Mirabelle (Sidekick Editor)

DOWNLOAD
IN PROGRESS

Burma Shave

Download in Progress

I arrived at the D.A.'s office at 9:15 that morning and blamed Daylight Savings Time. In reality I planned to be late so that they'd sweat it out for a change. The D.A. was impatiently waiting for me, and I got an ear full.

"You're late! I told you to be at nine sharp." He said, resplendent in his cardinal red robes and van dyke beard.

"Spring forward, fall back, I always get confused. Sorry Richelieu." I faked an apology.

"You're not the only game in town, Sartre. I have other cases to work on. Important cases. Last night someone broke into the palace at Versailles and stole a bunch of furniture." He complained.

I didn't know where to look.

"OK, so you're a busy guy. So I'm a busy guy. So everybody's a busy guy who don't know where they put their last pair of clean underwear." I snapped at him.

"Alright, don't pop off. I just wanted to have a quiet friendly chat with you about your partner." Richelieu indicated as he sat back in his chair looking more relaxed.

"In my experience, there's no such thing as a quiet friendly chat with the D.A." I said

"Man, don't hit me with that existential crap this early in the morning. I just had Kierkegaard in here yesterday, and my headache hasn't gone away yet."

"He's good at generating angst in absurd situations." I noted.

"You don't respect me much, Sartre. That's OK, but I hope you respect the job I'm trying to do here." He leveled his eyes at me.

Lincoln assassinated by Illuminati because he learned secret word that rhymed with orange. :::::

Download in Progress

"As I told my girlfriend in the back seat of my car at the drive in—'I respect you like crazy'. I said.

Then I went on, "I respect how you can wear that color red this late into the season. I respect how you think you're going to bring the van dyke beard back into style. You make it work, but the look is too retro for everybody else's taste, and I respect how you can forgive sins, but still root for the Cubs when you're a Cardinal." I kept rattling things at him.

"Alright, Sartre, you got me there. I just need to know if you have anything on your partner's murder." Asked Richelieu.

"Murder? Your department claims he died of natural causes. Sounds like you boys are having doubts like a groom thinking marriage may be a big step after all?" I told him.

Before we could discuss the point, his phone rang and I was sitting there listening to his half of the conversation.

"What!? How could a seventeen foot statue just disappear? How could he get it past security? Come on, nobody wears a size 957 Husky. Alright, keep me informed." Richelieu concluded as he hung up.

"Another dippy case, Cardinal?" I asked.

"Never mind. You don't have to talk to me, but if I find you were hiding evidence…"

"Like a 17 foot statue?" I took a gamble to push him off the trail.

"Get out of here, Sartre." Richelieu ordered. And so I left, feeling things were getting tighter than the waist band on your pants after a six course Italian dinner.

with orange. ::::: Mouthwash kills 99.9% of germs- and then self. No motive for murder/suicide. :

Download in Progress

I decided to move the statue to my flat for the night. I had to bust a hole in the ceiling to give it some head room.

Needless to say, my upstairs neighbor wasn't too happy about David's head poking up through the floor of his bathroom. Some people are touchy when it comes to privacy.

I already made the calls I needed to, and the D.A. was off my back—for now. It was about nine o'clock that night when one by one my guests started arriving as expected.

First received was Otto Von Bismarck and his now wheelchair bound gunsel, Bonaparte. In addition to his feet, now both hands and his head were in casts.

Bismarck didn't fail to notice the 17 foot statue standing in my living room.

"I see you have located David. Excellent, sir, excellent. I will gladly relieve you of it at the agreed upon fee." He offered.

"About that." I said. "There may be some negotiating that we have to do."

"What do you mean, sir? Negotiating?" This is most irregular!" Bismarck protested.

"You failed to mention there are other interested parties in this matter, Bismarck. And I'd be remiss if I didn't give them an equal chance at going home with the brass ring." I indicated.

"An innocent oversight I assure you. By the by, what other parties do you refer to, sir? If you don't mind my inquiry?" Bismarck probed.

"I don't mind at all. In fact, they should be here any minute. Say, what happened to Junior' here?" I asked Bismarck.

No motive for murder/suicide. ::::: Antelope Freeway 1/8 mile. ::::: IUCN: Splendid Poison Frog now ext

Download in Progress

"A most unfortunate event, sir. A most obnoxious fellow by any measure, if I may add, tied poor Bonaparte to that wheelchair and thrust him down a flight of stairs. He bounced along very merrily, sir, until he splattered into the wall at the bottom."

Too bad for the gunsel. Sure, the Kid was a punk, but he got a bad break. This wasn't just a Trust Exercise that went wrong. Somebody went out of the way to get him. On the flip side, that's what you get when you put yourself in a wheelchair. Every two bit sadistic Tommy Udo type is going to throw you down a flight of stairs, into the path of a bus, or out a window. You didn't have to like it, but that's just where the chips fell.

"He's a creep, and I squash out creeps." Bonaparte could barely get the words out of his wired jaw. He was filled with an impotent rage.

"Relax, Kid. You can't even use a spoon in your condition. Let it go." I advised.

"Nobody gets away with that! I'm the Emperor. I'm going to fix this guy but good. Does anybody have an aspirin?" Raved Bonaparte.

"As harsh as it may seem, Mr. Sartre, I don't believe we are here to commiserate about poor Bonaparte's dreadfully fatal condition." Bismarck attempted to bring the conversation back to business.

"Hold your horses, Otto. Not everybody is here yet." I told him.

"Wait, what do you mean—fatal?" The Kid caught Bismarck's last word.

A few minutes later, a knock on the door announced my next guest(s). The last time I saw her Eleanor Roosevelt was making eyes at me. I couldn't wait to see who she was bringing with her tonight.

mile. ::::: IUCN: Splendid Poison Frog now extinct. Last one killed in gun battle with police ::::::

Download in Progress

"Hello!" Was her chipper greeting. "I'm Helen Keller, and I'm selling bibles with Jesus on the cover. If you observe, his eyes follow your every move, just as if you were dealing him three card monte."

"You're holding a 1942 copy of Time Magazine with Joseph Stalin on the cover." I corrected.

"Did I say bibles? I meant encyclopedias. No, vacuum cleaners. Hi! My name is Amelia Earhart. I just flew in. Boy are my arms tired." She rambled.

"Come on in, baby. Meet my other guests. I have a suspicion that you may already know them." I announced.

"Good evening, Miss Dietrichson." Bismarck greeted one of the many faces of Eve.

"You obviously have mistaken me for the wrong Barbara Stanwyck character, Chancellor Von Bismarck. My name is Martha Ivers. What's yours?" Her tone didn't hide her ruffled feathers.

"The real issue, my dear Miss Ivers, is not names. It is the conditions under which we meet. Perhaps Mr. Sartre would be so kind as to enlighten us." Bismarck was anxious to know.

police. ::::: AP: Jesus makes-blind see, deaf hear, mimes speak. Mimes to sue. ::::: Antelope Fre

DOWNLOAD
<u>COMPLETED</u>

:::: Antelope Freeway 1/16 mile. ::::: Tooth Fairy implicated in denture scam. ::::: Vikings sue C

EDITOR'S NOTE

The 2.0 Download has completed and it looks like we are back up and running. I apologize for the technical problems and any inconveniences. Once again thank you for your patience.

Menu
Sub-Titles: ON
Commentaire: OFF

Pitch Mirabelle (Sidekick Editor)

"In a moment, Otto. There's still one more guest I'm expecting." I informed Bismarck.

However, before a knock on the door came, my upstairs neighbor's annoyed voice shouted down from the hole in the ceiling.

*"Hey, Sartre! I got to pee, and I can't do it while this thing's head is looking at me. You want to at least turn him around for C*****'s sake?" He complained.*

"I'm busy now, Marlowe. Can't you hold it?" I tried to brush him off because that next knock on the door was coming soon. When it came, it announced someone I wasn't expecting.

It had just started to rain and two soaked figures stared at me from the doorway. One of them was dead.

"B.B.! What are you doing here?" I said, genuinely surprised.

"You mean why am I lugging this 300 pound corpse around in the pouring rain?" She said, and in a completely irritated voice.

"Well, now that you put it that way, yeah, I'm curious." I responded.

"I'll tell you when you let me in, or do you want me to leave this two ton sperm whale on your doorstep."

"Is that a whale she is carrying or is she just glad to see us?" Asked Bismarck.

"OK, come in, but don't drip on my carpet. I haven't finished paying the installments yet." I insisted.

Editor's Note

F***! The G** D*** download didn't work. I'm just going to kick the living s*** out of this f***ing thing and see how that works! Maybe that's what it likes. The son-of-a-b****!

> Menu
> *Sub-Titles: ON*
> *Commentaire: OFF*

Pitch Mirabelle (Sidekick/Editor)

KICKING THE S*** OUT OF THIS THING

B.B. struggled getting through the door way. She dropped the sperm whale on my new carpet.

"What did I just say about the installments, .B.B.?" I complained futilely.

"I can't keep him at my place anymore. He's freaking out my cats." B.B. began.

"They just sit in front of him and either claw at his coat or just stare. He's like a big treat of catnip to them. This guy has got to go. I promised the cats.

B.B. suddenly realized there were people in the room.

"Oh, hello. I didn't realize you had company." Apologized B.B. "Is this a bad time?"

In consideration to the rug, everybody helped to move the big fat whale to the sofa. However, they were naturally curious about the huge aquatic mammal.

"Forgive me for asking, sir, but can you introduce us to your enormously wet friend on the sofa?" Bismarck inquired.

"It looks like he's wearing a doorman's uniform." Observed the Femme Fatale.

"I observed the dead man's outfit myself, and came to my own conclusion.

"Not a doorman, but a sea captain." I noted.

"Captain Kangaroo?" B.B. chimed in.

bowl victory.::::: CDC confirms Covid virus is mutated variant of Marjorie Taylor Greene. :::::

KICKING THE S*** OUT OF THIS THING

"Nice guess, Mr. Green Jeans." I answered.

"No, it's the Captain and Tennille!" Miss Ivers contributed, and began a brief version of Love Will Keep Us Together to which everyone joined in.

Everyone, that is, but Junior. "What do you mean—fatal?" Bonaparte cried.

"Did you know how Tennille divorced him? It was cold." The Femme Fatale remarked.

"William Thomas Turner, Captain of the Lusitania." Bismarck dramatically presented his guess after the singing stopped. "Final answer."

"Wait that was on Jeopardy in Maritime Disasters for $500—'What ship was sunk by one of Bismarck's U-boats, and precipitated the American entry into World War 1?'. Responded the Femme Fatale who might have been Alex Trebek in a previous life.

"No, I'm sorry. The correct response would be—What was the Zimmerman telegram? How much did you wager, Martha?" I asked.

"All of it." Came her bitter response.

*Then the voice from upstairs rang down upon us again. "Are you going to turn this God D*** statue around. I have to pee so badly, but I can't do it. He's staring right at me!"*

"Throw a towel over his head, Marlowe." I said. Then came another knock on the door.

B.B. answered it this time to greet the odd little man that ran me out of toilet paper.

"Good evening, Too-Loose. Glad you could make it. The bathroom is free" I said.

Taylor Greene. ::::: AP: Louis Pasteur milks dairy sterilization into Nobel Prize. ::::: French

KICKING THE S*** OUT OF THIS THING <u>COMPLETED</u>

sterilization into Nobel Prize. ::::: French Revolution comes to a head. ::::: Vatican declar

J'ai fait les presentations et mes invites ne se sont pas crache dessus.

Too-Loose ran past the guests and made a bee line for the head. After his usual five or more flushes he emerged saturated with the aroma of Fleur de Male. I then made introductions which were brief but cordial. A least they weren't spitting on each other.

"S'il vous plait dites nous Pourquoi vous nous avez reunis ice." Dit Bismarck.

"Now that you have gathered us all here, Mr. Sartre, would you be so kind as to enlighten us to your purpose, sir?" Asked a wary Bismarck.

"Merci de demander. C'est simple vraiment." Je dit.

"Thank you for asking. It's simple really. You're all paying me a lot of money to find something for you. Alright, I found it." I started off.

Je n'ai pas de serviettes. Je dois faire pipi." Marlowe s'est exclame.

"I don't have any towels that I can just throw over this thing's head. I can't hold it any longer!" Marlowe griped in a desperate voice.

"Ne sois pas un bebe, Marlowe. Homme debout." Je rale.

"Don't be such a baby, Marlowe. Man up!" I griped back.

Pardonnez l'interruption." Je me suis excuse.

"Sorry for the interruption." I apologized to my guests.

Ensuit, l'auteur a eu le culot d'amener un autre personnage a frapper a ma porte.

Before the apology was compete, there was another knock on my door. This one was unexpected. I had a good mind to tell the author to stop the dribble and just let everyone in at once, but that wasn't the smart thing to do in the middle of a wrap up.

comes to a head. ::::: Vatican declares- Jesus is 'woke', Pope gains street cred. ::::: Beer mogul cl

C'etait son altesse, l'ex femme de mon ex-conjoint, Madame XVI.

This time at the door, was Her Highness, Mrs. XVI. Louis's ex-wife was now mourning in a flamboyant blue party dress with pearls. She was sobbing.

"Jean Paul, je ne peux pas vivre sans toi. Faites vous une fete?" Elle demande.

"Oh, Jean Paul, I can't cope with the grief any longer. Can I stay here with you, at least until we run away together?" She begged as she snuck a peek inside. "Oh, you're having a party? Hi, everyone!" Then she burst into the room like it was her debutante ball.

Trop d'interruptions alors je les ai menaces avec mon flingue.

It was getting tough to deliver the final big wrap up speech for this case. Lucky I was trained in public speaking. So I gave everybody lesson one, and shoved a loaded US Army Issue Colt .45 automatic in their faces.

"Je tirerai sur le prochain qui interrompt." J'ai promis.

"OK, listen up. I'll shoot the next one of you that butts in again!" I threatened.

L'ecrivain a fait apparaitre un autre personnage dans mon appartement.

They all buttoned up so I guess they got the point. But I didn't figure on one who the author had just planted in the apartment. Evidently, she also finally got tired of having people come in through the door.

"Est ce une arme ou es tu juste le joyeux de me voir?" Javert dit snide.

"Well, peeper, is that a gun in your hand, or are you just happy to see me?" Javert wisecracked.

cred. ::::: Beer mogul claims rival stole recipes and formulas. Trouble brewing. :::::

"C'est une arme." Je snide alseau.

"It's a gun, and I'm never happy to see you, Javert. Now get over there with the rest of them." I commanded, but first I frisked him and took his police issued .38 pistol.

Javert est un imbecile. Mais il n'a pas negliger la statue de 17 feet.

Whatever you could say about Javert, he didn't miss obvious stuff. One of the first things he noticed was the objet d'art in the room.

"Qui est le grand gui avec la waxe Europeenne?" Il inquire.

"OK, gumshoe, who's this big guy with the European Wax job standing with his head through the roof?" Quizzed the Inspector.

Javert n'est pas tres cultive.

Javert, wasn't too cultured, so I had to give him a crash course on Italian 17th century sculpture.

"C'est la statue de David par Michelangelo, tu retarde." Je lecture.

"For your education, Inspector, that's the statue of David made by Michelangelo." I told him.

"Porquoi est il createz sans pantalon?" Javert desapprouve.

"Yeah, why'd he make him with no pants?" Javert asked with a touch of disapproval.

"Il juste evacuee de la shouwere. Je desiree au explique mon solutione."

"David was just getting out of the shower when Michelangelo was carving. See that's a towel over David's shoulder." I said.

"Ca devait etre une douche froide." Javert specula-t-il.

"Must have been a cold shower, hey?" Javert speculated.

There once was a man from Nantucket

"Sure." Je dit.

"Sure." I said trying to disengage from the conversation.

Marlowe crie. "Je vais pee sur ta statue et ton nouveau carpete!"

Marlowe yelled down once again. "I'm going to pee on the statue and your carpet!"

"Bastarde!" Je crie et je au il shotte.

"You bastard!!" I yelled back, and fired a couple shots through the ceiling.

Nous au la statue shotte. Toutes les personnes releaser les gasps.

There were chunks of marble coming off what was considered one of the world's greatest works of sculpture. A horrified gasp rose from everyone's throats.

"Ne vous alarmez pas. La statue est un faux." J'informe.

"Nothing to be alarmed about." I tried to console. "The statue is a fake."

"Quel!?"

A universal "What?" Echoed through the room.

"J'explique, et je la shoote la premiere personne que interrompra." Je warner.

"That's right it's a fake. And here's how I know." I was about to reveal the big secret. "And remember, I still shoot the next one who interrupts.

Un podiatrist demente breaker la toe de la statue.

"I read this on a scrap of newspaper that the statue was wrapped in. A while back some kook, took a hammer and chipped off a toe from the statue of David. This joker said the statue told him to do it. Truth is he was a demented podiatrist.

Whose foot was stuck in a bucket

Mais la statue a un douzen les orteils.

Anyway, that should have left David with nine toes. But, if you look carefully at his feet, you'll see he has twelve. Now, does he carry around a few spares with him? Not in that outfit, I'm guessing.

"Est la statue un mutant radioactive? Non, la statue est un faux." Je dit.

Or maybe this sculpture represents the fate of man mutated by radioactive contamination. You have to swallow hard to get an idea like that down your throat. The simplest answer is that it's a fake." I continued.

Je acute Marlowe et me il shotte a encore.

I suddenly heard Marlowe moving upstairs and let go a few rounds to quiet him.

"Ca m'a smack comme un sac de nickels smack un aged homme en au visage.

"Anyway, why go out of the way to steal a fake flawed masterpiece, and set off a major search to find it? Then it hit me, like a bag of nickels in the face of an old man who's driving thirty miles an hour in a sixty MPH zone on a busy highway. I had no idea."

He couldn't get free

Editor's Note

Yes, the kicking seemed to work.

Sorry I was called away. I'm elated that the problem is now fixed.

Hopefully, we can look forward to the uninterrupted conclusion to our story.

Once again, thank you for your patience.

Menu
Sub-Titles: **ON**
Commentaire: **OFF**

Pitch Mirabelle (Sidekick/Editor)

When he needed to be

"Vengeance pour le hole en mon floore." Marlowe menace. Il est encore en vie.

"I'm going to get you for putting a hole in my bathroom floor, a**hole." Marlowe threatened. I was glad he was still alive.

"Oui, est un hole en mon ciel, Marlowe. Nous sommes le 'even steven'."

"Yeah, well I had to put a hole in my ceiling to do it, jerk. So we're even." I replied.

Il etait calme pour le reste de la nite.

Maybe he had to think that one over, or maybe he just lost too much blood and passed out. Anyway, I figured we reached some kind of impasse.

"Qu'en est-il le Capitan Crunch?" B.B. inquire.

"What about, the dead whale here." Asked B.B. with some interest.

"Ne t'attache pas. Laisse le partir." Je advice.

"I know you've grown attached to him, baby, but sometimes you just have to let go. And this is one of those times." I tried to soothe her.

"Porquoi le petit truc?" Demande la Femme Fatale.

"And what is the vast under representation on the statue all about? And you all know what I'm talking about." Asked the Femme Fatale.

"Mary Ann est plus sexy que Ginger." B.B. dit.

"Don't count on it Madame Curie. They're men and all they know for sure is that Mary Ann is sexier than Ginger." B.B. adds.

Les hommes sont d'accord.

All the men nod in agreement.

So he just gave up and said "F*** it"!

"Qu'est le tout signifie?" Javert demander.

"What does any of this mean, gumshoe?" Javert launched a pointed question at me.

"Zip." Je dit. "Nous muste discouver que murdeur Louis XVI."

"It means we find out who murdered my partner." I said.

"Pensez vous que l'un murdeur Louis XVI?" La Femme Fatale gaspe.

"Do you believe one of us killed your partner?" the Femme Fatale gasped.

"Pour toi il y a une douzaine de suspects." Je explique.

"In your case alone I have a dozen suspects. And the rest of you aren't out of the woods so keep your putters in the bag. This is how I figure it." I said that with a more than a little irritation.

"Vous engage Louis en premier. Pourquoi, parce il est le roi de France?"

"Before you came to me, you all hired Louis to find your statue. Why him? Maybe because he looked more respectable because he wore silk shirts, bouffant breeches, white silk stockings, and a full bottom past the shoulders powdered wig.

Mais, il vous double crosse et vous il l'arreter.

That was on the one hand. On the other hand, he got greedy, and went into business for himself. That was taboo. So any one of you treasure hunters had a motive for murder.

Louis a shotte en la tete. Mais le bullettes son minuscule fromme petite pistolet.

My partner was shot, stabbed, poisoned, and run over by a bus. They called it a natural death for a detective. OK, fair enough. He was shot in the head three times. That should have been enough, except the bullets were fired from a tiny gun, one small enough to carry in a woman's purse. A purse like yours Marie Curie.

Burma Shave

Oups, Annie Oakley a des armes.

"But we don't carry a gun. Sure, Lizzy Borden is a serial killer but she uses an axe. OK, correction, Annie Oakley has guns. Sorry, oversight. My bad.

Tu n'es pas un psycho. Tu es un liar pathologique. Quel est ton nom, baby?"

"True, baby, but Annie's guns are big ones." I said. "And by the way, you're not a multiple personality nut case. That story has more holes than it takes to fill the Albert Hall. You're just a pathological liar. Now who are you, baby, and this time I'd like it straight?"

"Je suis ma soeur."

With tears in her eyes she whimpered out. "I'm my sister."

Elle slappe Bonaparte encore et dit. "Ma fille."

Then she slapped Bonaparte, and cried out. "My daughter." She dealt another slap to the defenseless gunsel. She didn't stop there.

Continuer. Slappe—"Ma soeur." Slappe "Ma Fille." Etc.

"My sister." Slap. "My daughter." Slap.

Je l'ai arrete.

"Break it up and go to your corners." I said getting between them. "Alright Madame Curie, I guess straight isn't your game."

Poore Bonaparte. Ne pouvait pas faire un pause chez les garcons Pep Boys.

Bonaparte was just a cheap punk and unlucky gunsel. He couldn't get a brake if he walked into Pep Boys with a million dollars. But the kid took Marie Curie's beating OK. He may not have liked it, but he took it all the same. I respected him for that, at least.

The world's first 'Man from Nantucket' limerick, by William Shakespeare (Bard of Avon). :::

"Bismarck utiliserait un casque de piclehaube." Je dit.

"Then there were the stabs in the back. You, Bismarck or you, Lautrec could have done those. Except the stab wounds were from a knife. Bismarck would have done it with a Pickelhaube helmet. The only sharp instrument he was familiar with." I said

Bismarck ne peut pas utiliser un couteau a steak."

"This is true. I don't even know how to use a steak knife." Bismarck confessed.

"L'odeur de Lautrec avertirait qu'il etait dans les parages." Je dit.

"And Lautrec, with your Fleur de Male aroma, you couldn't sneak up on anyone from behind." I continued.

"OK, j'ai des intestins irritables." Lautrec dit.

"That's right, I have irritable bowels. Speaking of which I must be excused." Lautrec said as he scampered off to the bathroom.

"Le poison au mercure provident du thon." Je dit.

"But then there was a note on the bottom of the autopsy report that everyone ignored. It talked about mercury poisoning. A common result of eating tuna." I said. "The tuna that everyone overlooked—until now."

"Et el bus?" Javert demande.

"Wait, what about the bus?" Javert asked.

"Je n'ai aucune idee." Je dit.

"Again, no idea. I'll leave that one up to the D.A. The clincher is the tuna." I said.

"Et le thon?" Javert demande.

"What about the tuna?" Javert asked.

:: 65 million BC dinosaurs go extinct. Columbus blamed. His day removed from calendar. ::

"Le tour du demi-thon de la Resistance francaise." Je dit.

"It was the half tuna sandwich. A way the French Resistance used to ID each other in the war against the Germans." I relayed.

"De quelle guerre?" Demande Bismarck.

"Which one?" Bismarck asked.

Comment ca marche est de mordre un sandwich au thon et de le couper en deux.

"Here's how it works. You get a tuna sandwich and one guy takes a bite. Then you cut it in half so that each half has part of the bite mark. Each guy gets a half. When they meet up, they put the halves together and if the bite marks match, you know you have the right guy. The only problem was if you got hungry." I explained.

"Pas etonnant que nous ayons toujours gagne les guerres." Dit Bismarck.

"No wonder we always won." Bismarck commented.

"Louis la moitie du sandwich n'avait pas de bouchees." Je dit.

"But the half of the tuna sandwich that Louis had didn't have bite marks. He didn't like tuna so I know he didn't eat it." I noted.

"Ou sont les deux moities du sandwich?" demande Marie Curie.

"So where did the halves go?" Marie Curie asked.

"Le gros mort en a un." Je dit.

"I'm sure our dead whale has one of them." I said as I preceded to check his jacket. I was rewarded by finding a moldy half of a tuna sandwich with a bite mark. I presented the exhibit to the room.

calendar. ::::: Wright brothers first non-stop flight - 90 feet. Restrooms added to plane. ::

"Oh, ca explique les chats." B.B. dit.

"Oh, that explains the cats." B.B. said.

"Ou est l'autre moitie? Lautrec demande.

"Where's the other half?" Lautrec asked just after he returned from and just before he returned to the bathroom.

"Ou en effect, Mme XVI!" Je dit.

"We find that, children, and we find our murderer. Don't we, Mrs. XVI?" I claimed

"Que veux tu dire?

"What do you mean, Jean Paul?" Asked Marie Antoinette.

"Je veux dire que tu as tue Louis." J'ai accuse.

"I means you killed Louis and here's the half of the tuna sandwich to prove it." I said as I pulled the sandwich from her purse. "I could smell it on you every time you came up close to me."

"Louis vous a fait confiance. Une grosse erreur." Je dit.

"First of all, Louis wouldn't be stupid enough to go down a dark alley alone. But he was just stupid enough to go down one with somebody he trusted and that would either be you or the blonde sales clerk at the shoe store. Oops, sorry. I didn't mean to spill that while you were still in morning. However, she didn't have half a tuna sandwich on her. So it was you he trusted down that alley. It was you he trusted with the story of how he was going to score big with the statue."

"Pas vrai. J'ai adore Louis." Dit Marie Antoinette

"No, it's not true. I loved Louis." The queen said.

::::: This is a test of the Civil Air Defense Warning System. If this were a real emergency, you'd be dead.

"Bien sur que tu l'as fait." Je dit.

"Sure you did, baby. I could tell that when you tried to jump my bones. But the truth was you were tired of Louis. Tired of meat loaf, and tired of making bad loans, and bad bets on races against squirrels running in the park." I said.

"Rien de tout cela n'est vrai." Dit Mrs. XVI.

"None of this is true, Jean Paul. You know it's not." Marie Antoinette said.

"Pensiez vous que votre mari etait Raspoutine? Je demande.

"What's true, baby, is that in that dark alley, you saw a way to get rich, get rid of Louis, and get away with murder. You shot, stabbed, and poisoned him. You're pretty thorough. Did you think he was Rasputin?" I accused her.

"No! Ce n'est pas valide. J'aime tu." La Reine a reclame.

"Oh, Jean Paul, none of that is true. Don't do this. I love you." Mrs. XVI pleaded.

"Desole, bebe. Je vous envoie tous les deux en prison." Je dit

"Keep saying that, baby. I like the gleam in your eyes when you do. But you're going over, and I'm sending you there first class, postage paid.

"No, no! J'ai mon tears, et le ma nose est runnez le boogers." Elle pleade.

"No, Jean Paul, No, No. Not me. You'll never do that to me." Her Highness said through a rain of tears.

"Je suis, poupee. Je le fais parce que je deteste les mimes." Je dit.

"I can't tell if those tears are real or not. They look good either way. But I am doing it, baby. I'll hate it worse than watching a mime act. You know those guys can talk, but all they do is pretend they can't get out of boxes or walk against the wind. I just want to punch their teeth out.

"Pourquoi, mon ami, Pourquoi?" Marie Antoinette demande.

But why? Why, Jean Paul? Why? Her majesty pleaded.

:: Both Henri's and Louise's parents divorced. They propose wife swap. ::::: RANON: Mitch M

"Quand le partenaire d'un homme est tue, cela signifie que le gars est mort."

I'll try to explain this once and only once. When a man's partner is murdered it usually means the guy is dead. Maybe for a good reason, maybe not. It doesn't matter if you didn't like the way he put whipped cream on his French fries, or talked with his mouth full slobbering crud all over the office. He's still dead and you hope he stays that way to keep your heating bill low. But because he was your partner, past tense, you have to do something about it. I hope you understand."

"Je n'ai acune idee de ce que tu as dit." Mme XVI dit.

"Sorry, not even close." Mrs. XVI said.

"Je t'arrete, Mme XVI." Dit Javert.

"That's it, Mrs. XVI. I'm taking you and this size 957 jacket in. With some tailoring, I think it would look good on me." said Javert.

"Tiens la tete haute, bebe." Je dit.

"This is it, baby." I told the Queen. "When they take you away, hold your head up high, or someone else will do it for you."

Elle a pleure.

She whimpered a little bit, but took it as well as anyone that was going to spend the rest of her life in solitary confinement with a toilet that didn't have a seat. She walked out the door and waded into the swarming crowd of press people with their cameras flashing and mics pointing. I remember the last thing she said.

swap. ::::: RANON: Mitch McConnell controlled by miniature alien beings in his jowls. :::::

"Prends ma photo, Mssr. DeMille."

"I'm ready for my close up now, Mr. DeMille."

La dame pourrait faire une sortie.

The dame knew how to make an exit.

"Nos reves sont aneantis monsieur. Et maintenant." Dit Bismarck.

"Well, sir. What do we all do now that you've dashed all of our dreams? "Bismarck asked the million dollar question.

"Suggestiones? Demande Lautrec.

Lautrec, seconded the thought with his nasally voice. "Yes, do you have any suggestions? Please inform us, Mr. Sartre."

"Serons nous des personnages mineurs dans d'autres histoires?" Dit la Femme Fatale.

"Yes, please do, Mr. Sartre, or are we all doomed to become secondary characters in someone else's story?" The Femme Fatale added her inquiry.

"C'est la vie." Je dit.

"You know what they say, 'Easy come, easy go'." I remarked.

"Je me demande qui a dit un statement si ridicule." Ponder Lautrec.

"I wonder who would say such a ridiculous thing." Wondered Lautrec aloud.

"Je pense que c'etait Voltaire." Je informe.

"I think it was Voltaire." I responded.

Epilogue

B.B. m'a dit, "Oubliez ca patron. C'est le quartier chinois."

They all slowly filed out of my apartment, heads down and dreams broken. Sometimes you learn the hard way—like when a sadistic nun with bad teeth who drinks too much sacramental wine hits you across the knuckles with a metal ruler. You take life as it comes, and you don't look back. Maybe I looked back this one time. That's when B.B. put her arms around me and said: "Forget it, Boss. It's Chinatown."

FIN

Medical Hospital

Introduction

The Empress Dowager Cixi was a Chinese noblewoman, and regent who controlled the government in China from 1861 to 1908 under the Qing dynasty. China, during her reign, experienced several capital events including, the Tongzhi Restoration, the Boxer Rebellion, and the creation of the National Mah-Jongg League.

While Cixi refused to support social changes based upon Western ideals, she did promote Western technological, military, and soap opera reforms. Her reign saw a widespread growth in soap operas at court and they quickly became the dowager empress's favorite entertainment. During this period Cixi rigorously also promoted the development of original Chinese soap operas among the literary artists in her realm.

So enamored of the soap opera was she that it has been claimed the Boxer Rebellion failed when Cixi withdrew support for their movement in order to watch her shows. I now present one of the recently discovered Soap Operas of Cixi.

PD-US-expired

T. E. Winchester, Esq.

EXT—FRONT OF HOSPITAL—DAY
Establishing shot of hospital. Sign on in front reads 'THE HOSPITAL'.

ANNOUNCER   In the never ending battle between sickness and
health, life and death, and outlandish medical bills
and insurance claims, health care workers fight the
good fight against disease at an institution they call
Medical Hospital.

Medical Hospital is brought to you by Constabate
the only laxative in a soup that comes with patented
Poop-Flo 21—the castor oil of physics.

And now, Medical Hospital.

Opening with an **ORGAN FLORISH THEME.**

INT—HOSPITAL—DAY
Busy halls of hospital. Doctors, nurses, and staff walk purposefully to their
tasks. Pathetic looking patients in wheel chairs, gurneys, or benches are
ignored or tripped over. Each patient has attached some medical device on
a pole (saline solution, monitor, and one has a circulating radar antenna
which sends blips to its monitor).

ENTER DR. MEL PRACTISS and **DR. PAM DEMIC**, Hospital
Administrator. They walk down the hall in conversation.

DR. DEMIC   We've had two more cases of missing brains this
morning, Dr. Practiss. That makes six patients this
week with Vanishing Cerebral Syndrome, (VCS).

DR. PRACTISS   It's an epidemic.

DR. DEMIC   Exactly, as an administrator of this facility, I must
take action. Therefore I'm opening a Missing Brain
ward and I'd like you to head it.

PA SYSTEM	Will the person driving a blue Ranger, license HITNRN please move your car. There is a porter pinned beneath it. Thank you.
DR. PRACTISS	This VCS reminds me of the Tonsil Displacia scare in the 1950s.
DR. DEMIC	Where they thought the tonsils were migrating to a different part of the body? The physician who diagnosed that didn't realize his subjects all had tonsillectomies. No this is real, Doctor. People are missing their brains. They may not think much about it now, but sooner or later it will cross their minds. Please step into my office where we can discuss the plans for the new ward.

Dr. Demic and Practiss go into the office and close the door behind them. They are unaware that it does not close all the way. However, as soon as they think they have privacy the two doctors **FALL** into each other's arms and **KISS** passionately.

DR. DEMIC	Oh, Mel, I love you so much. I wish we could go away and be together forever.
DR. PRACTISS	I can't live without you, Pam, but we have the Brain ward to consider. That and your husband who won't grant you a divorce.
DR. DEMIC	Him! I can't believe I once cared for him, but now that's how much I hate him. I wish he were dead.
DR. PRACTISS	So we could be free.
DR. DEMIC	Well, yes, but mostly because he would be dead.

DR. PRACTISS	If only there were a way. A magic way that would make wishes come true.
DR. DEMIC	There are no fairy godmothers, Mel. It's up to us.
DR. PRACTISS	We're doctors, Pam. We must remember our oath.
DR. DEMIC	The Pledge of Allegiance?
DR. PRACTISS	No, an older oath than that—'For Duty and Humanity'.
DR. DEMIC	Oh yeah, that one. Well, you have to make your rounds and I have a meeting with the board. We can't afford to arouse suspicions about us, darling.
DR. PRACTISS	You're right as always, Pam. We need to go. For now.

Dr. Practiss and Demic have a final embrace and kiss before they exit the office. Dr. Practiss barely notices the door is cracked open a smidge but pays it no mind. The two merge into the hallway traffic going their separate ways. Meanwhile, back at the door, a figure, whose head is supposedly buried in some paperwork, turns with a sinister look and his one eye follows the trail of Dr. Practiss and Demic. His other eye is covered with a patch. This is **LEBORGNE PERFIDIOUS.**

PLAY single dramatic **ORGAN NOTE.**

CUT TO
INT—AMNESIA WARD—DAY

Handsome heartthrob **DR. TRENCH FEVER** and **ACUTE NURSE LOUISE LUPUS** examine amnesia patient **FUGUE SIBLING**, While Dr. Fever's fiancé and Fugue's sister **SOEUR SIBLING** looks on.

NURSE LUPUS	Is it what we suspected, doctor?
DR. FEVER	I'm afraid so.
FUGUE	Give it to me straight, Doc. What do I have?
DR. FEVER	You've got the first diagnosed case of Gyroglobal extro-molly amnesia. The most severe example I've ever seen.

PLAY single dramatic **ORGAN NOTE.**

FUGUE	Give it to me straight, Doc. What do I have?
SOEUR	Trench, what does this mean?
DR. FEVER	It is an amnesia so severe that it makes other people forget.
SOEUR	Forget what?
NURSE LUPUS	Like your own name.
SOEUR	Which is? Come on, give me a hint.
FUGUE	Give it to me straight, Doc. What do I have?
DR. FEVER	What was the question?
NURSE LUPUS	We better move a few feet away from him.
DR. FEVER	Good idea.

Dr. Fever, Nurse Lupus, and Soeur step away from Fugue to the other side of the room. Where they converse in private.

DR. FEVER	There's something else, Soeur.
SOEUR	Please, don't keep anything from me.
DR. FEVER	OK, well there was this time in high school after gym in the showers and you know how young men like to experiment sexually sometimes…
SOEUR	No, No, No. I mean about my brother.
DR. FEVER	Oh, right.
NURSE LUPUS	Well, I'd like to hear about the shower thing later. And don't keep anything from me either.
DR. FEVER	According to the brain scans, your brother also seems to be suffering from Dissociative Identity Disorder, DID.
SOEUR	Did what?
DR. FEVER	No, D-I-D. More commonly known as Multiple Personalities.
SOEUR	Is one of those personalities, Walter Ego?
DR. FEVER	According to the brain scan, yes.

PLAY single dramatic **ORGAN NOTE.**

FADE OUT

| ANNOUNCER | Medical Hospital will be right back, but first an important message from one of our sponsors. |
| | Do you need a full strength, full time adhesive for your home or home projects? If so you need Stick-2-It glue. Strong, dependable, and durable. Stick-2-It lasts forever so don't get it on the kids. It is the only glue that is made of natural fluids from the reproductive organs of grown horses. The same fluids used in advanced medical products like Poop-Flo 21. So if you need an adherent, stick to the best—Stick-2-It. And now back to Medical Hospital. |

PLAY an **ORGAN FLORISH THEME**.

INT—HOSPITAL—DAY

ENTER DR. COQUETTE SIREN the raven haired, dark eyed beauty and chief of the medical staff. She is walking down the hospital hallway reading a patient chart when an arm reaches out and pulls her into a supply closet.

| LEBORGNE | Dr. SIREN, it's me, Leborgne Perfidious. |

| DR. SIREN | I can see that, you idiot. I have two eyes. And I told you to never come here to meet. |

Dr. Siren then slaps Leborgne which causes his eye patch to shift out of place. He clumsily straightens it out.

| LEBORGNE | Sorry, but my father has been brought in and I found out something you need to know. |

Dr. Siren then knees Leborgne in the groin. Leborgne doubles over and grimaces in great pain.

| DR. SIREN | I'll decide what I need to know. You got that, worm. Now what is it you found out? |

LEBORGNE	My father was brought in with his business partner, who claims my father embezzled hundreds of millions from their company. If he sues, and he will, and if my father is guilty, and he is, the old man is broke.
DR. SIREN	Broke? Let me think, what can be done? If your father dies before any law suit. You are still in the will for half. The other half goes to that bitch, his wife, Dr. Pam Demic. We'll not be greedy. We'll take our half, that's nearly three-hundred million. Leave the country to someplace with tropical drinks that have little umbrellas in them and no extradition agreements. Still a sweet deal.

Dr. Siren then softly runs her fingers through Leborgne's hair, but at her next thought she slams his head a few times against the door.

DR. SIREN	But how to kill him? How? How? How?
PA SYSTEM	Calling Doctor Howard, Doctor Fine, Doctor Howard. Calling Doctor Howard, Doctor Fine, Doctor Howard.

Leborgne staggers and tries to shake his head clear.

LEBORGNE	Maybe this will answer your question.
DR. SIREN	What!?

Dr. Siren's response snaps at Leborgne and he now instinctively covers up in a defensive posture. In a moment, when he realizes he is not going to be pummeled, he unfolds. That is just when he gets slapped.

DR. SIREN	What!? Come on, out with it.

LEBORGNE   It turns out our Dr. Demic and Dr. Practiss are
                       having an affair. My father won't give her a divorce.
                       And in her office the two were considering an option
                       for murder. If we find a way to pin this on them,
                       she can't inherit and I will get all my father's money.

DR. SIREN   Very interesting. That such a thought could percolate
                       up from that tangled mass of cabbage that you call
                       a brain. Well, my love let me consider this and I'm
                       sure we can put together a plan.
                       By the way, how is your brain stealing caper coming
                       along?

LEBORGNE   Hit a snag. My partner has developed amnesia and
                       doesn't remember where he hid the brains.

DR. SIREN   Who is your partner?

LEBORGNE   Walter Ego.

PLAY single dramatic ORGAN NOTE.

CUT TO
INT—EMERGENCY ROOM

TRUHART H. PERFIDMIOUS, husband of Dr. Demic and father of
Leborgne, and another, as of yet, unnamed man are wheeled in. Dr. Practiss
is there to meet them. He reads their charts with a serious face.

PERFIDIOUS   What is it, Dr. Practiss? Yes, I know who you are.

DR. PRACTISS   According to this chart, Mr. Perfidious, you have
                       DeFraude's Syndrome, and he wants it back.

Suddenly the other old man, VIC DEFRAUDE, shouts out.

DeFRAUDE	You're God D*** right I want it back! This b****** has stolen everything from me and now he's taking my disease! You should die you son-of-a-b****, but not from my disease! Over my dead body!

Dr. Siren, Dr. Demic, and Leborgne join the group in the Emergency room. A beat later, Nurse Lupus also arrives.

DR. SIREN	What so we have here, Dr. Practiss?
DR. PRACTISS	A case of DeFraude's Syndrome, but we're trying to figure out which of these two men it belongs to.
DR. SIREN	Who has it now?
DR. PRACTISS	Mr. Perfidious.
DR. SIREN	Finders' keepers. Aide, wheel this other gentleman out.

An aide comes over and roughly wheels Mr. DeFraude out of the Emergency room, banging his head against the swinging doors. With a final push, DeFraude is shoved out into the parking lot. We hear a **SCREAM** and **CAR CRASH**, and the sound of a **ROLLING HUB CAP**.

DR. SIREN	Dr. Practiss, Mr. Perfidious requires immediate brain surgery. I'm assigning you to as primary surgeon.
DR. PRACTISS	Dr. Siren, I'm a urologist. I've never operated on anything above the waist. I'm not qualified.
PERFIDIOUS	I think he makes a good point, Dr. Siren, if you think about it.

DR. SIREN	Dr. Practiss, this man needs an immediate operation, any delay and the patient will die. It's time to put away your insecurities and think about saving this man's life.
DR. DEMIC	Dr. Practiss, I have every confidence in you operating on my husband and I think the outcome will be very satisfactory, if you know what I mean.
DR. PRACTISS	Doctors, I am a urologist. I specialize in 'you know whats'. Not brains. Look the closest I ever get to the brain is when I shove my finger up the poop shute for a prostate exam. Just because the 'you know whats' sometimes override the brain doesn't mean I can just pop in to somebody's skull and dig around.
PERFIDIOUS	That really makes a lot of sense to me. Don't you have a couple brain surgeons hanging around that can do the job?
DR. SIREN	They're on break.
LEBORGNE	Don't be such a baby, dad. It will all be over before you know it.

Dr. Siren stomps on Leborgne's foot before he can say anything more. Leborgne hops away in agony.

DR. SIREN	Dr. Practiss, no further delays. Report to the operating room immediately. For duty and humanity!

Everyone echoes that chant 'FOR DUTY AND HUMANITY!'

NURSE LUPUS	Dr. Practiss, a word aside, please.

Dr. Practiss and Nurse Lupus step away from the group to have a private word.

NURSE LUPUS Dr. Practiss, the amnesia patient Fugue Sibling. Under his bed I found these.

Nurse Lupus then holds out her hands which contain two fresh brains.

PLAY single dramatic **ORGAN NOTE**.

LATER
INT—OPERATING ROOM—DAY

We see the PA loud speakers on the hallway ceiling as announcements are made.

PA SYSTEM 1 Attention. The white hospital zone is for loading and unloading only.

PA SYSTEM 2 Don't start with the 'white zone' s*** again!

PA SYSTEM 1 Well I still have a porter pinned under a parked car in the white zone, a**hole.

Dr. Prentis accompanied by Nurse Lupus and Dr. Demic wheel Mr. Perfidious into the operating room. Just before anesthesia is applied Perfidious issues a warning.

PERFIDIOUS Dr. Practiss, just because you are not qualified to operate on my brain and a simple slip could be fatal to me but no one will blame you for murder, thus negating the need for a divorce so that you can marry my wife who will inherit hundreds of millions of dollars that you can both use to live lives of luxury— don't get any ideas.

DR. DEMIC Don't think of such things at a time like this.

NURSE LUPUS   It's not the operation you have to worry about, it's the hospital food that will probably get you.

DR. PRACTISS   Nurse Lupus, bring out the surgical instruments.

NURSE LUPUS   There are no instruments, doctor. Dr. Siren sent them all out to be sterilized.

DR. PRACTISS   What!? All of them? Where are they now?

NURSE LUPUS   Cleveland.

DR. DEMIC   Looks like we're going to have to do this with our bare hands.

PERFIDIOUS   This is not how I planned my day when I woke up this morning.

DR. PRACTISS   OK, find me something big and heavy to open the cranium.

PERFIDIOUS   Is that really the best way to go?

DR. DEMIC   Yes, the impact will not only open the cranium, but also serve as an anesthetic to put you under.

PERFIDIOUS   Don't I have to sign a consent form?

DR. DEMIC   No, you have a patient validated parking ticket.

PLAY single dramatic **ORGAN NOTE.**

FADE OUT

ANNOUNCER	Medical Hospital will be back in a moment, right after this important message.
	SUDS—is the first product that is both a dish detergent and a light beer. Experience dishwashing like it was meant to be—more fun and less filling. SUDS—clean on the outside, wet on the inside.
	And now back to Medical Hospital.

PLAY AN ORGAN FLOURISH THEME.

INT—HOSPITAL—DAY

Dr. Fever and Soeur walk down the hall in conversation.

DR. FEVER	Soeur, I feel there's something you want to tell me about Walter Ego.
SOEUR	Yes, but it's so very difficult to talk about.
DR. FEVER	You can tell me anything, Soeur. You know I love you.
SOEUR	I'm pregnant with Walter Ego's child.

PLAY single dramatic **ORGAN NOTE.**

DR. FEVER	J**** C*****! Don't tell me that! He's your brother! That's incest for C*****'s sake. How? Why?
SOEUR	His amnesia made us both forget who we were and when his other personality, which would be Walter Ego…
DR. FEVER	I know who it is!

SOEUR   Well, we just forgot everything and got lost in a pas-
                 sionate moment. You said yourself this could happen
                 with that polly-wolly amnesia disease thing.

DR. FEVER   I was talking about forgetting your name or address,
                 not something like incest and with our wedding just
                 a month away! Couldn't you keep it in your pants
                 for thirty more days?

SOEUR   I'm so sorry, darling. I still love only you and I've
                 already picked the flower arrangement for the recep-
                 tion. I got the yellow beaded lily rose bouquet. It's a
                 very soft color that goes with the bridesmaids' gowns
                 and they're not very expensive. I know you wanted
                 to keep costs down.

DR. FEVER   Your brother is even in the wedding party. Well,
                 he's not giving any toast. I'm putting my foot down
                 on that!

PLAY single dramatic ORGAN NOTE.

LATER
INT—HOSPITAL—DAY
Dr. Practiss, Dr. Demic, and Nurse Lupus emerge from the operating room.
Their white operating gowns, faces, and hands are covered in dripping blood.
A gurney is wheeled out of the OR, upon it is a blood soaked sheet that
covers a body, presumably that of Truhart H. Perfidious. It is wheeled past
the distraught Dr. Fever and Soeur as they join the others.

DR. DEMIC   Well we almost saved him. Boy, I will say this much,
                  he was a real fighter. He hung on longer than I
                  expected.

NURSE LUPUS   I still say we should have used one of those spare
                  brains to replace his.

DR. PRACTISS	That would have been unethical.
DR. FEVER	What's going on and who was on that gurney?
DR. DEMIC	My husband. Er, ex-husband.
DR. PRACTISS	We almost saved him.
NURSE LUPUS	He hung on longer that we expected.
DR. DEMIC	A real fighter.
DR. FEVER	But Mel, you're a urologist. You specialize in 'you know whats' not brains. You forgot your oath not to do harm. Never to do harm.

Fugue Sibling/Walter Ego arrives in his wheel chair and adds his presence to the group. He is immediately attacked by Dr. Fever. It takes several people to tear the two apart.

DR. FEVER	You dirty Son-of-a-B**** of a B******! Doing my fiancé! Your own sister! You motherf***ing piece of s***! There were only thirty days left before the wedding! You're not giving any f***ing toast, you f***!
FUGUE	Sister? I don't know what you're talking about, you maniac. My name is Walter Ego.
STRANGER	Walter Ego, Junior.

PLAY single dramatic **ORGAN NOTE**.

Everyone snaps their attention to the **STRANGER** that has just silently walked in among them. They are shocked by what they see. The Stranger is the spitting image of Truhart H. Perfidious. Everyone gasps in shock.

Leborgne faints straight away and hits the deck hard.

STRANGER	Allow me to introduce myself. I am Walter Ego, Senior although I was born Truhart H. Perfidious. The Perfidious that you just wheeled out of here was my evil twin, Mordecai H. Perfidious. Let me explain. In my youth I was married to Amanda Reckonwith, your mother Dr. Siren. While I had temporarily become the personality of Walter Ego, senior, we had a son. The boy ran away to the circus when he was four and was raised in a tiny car by thirty-six clowns.
DR. SIREN	Married to my mother? Having a child. Outlandish.
STRANGER	We would have told you except Amanda lost your address at school. Part of the collateral memory issues caused by my Gyroglobal extro-molly amnesia, I suppose.
SOEUR	What about me? Am I your daughter?
STRANGER	No, but I better let Dr. Siren explain whose child you are.
DR. SIREN	How should I know? (a beat) Unless. Unless. When I was seven my parents had another daughter. I became jealous of the baby getting all the attention so I put her in a laundry basket set it out on the porch where a mime from a traveling circus made off with it. The same mime later left the circus.
SOEUR	Why?
DR. SIREN	He didn't say.

PLAY single dramatic **ORGAN NOTE**.

SOEUR	This would explain my obsession with laundry baskets and detergents
DR. FEVER	Wow, what a break.
STRANGER	That brings us to you Pam. It was me that you married ten years ago but my brother, Mordecai, consumed by his overwhelming lust and desire for you, had me kidnapped and marooned deep in the jungles of New Guinea so that he alone could possess you.
DR. DEMIC	How did you survive in the jungles for ten years?
STRANGER	By eating cannibals and perhaps I told them my name was Margret Mead. There I studied the social and sexual mores of Central Pacific cultures. Man, you think Hugh Hefner was wild. He's got nothing.
	And did you know they drive on the left there. Also it is illegal to bring a horse into a bar in Port Moresby. So when you start telling a joke like 'This horse walks into a bar', people look at you like you're crazy.
DR. SIREN	If you're here to collect your brother's fortune, you're in for a sad disappointment. It is all bequeathed to Dr. Demic and his unconscious son…

Dr. Siren gives Leborgne a few stout kicks to verify he is unconscious

DR. SIREN	Yep, he's out cold.

STRANGER	There is no fortune, Dr. Siren. My brother died penniless. Who do you think tipped the authorities that he was embezzling funds? All his wealth was confiscated long ago. His riches were an illusion to everyone but greedy parties. I, on the other hand, have saved and invested wisely. I've doubled any money my brother ever had by dealing in the black market brain business and betting on sports.
DR. PRACTISS	Side issue, if I may? Don't you find it ironic that baseball condones wagering hundreds of millions of dollars in sports gambling franchises, but refuses to admit Pete Rose into the Hall of Fame for betting on his own team?
DR. DEMIC	Now we can be together without any obstacles, Mel. It's like a heavy weight has been lifted.
SOEUR	Now we can get married without any stigma of incest, Trench.
DR. FEVER	Well, OK, since you've already picked out the flowers.
FUGUE	Give it to me straight, Doc. What do I have?
DR. SIREN	Dear Mr. Perfidious, may I call you Truhart? Have you had a complete physical since you've arrived back in the country? I would be happy to conduct one for you. Let's say seven, tonight at my place.
STRANGER	What about your friend on the floor there?

Dr. Siren calls an aide over and gives him directions on what to do with the knocked out Leborgne sprawled on the floor.

DR. SIREN   Aide, pick this man off the floor and bring him to the brain surgeons when they get back to lunch. Have them give this fellow a thorough lobotomy.

Leborgne is wheeled off for his lobotomy. Dr. Siren walks off arm in arm with the real Truhart H. Perfidious. Dr. Practiss and Dr. Demic embrace and kiss. Soeur and Dr. Fever look at table seating for their reception. Fugue and Nurse Lupus make plans to steal more brains.

Over the PA system we hear 'THE JAPANESE FAREWELL SONG (SAYONARA)."

FADE OUT

THE END

MEDICAL HOSPITAL CAST

Dr. Mel Practiss	**Zhou Enlai**
Dr. Pam Demic	**Mulan**
Dr. Coquette Siren	**Madam Deal**
Leborgne Perfidious	**Keye Luke**
Dr. Trench Fever	**Dr. Lao**
Soeur Sibling	**Sai Zhenzhu**
Fugue Sibling/Walter Ego	**Puyi/Puyi**
Truhart/Mordecai Perfidious	**Sun Tzu/Richard Loo**
Vic DeFraude	**Warner Oland**
Aide	**Hop Sing**

Petite Pierres Precieuses
(Small Gems)

Introduction

The fruits of my search for lost works uncovered small gems (petite pierres precieuses) of great value and interest. While the size of these works may be diminutive, their importance is not. Any find of the type our research seeks out opens the curtains on the windows of knowledge and brings light to illuminate the unlit knowledge that is now illuminated by the light from the open windows if it is sunny or just daytime out. You know what I mean.

Two such petite pierres precieuses are presented in this section. The first is an opening passage written by the Byzantine emperor Konstantinos V. The other is a preserved comment copy of Hammurabi's Code of laws.

KONSTANTINOS—BYZANTINE EMPEROR

Prior to this find, the only thing known about Konstantinos was that he died. It is assumed that he was alive prior to that somewhere between the years 385 to the Beatles first US visit in 1964, with his death coming somewhere in the middle.

More interesting than his tenure as Byzantine emperor or, perhaps, even his literary ambitions, is the curiosity of what lay under his enormous hat. Speculations include a poodle, a massive bouffant hairdo, a serious cranial malfunction, the first hot air balloon, or Texas. The small opening passage shown here indicates that Konstantinos had ambitions of becoming a gothic mystery writer.

PD-US

Konstantinos V

OPENING PASSAGE OF KONSTANTINOS V's UNDISCOVERED NOVEL

Sunday, December 7, 1941, but in a galaxy far, far away.

It was a bright cold day in April when the dark and stormy night brought the winter of our incontinence, and a truth universally acknowledged that I would soon find whether I would be the hero of my life, or the fire of my loins which burned someplace in La Mancha where Mother died today like the old man who fished alone against the infinite sea. The moral being he needed a bigger boat. So upon him now falls the night, and a dark time for a soul laid waste in the poverty and servitude of existence. For me, life holds nothing except hard work and absent joys. I was born Amanda Rekonwith. Call me Ishmael. In my life I looked not for trouble—it knew where to find me.

Hammurabi—King of Mesopotamia and the Greater Babylon Area

The other item in this section comes from ancient Mesopotamia and the court of Hammurabi, Sixth King of the First Dynasty of Babylonia, Conqueror of the Eshnunna and Elamites, and Lord of the powerful Assyrians. Hammurabi is most famous for his code of laws established in the mid-1700s BC, but was also a very popular Mesopotamian DJ (aka DJ Hammbone King).

Our find from the Tigris-Euphrates region shows a small section of a comment copy for the Hammurabi codes. This find demonstrates that Hammurabi was actively involved in the final version of the laws and did not think there was a serious chicken-stealing problem in Mesopotamia at the time. It was an oversight which led to the war against the city of Ur, the Chicken-Stealing Capital of the Fertile Crescent.

Following his victory over Ur, Hammurabi banned the troublesome chickens from his empire and mandated that all cities henceforth must have at least three letters in their name. This effectively destroyed Ur as a regional power until the time of the Sumerians and their god Gozer.

PD-US

Hammurabi—King of Babylon

COMMENT COPY OF PROPOSED HAMMURABI CODES

- If a man hath 2 chickens and his neighbor has 1, the man with the 1 cannot steal the chicken from the man with 2 chickens or he will have his eyes plucked.

  The neighbor has 1 what? Chicken? Clarify. Also do we really have a big enough chicken stealing problem to warrant a separate code? H

- If a man hath 2 chickens and his neighbor has none, if the one with none takes one so they both have one and none have none, it will be considered a tie to be resolved by a 5 minute overtime period?

  Not sure why you think we have a chicken problem. We are an arid climate zone and don't have many chickens running around. BTW—no ties! H

- If a man, who by the way has two chickens, fails to pay his bills to a man, who incidentally has no chickens, the man with no chickens can take the two chicken man to the courts to receive fair payment, perhaps in the form of a chicken.

  What is it with you and chickens? H

- If there are fewer than 2 outs and there is a force at third base, if the batter hits a fly ball that in the opinion of the umpire can be fielded by an infielder, the batter is automatically out and will be stoned to death. However, if the stone throwers are found to use any foreign substance that improves grip or increases spin rate, then they also will be stoned.

  I like it! H